STATUTORY AND DOCUMENTARY SUPPLEMENT TO CASES, MATERIALS AND PROBLEMS ON

SPORTS AND THE LAW

Third Edition

By

Paul C. Weiler
Friendly Professor of Law
Harvard Law School

Gary R. Roberts
Deputy Dean, Sumter Davis Marks Professor of Law
Tulane Law School

AMERICAN CASEBOOK SERIES®

Mat #40183954

American Casebook Series and West Group are trademarks
registered in the U.S. Patent and Trademark Office.

COPYRIGHT © 1993 WEST PUBLISHING CO.
COPYRIGHT © 1998 WEST GROUP
© 2004 West, a Thomson business
      610 Opperman Drive
      P.O. Box 64526
      St. Paul, MN 55164–0526
      1–800–328–9352

Printed in the United States of America

ISBN 0–314–15021–8

TEXT IS PRINTED ON 10% POST CONSUMER RECYCLED PAPER

Preface

Sports, like any industry or walk of life, is governed by law. What is unusual about the sports industry, however, is its enormous body of privately-created law—i.e., law other than statutes and regulations enacted or adopted by various governmental bodies. Of course, the Sherman and Clayton Antitrust Acts, the National Labor Relations Act, the Amateur Sports Act, Title VII and Title IX, the Americans With Disabilities Act, federal trademark and copyright laws, state and federal tax codes, state legislation regulating agents, and the common law of torts and contracts, all have played a vital role in the evolution of American sports. But participants in the day to day life of the sports world are even more preoccupied with the large array of privately-written rules defining what they can and cannot do—rules contained in constitutions and by-laws governing professional sports leagues, sports governing bodies, and individual sports tours, collective bargaining agreements between leagues and players associations, agent regulations promulgated by player unions, the voluminous NCAA Manual, and the standard contracts that shape hundreds of different types of relationships in sports.

As we were preparing the manuscript for this edition of *Sports and the Law,* as with the first two editions, it quickly became apparent that for readers to grasp the full scope of the many issues raised in the book, they would need to have access to a representative sampling of these underlying legal documents that frame real world sports conflicts. Rather than expand the book itself with lengthy documentary excerpts that would break the flow of the text, we decided the best approach would be to include in the standard statutory Supplement key portions of the most important private sources of law. Thus, this volume.

We do note, however, that the materials incorporated in this Supplement cover only a tiny portion of this private legal regime. League, NCAA, and other sports constitutions sometimes run for hundreds of pages, as do the various collective bargaining agreements. We have included those excerpts that will be of greatest assistance to readers reflecting on the questions posed in the casebook. At the same time we have had to edit out many of the qualifications or limitations to the rules set forth in this volume. Furthermore, these private sports agreements are constantly changing as relationships in the industry evolve. Lawyers or agents practicing in the area must rely, then, not on this Supplement but on the full text of the most recent and unedited versions of the relevant documents. We hope that our intended audience of students of sports law will find that this Supplement provides a useful and easy-to-read glimpse of the most important legal rules shaping the world of sports.

Paul C. Weiler

Gary R. Roberts

May 2004

Table of Contents

STATUTORY AND DOCUMENTARY SUPPLEMENT TO CASES, MATERIALS AND PROBLEMS ON

SPORTS AND THE LAW

Third Edition

*

A. CONSTITUTIONAL, STATUTORY, AND ADMINISTRATIVE MATERIALS

UNITED STATES CONSTITUTION

Article 1, § 8

(1) The Congress shall have Power to lay and collect Taxes ..., to pay the Debts and provide for the common Defense and general Welfare of the United States; ...;

(3) To regulate Commerce with foreign Nations, and among the several States, and with the Indian Tribes;

(18) To make all Laws which shall be necessary and proper for carrying into execution the foregoing powers, and all other Powers vested by this Constitution in the Government of the United States, or in any Department or Officer thereof.

Amendment XIV (1868)

Section 1. All persons born or naturalized in the United States, and subject to the jurisdiction thereof, are citizens of the United States and the state in which they reside. No state shall make or enforce any law which shall abridge the privileges and immunities of the citizens of the United States; nor shall any state deprive any person of life, liberty or property, without due process of law; nor deny any person within its jurisdiction the equal protection of the laws.

———

SHERMAN ACT (1890)

Section 1 (15 U.S.C. § 1). Trusts, etc. in restraint of trade illegal; penalty

Every contract, combination in the form of trust or otherwise, or conspiracy, in restraint of trade or commerce among the several States, or with foreign nations, is declared to be illegal. Every person who shall make any contract or engage in any combination or conspiracy hereby declared to be illegal shall be deemed guilty of a felony....

Section 2 (15 U.S.C. § 2). Monopolization; penalty

Every person who shall monopolize, or attempt to monopolize, or combine or conspire with any other person or persons, to monopolize any part of the trade or commerce among the several States, or with foreign nations, shall be deemed guilty of a felony. . . .

———

CLAYTON ACT (1914)

Section 4 (15 U.S.C. § 15). Suits by persons injured

(a) Amount of recovery; prejudgment interest— . . . [A]ny person who shall be injured in his business or property by reason of anything forbidden in the antitrust laws may sue therefor in any district court of the United States in the district in which the defendant resides or is found or has an agent, without respect to the amount in controversy, and shall recover threefold the damages by him sustained, and the cost of the suit including a reasonable attorney's fee. The court may award under this section . . . simple interest on actual damages for the period beginning on the date of service of such person's pleading. . . .

Section 6 (15 U.S.C. § 17). Antitrust laws not applicable to labor organizations

The labor of a human being is not a commodity or article of commerce. Nothing contained in the antitrust laws shall be construed to forbid the existence and operation of labor, agricultural or horticultural organizations, instituted for the purposes of mutual help, . . . or to forbid or restrain individual members of such organizations from lawfully carrying out the legitimate objects thereof; nor shall such organizations, or the members thereof, be held or construed to be illegal combinations or conspiracies in restraint of trade under the antitrust laws.

Section 20 (29 U.S.C. § 52). Depositions for use in suits in equity; proceedings open to the public

No restraining order or injunction shall be granted by any court of the United States, or a judge or the judges thereof, in any case between an employer and employees, or between employers and employees, or between employees, or between persons employed and persons seeking employment, involving, or growing out of, a dispute concerning terms or conditions of employment, unless necessary to prevent irreparable injury to property, or to a property right, of the party making the application, for which injury there is no adequate remedy at law. . . .

———

THE CURT FLOOD ACT OF 1998

15 U.S.C. § 27a. Application of the Antitrust Laws to Professional Major League Baseball.

(a) Major League Baseball subject to antitrust laws

Subject to subsections (b) through (d), the conduct, acts, practices, or agreements of persons in the business of organized professional major league baseball directly relating to or affecting employment of major league baseball players to play baseball at the major league level are subject to the antitrust laws to the same extent such conduct, acts, practices, or agreements would be subject to the antitrust laws if engaged in by persons in any other professional sports business affecting interstate commerce.

(b) Limitation of section

No court shall rely on the enactment of this section as a basis for changing the application of the antitrust laws to any conduct, acts, practices, or agreements other than those set forth in subsection (a). This section does not create, permit or imply a cause of action by which to challenge under the antitrust laws, or otherwise apply the antitrust laws to, any conduct, acts, practices, or agreements that do not directly relate to or affect employment of major league baseball players to play baseball at the major league level, including but not limited to—

(1) any conduct, acts, practices, or agreements of persons engaging in, conducting or participating in the business of organized professional baseball relating to or affecting employment to play baseball at the minor league level, any organized professional baseball amateur or first-year player draft, or any reserve clause as applied to minor league players;

(2) the agreement between organized professional major league baseball teams and the teams of the National Association of Professional Baseball Leagues, commonly known as the 'Professional Baseball Agreement', the relationship between organized professional major league baseball and organized professional minor league baseball, or any other matter relating to organized professional baseball's minor leagues;

(3) any conduct, acts, practices, or agreements of persons engaging in, conducting or participating in the business of organized professional baseball relating to or affecting franchise expansion, location or relocation, franchise ownership issues, including ownership transfers, the relationship between the Office of the Commissioner and franchise owners, the marketing or sales of the entertainment product of organized professional baseball and the licensing of intellectual property rights owned or held by organized professional baseball teams individually or collectively;

(4) any conduct, acts, practices, or agreements protected by Public Law 87–331 (15 U.S.C. § 1291 et seq.) (commonly known as the 'Sports Broadcasting Act of 1961');

(5) the relationship between persons in the business of organized professional baseball and umpires or other individuals who are

employed in the business of organized professional baseball by such persons; or

(6) any conduct, acts, practices, or agreements of persons not in the business of organized professional major league baseball.

(c) Standing to sue

Only a major league baseball player has standing to sue under this section. For the purposes of this section, a major league baseball player is—

(1) a person who is a party to a major league player's contract, or is playing baseball at the major league level; or

(2) a person who was a party to a major league player's contract or playing baseball at the major league level at the time of the injury that is the subject of the complaint; or

(3) a person who has been a party to a major league player's contract or who has played baseball at the major league level, and who claims he has been injured in his efforts to secure a subsequent major league player's contract by an alleged violation of the antitrust laws: Provided however, That for the purposes of this paragraph, the alleged antitrust violation shall not include any conduct, acts, practices, or agreements of persons in the business of organized professional baseball relating to or affecting employment to play baseball at the minor league level, including any organized professional baseball amateur or first-year player draft, or any reserve clause as applied to minor league players; or

(4) a person who was a party to a major league player's contract or who was playing baseball at the major league level at the conclusion of the last full championship season immediately preceding the expiration of the last collective bargaining agreement between persons in the business of organized professional major league baseball and the exclusive collective bargaining representative of major league baseball players.

(d) Conduct, acts, practices, or agreements subject to antitrust laws

(1) As used in this section, 'person' means any entity, including an individual, partnership, corporation, trust or unincorporated association or any combination or association thereof. As used in this section, the National Association of Professional Baseball Leagues, its member leagues and the clubs of those leagues, are not 'in the business of organized professional major league baseball'.

(2) In cases involving conduct, acts, practices, or agreements that directly relate to or affect both employment of major league baseball players to play baseball at the major league level and also relate to or affect any other aspect of organized professional baseball, including but not limited to employment to play baseball at the minor league level and the other areas set forth in subsection (b), only those components, portions or aspects of such conduct, acts, practices, or agreements that directly relate to or affect employment of major league players to play baseball at the major league level

may be challenged under subsection (a) and then only to the extent that they directly relate to or affect employment of major league baseball players to play baseball at the major league level.

(3) As used in subsection (a), interpretation of the term 'directly' shall not be governed by any interpretation of section 151 et seq. of title 29, United States Code (as amended).

(4) Nothing in this section shall be construed to affect the application to organized professional baseball of the nonstatutory labor exemption from the antitrust laws.

(5) The scope of the conduct, acts, practices, or agreements covered by subsection (b) shall not be strictly or narrowly construed.

———

NORRIS–LaGUARDIA ACT (1932)

29 U.S.C. § 101.　Issuance of restraining orders and injunctions; limitation; public policy

No court of the United States . . . shall have jurisdiction to issue any restraining order or temporary or permanent injunction in a case involving or growing out of a labor dispute, except [under section 107 when irreparable property damage is threatened, there is no adequate remedy at law, and law enforcement officials are unable or unwilling to prevent the damage] . . . .

29 U.S.C. § 102.　Public policy in labor matters declared

In the interpretation of this chapter . . . , the public policy of the United States is as follows:

Whereas under prevailing economic conditions developed with the aid of governmental authority for owners of property to organize in the corporate and other forms of ownership association, the individual unorganized worker is commonly helpless to exercise actual liberty of contract and to protect his freedom of labor, and thereby to obtain acceptable terms and conditions of employment, wherefore, though he should be free to decline to associate with his fellows, it is necessary that he have full freedom of association, self-organization, and designation of representatives of his own choosing, to negotiate the terms and conditions of his employment, and that he shall be free from the interference, restraint, or coercion of employers of labor, or their agents, in the designation of such representatives or in the self-organization or in other concerted activities for the purpose of collective bargaining or other mutual aid or protection; therefore, the following definitions of and limitations upon the jurisdiction and authority of the courts of the United States are enacted.

29 U.S.C. § 104. Enumeration of specific acts not subject to restraining orders or injunctions

No court of the United States shall have jurisdiction to issue any restraining order or temporary or permanent injunction in any case involving or growing out of any labor dispute to prohibit any person or persons participating or interested in such dispute (as these terms are herein defined) from doing, whether singly or in concert, any of the following acts:

(a) Ceasing or refusing to perform any work or to remain in any relation of employment;

(b) Becoming or remaining a member of any labor organization or of any employer organization . . . ;

(e) Giving publicity to the existence of, or the facts involved in any labor dispute, whether by advertising, speaking, patrolling or by any other method not involving fraud or violence;

(f) Assembling peaceably to act or to organize to act in promotion of their interests in a labor dispute.

29 U.S.C. § 105. Doing in concert of certain acts as constituting unlawful combination or conspiracy subjecting person to injunctive remedies

No court of the United States shall have jurisdiction to issue any restraining order or temporary or permanent injunction upon the ground that any of the persons participating or interested in a labor dispute constitute or are engaged in an unlawful combination or conspiracy because of the doing in concert of the acts enumerated in § 104 of this title.

29 U.S.C. § 113. Definitions of terms and words used in this chapter

When used in this chapter, and for the purposes of this chapter—

(a) A case shall be held to involve or to grow out of a labor dispute when the case involves persons who are engaged in the same industry, trade, craft, or occupation; or have direct or indirect interests therein; or who are employers or employees; whether such dispute is (1) between one or more employers or associations of employers and one or more employees or associations of employees; (2) between one or more employers or associations of employers and one or more employers or associations of employers; (3) between one or more employees or associations of employees and one or more employees or associations of employees; or when the case involves any conflicting or competing interests in a "labor disputes" (as defined in this section) of "persons participating or interested" therein (as defined in this section).

(b) A person or association shall be held to be a person participating or interested in a labor dispute if relief is sought against him or it, and if he or it is engaged in the same industry, trade, craft or occupation in which such dispute occurs, or has a direct or indirect interest therein, or is a member, officer, or agent of any association composed in whole or in part of employers or employees engaged in such industry, trade, craft, or occupation.

(c) The term "labor dispute" includes any controversy concerning terms or conditions of employment, or concerning the association or representation of persons in negotiating, fixing, maintaining, changing, or seeking to arrange terms or conditions of employment, regardless of whether or not the disputants stand in the proximate relation of employer and employee.

————

THE NATIONAL LABOR RELATIONS ACT

(The Wagner Act of 1935, amended by
The Taft–Hartley Act of 1978)

29 U.S.C. § 151.   Findings and declaration of policy

The denial by some employers of the right of employees to organize and the refusal by some employers to accept the procedure of collective bargaining lead to strikes and other forms of industrial strife or unrest, which have the intent or the necessary effect of burdening or obstructing commerce. . . .

The inequality of bargaining power between employees who do not possess full freedom of association or actual liberty of contract, and employers who are organized in the corporate or other forms of ownership association substantially burdens and affects the flow of commerce, and tends to aggravate recurrent business depressions, by depressing wage rates and the purchasing power of wage earners in industry and by preventing the stabilization of competitive wage rates and working conditions within and between industries.

Experience has proved that protection by law of the right of employees to organize and bargain collectively safeguards commerce from injury, impairment, or interruption, and promotes the flow of commerce by removing certain recognized sources of industrial strife and unrest, by encouraging practices fundamental to the friendly adjustment of industrial disputes arising out of differences as to wages, hours, or other working conditions, and by restoring equality of bargaining power between employers and employees.

Experience has further demonstrated that certain practices by some labor organizations, their officers, and members have the intent or the necessary effect of burdening or obstructing commerce by preventing the free flow of goods in such commerce through strikes and other forms of industrial unrest or through concerted activities which impair the interest of the public in the free flow of such commerce. The elimination of such practices is a necessary condition to the assurance of the rights herein guaranteed.

It is declared hereby to be the policy of the United States to eliminate the causes of certain substantial obstructions to the free flow of commerce and to mitigate and eliminate these obstructions when they have occurred by encouraging the practice and procedure of collective-bargaining and by protecting the exercise by workers of full freedom of association, self organization, and designation of representatives of their own choosing, for the purpose of negotiating the terms and conditions of their employment or other mutual aid or protection.

29 U.S.C. § 152.   Definitions

(3) The term "employee" shall include any employee, and shall not be limited to the employees of a particular employer, unless this sub-chapter explicitly states otherwise, and shall include any individual whose work has ceased as a consequence of, or in connection with, any current labor dispute or because of any unfair labor practice, and who has not obtained any other regular and substantially equivalent employment, but shall not include any individual . . . having the status of an independent contractor, or any individual employed as a supervisor,

. . . .

(5) The term "labor organization" means any organization of any kind, or any agency or employee representation committee or plan, in which employees participate and which exists for the purpose, in whole or in part, of dealing with employers concerning grievances, labor disputes, wages, rates of pay, hours of employment, or conditions of work.

(9) The term "labor dispute" includes any controversy concerning terms, tenure or conditions of employment, or concerning the association or representation of persons in negotiating, fixing, maintaining, changing, or seeking to arrange terms or conditions of employment, regardless of whether the disputants stand in the proximate relation of employer and employee.

(11) The term "supervisor" means any individual having authority, in the interest of the employer, to hire, transfer, suspend, lay off, recall, promote, discharge, assign, reward, or discipline other employees, or responsibly to direct them, or to adjust their grievances, or effectively to recommend such action, if an connection with the foregoing the exercise of such authority is not of a merely routine or clerical nature, but requires the use of independent judgment.

29 U.S.C. § 157.   Right of employees as to organization, collective bargaining, etc.

Employees shall have the right to self-organization, to form, join, or assist labor organizations, to bargain collectively through representatives of their own choosing, and to engage in other concerted activities for the purpose of collective bargaining or other mutual aid or protection, and shall also have the right to refrain from any or all of such activities except to the extent that such right may be affected by an agreement requiring membership in a labor organization as a condition of employment as authorized in section 158(a)(3) of this title.

29 U.S.C. § 158.   Unfair labor practices

(a) Unfair labor practices by employer

It shall be unfair labor practice for an employer—

(1) to interfere with, restrain, or coerce employees in the exercise of the rights guaranteed in section 157 of this title;

(2) to dominate or interfere with the formation or administration of any labor organization or contribute financial or other support to it: Provided, That subject to rules and regulations made and published by the Board pursuant to section 156 of this title, an employer shall not be prohibited from permitting employees to confer with him during working hours without loss of time or pay;

(3) by discrimination in regard to hire or tenure of employment or any term or condition of employment to encourage or discourage membership in any labor organization: Provided, That nothing in this sub-chapter, or in any other statute of the United States, shall preclude an employer from making an agreement with a labor organization . . . to require as a condition of employment membership therein on or after the thirtieth day following the beginning of such employment or the effective date of such agreement, whichever is the later, . . .;

(4) to discharge or otherwise discriminate against an employee because he has filed charges or given testimony under this Act;

(5) to refuse to bargain collectively with the representatives of his employees, subject to the provisions of section 159(a) of this title.

(b) Unfair labor practices by labor organization

It shall be an unfair labor practice for a labor organization or its agents—

(1) to restrain or coerce (A) employees in the exercise of the rights guaranteed in section 157 of this title: Provided, That this paragraph shall not impair the right of a labor organization to prescribe its own rules with respect to the acquisition or retention of membership therein; or (B) an employer in the selection of his representatives for the purposes of collective bargaining or the adjustment of grievances;

(3) to refuse to bargain collectively with an employer, provided it is the representative of his employees subject to the provisions of section 159(a) of this title. . . .

(c) Expression of views without threat of reprisal or force or promise of benefit

The expressing of any views, argument, or opinion, or the dissemination thereof, whether in written, printed, graphic, or visual form, shall not constitute or be evidence of an unfair labor practice under any of the provisions of this subchapter, if such expression contains no threat of reprisal or force or promise of benefit.

(d) Obligation to bargain collectively

For the purposes of this section, to bargain collectively is the performance of the mutual obligation of the employer and the representative of the employees to meet at reasonable times and confer in good faith with respect to wages, hours, and other terms and conditions of employment, or the negotiation of an agreement, or any question arising thereunder, and the execution of a written contract incorporating any agreement reached if requested by either party, but such obligation does not compel either party to agree to a proposal or require the making of a concession: Provided, That where there is in effect as collective-bargaining contract covering employees in an industry affecting commerce, the duty to bargain collectively shall also mean that no party to such contract shall terminate or modify such contract, unless the party desiring such termination or modification—

(1) serves a written notice upon the other party to the contract of the proposed termination or modification sixty days prior to the expiration date thereof, . . . ;

(2) offers to meet and confer with the other party for the purpose of negotiating a new contract or a contract containing the proposed modifications;

(3) notifies the Federal Mediation and Conciliation Service within thirty days after such notice of the existence of a dispute, and simultaneously therewith notifies any State or Territorial agency established to mediate and conciliate disputes within the State or Territory where the dispute occurred, provided no agreement has been reached by that time; and

(4) continues in full force and effect, without resorting to strike or lock-out, all the terms and conditions of the existing contract for a period of sixty days after such notice is given or until the expiration date of such contract, whichever occurs later.

The duties imposed upon employers, employees, and labor organizations by paragraphs (2) to (4) of this subsection shall become inapplicable upon an intervening certification of the Board, under which the labor organization or individual, which is a party to the contract, has been superseded as or ceased to be the representative of the employees.... Any employee who engages in a strike within any notice period specified in this subsection, or who engages in any strike within the appropriate period specified in subsection (g) of this section, shall lose his status as an employee of the employer engaged in the particular labor dispute, for the purposes of sections 158, 159, and 160 of this title, but such loss of status for such employee shall terminate if an when he is reemployed by such employer.

29 U.S.C. § 159. Representatives and elections

(a) Exclusive representative; employees' adjustment of grievances directly with employer

Representatives designated or selected for the purposes of collective bargaining by the majority of the employees in a unit appropriate for such purposes, shall be the exclusive representatives of all the employees in such unit for the purposes of collective bargaining in respect to rates of pay, wages, hours of employment, or other conditions of employment: Provided, That any individual employee or a group of employees shall have the right at any time to present grievances to their employer and to have such grievances adjusted, without the intervention of the bargaining representative as long as the adjustment is not inconsistent with the terms of a collective-bargaining contract or agreement then in effect: Provided further, That the bargaining representative has been given opportunity to be present at such adjustment.

(b) Determination of bargaining unit by Board

The Board shall decide in each case whether, in order to assure to employees the fullest freedom in exercising the rights guaranteed by this subchapter, the unit appropriate for the purposes of collective bargaining shall be the employer unit, craft unit, plant unit, or subdivision thereof: Provided, That the Board shall not (1) decide that any unit is appropriate for such purposes if such unit includes both professional employees and employees who are not professional employees unless a majority of such professional employees vote for inclusion in such unit; . . . .

29 U.S.C. § 160. Prevention of unfair labor practices

(c) Reduction of testimony to writing; findings and orders of Board

. . . If upon the preponderance of the testimony taken the Board shall be of the opinion that any person named in the complaint has engaged in or is engaging in any such unfair labor practice, then the Board shall state its findings of fact and shall issue and cause to be served on such person an order requiring such person to cease and desist from such unfair labor practice, and to take such affirmative action including reinstatement of employees with or without back pay, as will effectuate the policies of this subchapter: Provided, That where an order directs reinstatement of an employee, back pay may be required of the employer or labor organization, as the case may be, responsible for the discrimination suffered by him: . . . . Such order may further require such person to make reports from time to time showing the extent to which it has complied with the order. If upon the preponderance of the testimony taken the Board shall not be of the opinion that the person named in the complaint has engaged in or is engaging in any such unfair labor practice, then the Board shall state its findings of fact and shall issue an order dismissing the said complaint. No order of the Board shall require the reinstatement of any individual as an employee who has been suspended or discharged, or the payment to him of any back pay, if such individual was suspended or discharged for cause. . . .

(j) Injunctions

The Board shall have power, upon issuance of a complaint . . . to petition [a] United States district court . . . for appropriate temporary relief or restraining order. Upon the filing of any such petition the court shall cause notice thereof to be served upon such person, and thereupon shall have jurisdiction to grant to the Board such temporary relief or restraining order as it deems just and proper.

COPYRIGHT ACT

(1976, as amended)

17 U.S.C. § 101.   Definitions

* * *

A "derivative work" is a work based upon one or more preexisting works, such as a translation, musical arrangement, dramatization, fictionalization, motion picture version, sound recording, art reproduction, abridgment, condensation, or any other form in which a work may be recast, transformed, or adapted. A work consisting of editorial revisions, annotations, elaborations, or other modifications which, as a whole, represent an original work of authorship, is a "derivative work."

To "display" a work means to show a copy of it, either directly or by means of a film, slide, television image, or any other device or process or, in the case of a motion picture or other audiovisual work, to show individual images nonsequentially.

A work is "fixed" in a tangible medium of expression when its embodiment in a copy or phonorecord, by or under the authority of the author, is sufficiently permanent or stable to permit it to be perceived, reproduced, or otherwise communicated for a period of more than transitory duration. A work consisting of sounds, images, or both, that are being transmitted, is "fixed" for purposes of this title if a fixation of the work is being made simultaneously with its transmission.

To "perform" a work means to recite, render, play, dance, or act it, either directly or by means of any device or process or, in the case of a motion picture or other audiovisual work, to show its images in any sequence or to make the sounds accompanying it audible.

"Publication" is the distribution of copies or phonorecords of a work to the public by sale or other transfer of ownership, or by rental, lease, or lending. The offering to distribute copies or phonorecords to a group of persons for purposes of further distribution, public performance, or public display, constitutes publication. A public performance or display of a work does not of itself constitute publication.

A "work made for hire" is—

(1) a work prepared by an employee within the scope of his or her employment; . . . .

17 U.S.C. § 102. Subject matter of copyright: In general

(a) Copyright protection subsists, in accordance with this title, in original works of authorship fixed in any tangible medium of expression, now known or later developed, from which they can be perceived, reproduced, or otherwise communicated, either directly or with the aid of a machine or device. Works of authorship include the following categories:

(1) literary works;

(2) musical works, including any accompanying words;

(3) dramatic works, including any accompanying music;

(4) pantomimes and choreographic works;

(5) pictorial, graphic, and sculptural works;

(6) motion pictures and other audiovisual works;

(7) sound recordings; and

(8) architectural works.

* * *

17 U.S.C. § 103. Subject matter of copyright: Compilations and derivative works

(a) The subject matter of copyright as specified by section 102 includes compilations and derivative works, but protection for a work employing preexisting material in which copyright subsists does not extend to any part of the work in which such material has been used unlawfully.

(b) The copyright in a compilation or derivative work extends only to the material contributed by the author of such work, as distinguished from the preexisting material employed in the work, and does not imply any exclusive right in the preexisting material. The copyright in such work is independent of, and does not affect or enlarge the scope, duration, ownership, or subsistence of, any copyright protection in the preexisting material.

* * *

17 U.S.C. 106. Exclusive rights in copyrighted works

Subject to sections 107 through 120, the owner of copyright under this title has the exclusive rights to do and to authorize any of the following:

(1) to reproduce the copyrighted work in copies or phonorecords;

(2) to prepare derivative works based upon the copyrighted work;

(3) to distribute copies or phonorecords of the copyrighted work to the public by sale or other transfer of ownership, or by rental, lease, or lending;

(4) in the case of literary, musical, dramatic, and choreographic works, pantomimes, and motion pictures and other audiovisual works, to perform the copyrighted work publicly; and

(5) in the case of literary, musical, dramatic, and choreographic works, pantomimes, and pictorial, graphic, or sculptural works, including the individual images of a motion picture or other audiovisual work, to display the copyrighted work publicly.

17 U.S.C. § 107. Limitations on exclusive rights: Fair use

Notwithstanding the provisions of sections 106 and 106A, the fair use of a copyrighted work, including such use by reproduction in copies or phonorecords or by any other means specified by that section, for purposes such as criticism, comment, news reporting, teaching (including multiple copies for classroom use), scholarship, or research, is not an infringement of copyright. In determining whether the use made of a work in any particular case is a fair use the factors to be considered shall include—

(1) the purpose and character of the use, including whether such use is of a commercial nature or is for nonprofit educational purposes;

(2) the nature of the copyrighted work;

(3) the amount and substantiality of the portion used in relation to the copyrighted work as a whole; and

(4) the effect of the use upon the potential market for or value of the copyrighted work.

The fact that a work is unpublished shall not itself bar a finding of fair use if such finding is made upon consideration of all the above factors.

* * *

17 U.S.C. § 110. Limitations on exclusive rights: Exemption of certain performances and displays

Notwithstanding the provisions of section 106, the following are not infringements of copyright:

* * *

(5) communication of a transmission embodying a performance or display of a work by the public reception of the transmission on a single receiving apparatus of a kind commonly used in private homes, unless—

(A) a direct charge is made to see or hear the transmission; or

(B) the transmission thus received is further transmitted to the public; . . . .

17 U.S.C. § 111. Limitations on exclusive rights: Secondary transmissions

* * *

(b) Secondary Transmission of Primary Transmission to Controlled Group.—Notwithstanding the provisions of subsections (a) and (c), the secondary transmission to the public of a primary transmission embodying a performance or display of a work is actionable as an act of infringement under section 501, and is fully subject to the remedies provided by sections 502 through 506 and 509, if the primary transmission is not made for reception by the public at large but is controlled and limited to reception by particular members of the public: . . . .

(c) Secondary Transmissions by Cable Systems.—

(1) Subject to the provisions of clauses (2), (3), and (4) of this subsection, secondary transmissions to the public by a cable system of a primary transmission made by a broadcast station licenses by the Federal Communications Commission or by an appropriate governmental authority of Canada or Mexico and embodying a performance or display of a work shall be subject to compulsory licensing upon compliance with the requirements of subsection (d) where the carriage of the signals comprising the secondary transmission is permissible under the rules, regulations, or authorizations of the Federal Communications Commission.

* * *

17 U.S.C. § 201. Ownership of copyright

(a) Initial Ownership.—Copyright in a work protected under this title vests initially in the author or authors of the work. The authors of a joint work are coowners of copyright in the work.

(b) Works Made for Hire.—In the case of a work made for hire, the employer or other person for whom the work was prepared is considered the author for purposes of this title, and, unless the parties have expressly agreed otherwise in a written instrument signed by them, owns all of the rights comprised in the copyright.

* * *

17 U.S.C. § 301. Preemption with respect to other laws

(a) On and after January 1, 1978, all legal or equitable rights that are equivalent to any of the exclusive rights within the general scope of copyright as specified by section 106 in works of authorship that are fixed in a tangible medium of expression and come within the subject matter of copyright as specified by sections 102 and 103, whether created before or after that date and whether published or unpublished, are governed exclusively by this title. Thereafter, no person is entitled to any such right or equivalent right in any such work under the common law or statutes of any State.

(b) Nothing in this title annuls or limits any rights or remedies under the common law or statutes of any State with respect to—

(1) subject matter that does not come within the subject matter of copyright as specified by sections 102 and 103, including works of authorship not fixed in any tangible medium of expression; . . . .

* * *

17 U.S.C. § 411.   Registration and infringement actions

* * *

(b) In the case of a work consisting of sounds, images, or both, the first fixation of which is made simultaneously with its transmission, the copyright owner may, either before or after such fixation takes place, institute an action for infringement under section 501, fully subject to the remedies provided by sections 502 through 506 and sections 509 and 510, if, in accordance with requirements that the Register of Copyrights shall prescribe by regulation, the copyright owner—

(1) serves notice upon the infringer, not less than ten or more than thirty days before such fixation, identifying the work and the specific time and source of its first transmission, and declaring an intention to secure copyright in the work; and

(2) makes registration for the work, if required by subsection (a), within three months after its first transmission.

———

COMMUNICATIONS ACT

47 U.S.C. § 605.   Unauthorized publication or use of communications

(a) **Practices prohibited.** Except as authorized by chapter 119, Title 18, no person receiving, assisting in receiving, transmitting, or assisting in transmitting, any interstate or foreign communication by wire or radio shall divulge or publish the existence, contents, substance, purport, effect, or meaning thereof, except through authorized channels of transmission or reception, [to various listed authorized persons]. No person not being authorized by the sender shall intercept any radio communication and divulge or publish the existence, contents, substance, purport, effect, or meaning of such intercepted communication to any person. No person not being entitled thereto shall receive or assist in receiving any interstate or foreign communication by radio and use such communication (or any information therein contained) for his own benefit or for the benefit of another not entitled thereto. No person having received any intercepted radio communication or having become acquainted with the contents, substance, purport, effect, or meaning of such communication (or any part thereof) knowing that such communication was intercepted, shall divulge or publish the existence, contents, substance, purport, effect, or meaning of such communication (or any part thereof) or use such communication (or any information therein contained) for his own benefit or for the benefit of another not entitled thereto. This section shall not apply to the receiving, divulging, publishing, or utilizing the contents of any radio communication which is transmitted by any station for the use of the general public, which relates to ships, aircraft, vehicles, or persons in distress, or which is transmitted by an amateur radio station operator or by a citizens band radio operator.

NEW YORK CIVIL RIGHTS ACT

§ 50. Right of Privacy

A person, firm or corporation that uses for advertising purposes, or for the purposes of trade, the name, portrait or picture of any living person without having first obtained the written consent of such person, or if a minor of his or her parent or guardian, is guilty of a misdemeanor.

§ 51. Action for injunction and for damages

Any person whose name, portrait, picture or voice is used within this state for advertising purposes or for the purposes of trade without the written consent first obtained as above provided may maintain an equitable action in the supreme court of this state against the person, firm or corporation so using his name, portrait, picture or voice, to prevent and restrain the use thereof; and may also sue and recover damages for any injuries sustained by reason of such use and if the defendant shall have knowingly used such person's name, portrait, picture or voice in such manner as is forbidden or declared to be unlawful by section fifty of this article, the jury, in its discretion, may award exemplary damages. But nothing contained in this article shall be so construed as to prevent any person, firm or corporation from selling or otherwise transferring any material containing such name, portrait, picture or voice in whatever medium to any user of such name, portrait, picture or voice, or to any third party for sale or transfer directly or indirectly to such a user, for use in a manner lawful under this article; nothing contained in this article shall be so construed as to prevent any person, firm or corporation, practicing the profession of photography, from exhibiting in or about his or its establishment specimens of the work of such establishment, unless the same is continued by such person, firm or corporation after written notice objecting thereto has been given by the person portrayed; and nothing contained in this article shall be so construed as to prevent any person, firm or corporation from using the name, portrait, picture or voice of any manufacturer or dealer in connection with the goods, wares and merchandise manufactured, produced or dealt in by him which he has sold or disposed of with such name, portrait, picture or voice used in connection therewith; or from using the name, portrait, picture or voice of any author, composer or artist in connection with his literary, musical or artistic productions which he has sold or disposed of with such name, portrait, picture or voice used in connection therewith. Nothing contained in this section shall be construed to prohibit the copyright owner of a sound recording from disposing of, dealing in, licensing or selling that sound recording to any party, if the right to dispose of, deal in, license or sell such sound recording has been conferred by contract or other written document by such living person or the holder of such right. Nothing contained in the foregoing sentence shall be deemed to abrogate or otherwise limit any rights or remedies otherwise conferred by federal law or state law.

———

CALIFORNIA CIVIL CODE

§ 3344. Use of another's name, voice, signature, photograph, or likeness for advertising, selling, or soliciting purposes

(a) Any person who knowingly uses another's name, voice, signature, photograph, or likeness, in any manner, on or in products, merchandise, or goods, or for purposes of advertising or selling, or soliciting purchases of, products, merchandise, goods or services, without such person's prior consent, or, in the case of a minor, the prior consent of his parent or legal guardian, shall be liable for any damages sustained by the person or persons injured as a result thereof. In addition, in any action brought under this section, the person who violated the section shall be liable to the injured party or parties in an amount equal to the greater of seven hundred fifty dollars ($750) or the actual damages suffered by him or her as a result of the unauthorized use, and any profits from the unauthorized use that are attributable to the use and are not taken into account in computing the actual damages. In establishing such profits, the injured party or parties are required to present proof only of the gross revenue attributable to such use, and the person who violated this section is required to prove his or her deductible expenses. Punitive damages may also be awarded to the injured party or parties. The prevailing party in any action under this section shall also be entitled to attorney's fees and costs.

(b) As used in this section, "photograph" means any photograph or photographic reproduction, still or moving, or any videotape or live television transmission, of any person, such that the person is readily identifiable.

(1) A person shall be deemed to be readily identifiable from a photograph when one who views the photograph with the naked eye can reasonably determine that the person depicted in the photograph is the same person who is complaining of its unauthorized use.

(2) If the photograph includes more than one person so identifiable, then the person or persons complaining of the use shall be represented as individuals rather than solely as members of a definable group represented in the photograph. A definable group includes, but is not limited to, the following examples: a crowd at any sporting event, a crowd in any street or public building, the audience at any theatrical or stage production, a glee club, or a baseball team.

(3) A person or persons shall be considered to be represented as members of a definable group if they are represented in the photograph solely as a result of being present at the time the photograph was taken and have not been singled out as individuals in any manner.

(c) Where a photograph or likeness of an employee of the person using the photograph or likeness appearing in the advertisement or other publication prepared by or in behalf of the user is only incidental, and not essential, to the purpose of the publication in which it appears, there shall arise a rebuttable presumption affecting the burden of producing evidence that the failure to obtain the consent of the employee was not a knowing use of the employee's photograph or likeness.

(d) For purposes of this section, a use of a name, voice, signature, photograph, or likeness in connection with any news, public affairs, or sports broadcast or account, or any political campaign, shall not constitute a use for which consent is required under subdivision (a).

(e) The use of a name, voice, signature, photograph, or likeness in a commercial medium shall not constitute a use for which consent is required under subdivision (a) solely because the material containing such use is commercially sponsored or contains paid advertising. Rather it shall be a question of fact whether or not the use of the person's name, voice, signature, photograph, or likeness was so directly connected with the commercial sponsorship or with the paid advertising as to constitute a use for which consent is required under subdivision (a).

———

LANHAM ACT (TRADEMARKS)

(1946, as amended)

15 U.S.C. §§ 1051, et seq.

15 U.S.C. § 1114.   Remedies; infringement; innocent infringement by printers and publishers

(1) Any person who shall, without the consent of the registrant—

(a) use in commerce any reproduction, counterfeit, copy, or colorable imitation of a registered mark in connection with the sale, offering for sale, distribution, or advertising of any goods or services on or in connection with which such use is likely to cause confusion, or to cause mistake, or to deceive; or

(b) reproduce, counterfeit, copy, or colorably imitate a registered mark and apply such reproduction, counterfeit, copy, or colorable imitation to labels, signs, prints, packages, wrappers, receptacles or advertisements intended to be used in commerce upon or in connection with the sale, offering for sale, distribution, or advertising of goods or services on or in connection with which such use is likely to cause confusion, or to cause mistake, or to deceive,

shall be liable in a civil action by the registrant for the remedies hereinafter provided. Under subsection (b) hereof, the registrant shall not be entitled to recover profits or damages unless the acts have been committed with knowledge that such imitation is intended to be used to cause confusion, or to cause mistake, or to deceive.

* * *

15 U.S.C. § 1125.   [Section 43(a) of the Act] False designations of origin, false descriptions, and dilution forbidden

(a) Civil action

(1) Any person who, on or in connection with any goods or services, or any container for goods, uses in commerce any word, term, name, symbol, or device, or any combination thereof, or any false designation of origin, false or misleading description or fact, or false or misleading representation of fact, which—

(A) is likely to cause confusion, or to cause mistake, or to deceive as to the affiliation, connection, or association of such person with another person, or as to the origin, sponsorship, or approval of his or her goods, services, or commercial activities by another person, or

(B) in commercial advertising or promotion, misrepresents the nature, characteristics, qualities, or geographic origin of his or her or another person's goods, services, or commercial activities, shall be liable in a civil action by any person who believes that he or she is or is likely to be damaged by such act.

* * *

(d) Cyberpiracy prevention

(1)(A) A person shall be liable in a civil action by the owner of a mark, including a personal name which is protected as a mark under this section, if, without regard to the goods or services of the parties, that person

> (i) has a bad faith intent to profit from that mark . . . ; and

> (ii) registers, traffics in, or uses a domain name that—(I) in the case of a mark that is distinctive at the time of registration of the domain name, is identical or confusingly similar to that mark; (II) in the case of a famous mark that is famous at the time of registration of the domain name, is identical or confusingly similar to or dilutive of that mark; or (III is a trademark, word, or name protected [by law for the American Red Cross or United States Olympic Committee].

§ 1127. Construction and definitions; intent of chapter

* * *

The term "trademark" includes any word, name, symbol, or device, or any combination thereof—

(1) used by a person, or

(2) which a person has a bona fide intention to use in commerce and applies to register on the principal register established by this chapter, to identify and distinguish his or her goods, including a unique product, from those manufactured or sold by others and to indicate the source of the goods, even if that source is unknown.

The term "service mark" means any word, name, symbol, or device, or any combination thereof—

(1) used by a person, or

(2) which a person has a bona fide intention to use in commerce and applies to register on the principal register established by this chapter, to identify and distinguish the services of one person, including a unique service, from the services of others and to indicate the source of the services, even if that source is unknown. Titles, character names, and other distinctive features of radio or television programs may be registered as service marks notwithstanding that they, or the programs, may advertise the goods of the sponsor.

* * *

The term "mark" includes any trademark, service mark, collective mark, or certification mark.

The term "use in commerce" means the bona fide use of a mark in the ordinary course of trade, and not made merely to reserve a right in a mark. . . .

A mark shall be deemed to be "abandoned" if either of the following occurs:

(1) When its use has been discontinued with intent not to resume such use. Intent not to resume may be inferred from circumstances. Nonuse for 3 consecutive years shall be prima facie evidence of abandonment. "Use" of a mark means the bona fide use of such mark made in the ordinary course of trade, and not made merely to reserve a right in a mark.

(2) When any course of conduct of the owner, including acts of omission as well as commission, causes the mark to become the generic name for the goods or services on or in connection with which it is used or otherwise to lose its significance as a mark. Purchaser motivation shall not be a test for determining abandonment under this paragraph.

The term "dilution" means the lessening of the capacity of a famous mark to identify and distinguish goods or services, regardless of the presence or absence of—

(1) competition between the owner of the famous mark and other parties, or

(2) likelihood of confusion, mistake, or deception.

The term "colorable imitation" includes any mark which so resembles a registered mark as to be likely to cause confusion or mistake or to deceive.

* * *

SPORTS BROADCASTING ACT OF 1961

15 U.S.C. § 1291. The antitrust laws * * * shall not apply to any joint agreement by or among persons engaging in or conducting the organized professional team sports of football, baseball, basketball, or hockey, by which any league of clubs participating in professional football, baseball, basketball, or hockey contests sells or otherwise transfers all or any part of the rights of such league's member clubs in the sponsored telecasting of the games of football, baseball, basketball, hockey, as the case may be, engaged in or conducted by such clubs. In addition, such laws shall not apply to a joint agreement by which the member clubs of two or more professional football leagues, which are exempt from income tax under section 501(c)(6) of Title 26, combine their operations in an expanded single league so exempt from income tax, if such agreement increases rather than decreases the number of professional football clubs so operating, and the provisions of which are directly relevant thereto.

15 U.S.C. § 1292. Section 1291 of this title shall not apply to any joint agreement described in the first sentence in such section which prohibits any person to whom such rights are sold or transferred from televising any games within any area, except within the home territory of a member club of the league on a day when such club is playing a game at home.

15 U.S.C. § 1293. The first sentence of section 1291 of this title shall not apply to any joint agreement described in such section which permits the telecasting of all or a substantial part of any professional football game on any Friday after six o'clock postmeridian or on any Saturday during the period beginning on the second Friday in September and ending on the second Saturday in December in a year from any telecasting station located within seventy-five miles of the game site of any intercollegiate or interscholastic football contest scheduled to be played on such a date if—

(1) such intercollegiate football contest is between institutions of higher learning both of which confer degrees upon students following completion of sufficient credit hours to equal a four-year course, or

(2) in the case of an interscholastic football contest, such contest is between secondary schools, both of which are accredited or certified under laws of the State or States in which they are situated and offer courses continuing through the twelfth grade of the standard school curriculum, or equivalent, and

(3) such intercollegiate or interscholastic football contest and such game site were announced through publication in a newspaper of general circulation prior to August 1 of such year as being regularly scheduled for such day and place.

15 U.S.C. § 1294. Nothing contained in this chapter shall be deemed to change, determine, or otherwise affect the applicability or nonapplicability of the antitrust laws to any act, contract, agreement, rule, course of conduct, or other activity by, between, or among persons engaging in, conducting, or participating in the organized professional team sports of football, baseball, basketball, or hockey, except the agreements to which section 1291 of this title shall apply.

———

EDUCATIONAL AMENDMENTS
OF 1972—"TITLE IX"

20 U.S.C. § 1681. Sex

(a) Prohibition against discrimination; exceptions—No person in the United State shall, on the basis of sex, be excluded from participation in, be denied the benefits of, or be subjected to discrimination under any education program or activity receiving Federal financial assistance except that: [*9 exceptions, none of which are relevant to athletic programs*].

(b) Preferential or disparate treatment because of imbalance in participation or receipt of Federal benefits; statistical evidence of imbalance—Nothing contained in subsection (a) of this section shall be interpreted to require any educational institution to grant preferential or disparate treatment to the members of one sex on account of an imbalance which may exist with respect to the total number or percentage of persons of that sex participating in or receiving the benefits of any federally supported program or activity, in comparison with the total number of percentage of persons of that sex in any community, State, section, or other area: *Provided*, That this subsection shall not be construed to prevent the consideration in any hearing or proceeding under this chapter of statistical evidence tending to show that such an imbalance exists with respect to the participation in, or receipt of the benefits of, any such program or activity by the members of one sex.

Accompanying Education Department Regulations (1975):

34 CFR § 106.41. Athletics.

(a) General. No person shall, on the basis of sex, be excluded from participation in, be denied the benefits of, be treated differently from another person, or otherwise be discriminated against in any interscholastic, intercollegiate, club or intramural athletics offered by a recipient, and no recipient shall provide any such athletics separately on such basis.

(b) Separate team. Notwithstanding the requirements of paragraph (a) of this section, a recipient may operate or sponsor separate teams for members of each sex where selection for such teams is based upon competitive skill or the activity involved is a contact sport. However, where a recipient operates or sponsors a team in a particular sport for members of one sex but operates or sponsors no such team for members of the other sex, and athletic opportunities for members of that sex have previously been limited, members of the excluded sex must be allowed to try out for the team offered unless the sport involved is a contact sport. For the purposes of this part, contact sports include boxing, wrestling, rugby, ice hockey, football, basketball and other sports the purpose or major activity of which involves bodily contact.

(c) Equal opportunity. A recipient which operates or sponsors interscholastic, intercollegiate, club or intramural athletics shall provide equal athletic opportunity for members of both sexes. In determining whether equal opportunities are available the Director will consider, among other factors:

(1) Whether the selection of sports and levels of competition effectively accommodate the interests and abilities of members of both sexes;

(2) The provision of equipment and supplies;

(3) Scheduling of games and practice time;

(4) Travel and per diem allowance;

(5) Opportunity to receive coaching and academic tutoring;

(6) Assignment and compensation of coaches and tutors;

(7) Provision of locker rooms, practice and competitive facilities;

(8) Provision of medical and training facilities and services;

(9) Provision of housing and dining facilities and services;

(10) Publicity.—Unequal aggregate expenditures for members of each sex or unequal expenditures for male and female teams if a recipient operates or sponsors separate teams will not constitute noncompliance with this section, but the Assistant Secretary may consider the failure to provide necessary funds for teams for one sex in assessing equality of opportunity for members of each sex.

(d) Adjustment period. A recipient which operates or sponsors interscholastic, intercollegiate, club or intramural athletics at the elementary school level shall comply fully with this section as expeditiously as possible but in no event later than one year from the effective date of this regulation. A recipient which operates or sponsors interscholastic, intercollegiate, club or intramural athletics at the secondary or post-secondary school level shall comply fully with this section as expeditiously as possible but in no event later than three years from the effective date of this regulation.

Department of Health, Education & Welfare, Office for Civil Rights, Policy Interpretation on Title IX and Intercollegiate Athletics

45 CFR, Part 26—December 11, 1979

* * *

VII. The Policy Interpretation

This Policy Interpretation clarifies the obligations which recipients of Federal aid have under Title IX to provide equal opportunities in athletic programs. In particular, this Policy Interpretation provides a means to assess an institution's compliance with the equal opportunity requirements of the regulation which are set forth at 45 CFR 88.37(c) and 88.4a(c).

A. Athletic Financial Assistance (Scholarships)

* * *

2. The Policy—The Department will examine compliance with this provision of the regulation primarily by means of a financial comparison to determine whether proportionately equal amounts of financial assistance (scholarship aid) are available to men's and women's athletic programs. The Department will measure compliance with this standard by dividing the amounts of aid available for the members of each sex by the numbers of male or female participants in the athletic program and comparing the results. Institutions may be found in compliance if this comparison results in substantially equal amounts or if a resulting disparity can be explained by adjustments to take into account legitimate, nondiscriminatory factors. Two such factors are:

a. At public institutions, the higher costs of tuition for students from out-of state may in some years be unevenly' distributed between men's and women's programs. These differences will be considered nondiscriminatory if they are not the result of policies or practices which disproportionately limit the availability of out-of-state scholarships to either men or women.

b. An institution may make reasonable professional decisions concerning the awards most appropriate for program development. For example, team development initially may require spreading scholarships over as much as a full generation [four years) of student athletes. This may result in the award of fewer scholarships in the first few years than would be necessary to create proportionality between male and female athletes.

3. Application of the Policy—This section does not require a proportionate number of scholarships for men and women or individual scholarships of equal dollar value. It does mean that the total amount of scholarship aid made available to men and women must be substantially proportionate to their participation rates.

* * *

B. Equivalence in Other Athletic Benefits and Opportunities

* * *

2. The Policy—The Department will assess compliance with both the recruitment and the general athletic program requirements of the regulation by comparing the availability, quality and kinds of benefits, opportunities, and treatment afforded members of both sexes. Institutions will be in compliance if the compared program components are equivalent, that is, equal or equal in effect. Under this standard, identical benefits, opportunities, or treatment are not required, provided the overall effects of any differences is negligible.

If comparisons of program components reveal that treatment, benefits, or opportunities are not equivalent in kind, quality or availability, a finding of compliance may still be justified if the differences are the result of nondiscriminatory factors. Some of the factors that may justify these differences are as follows:

a. Some aspects of athletic programs may not be equivalent for men and women because of unique aspects of particular sports or athletic activities. This type of distinction was called for by the "Javits Amendment" to Title IX which instructed HEW to make "reasonable (regulatory) provisions considering the nature of particular sports" in intercollegiate athletics.

Generally, these differences will be the result of factors that are inherent to the basic operation of specific sports. Such factors may include rules of play, nature/replacement of equipment, rates of injury resulting from participation, nature of facilities required for competition, and the maintenance/ upkeep requirements of those facilities. For the most part, differences involving such factors will occur in programs offering football, and consequently these differences will favor men. If sport-specific needs are met equivalently in both men's and women's programs, however, differences in particular program components will be found to be justifiable.

b. Some aspects of athletic programs may not be equivalent for men and women because of legitimately sex-neutral factors related to special circumstances of a temporary nature. For example, large disparities in recruitment activity for any particular year may be the result of annual fluctuations in team needs for first-year athletes. Such differences are justifiable to the extent that they do not reduce overall equality of opportunity.

c. The activities directly associated with the operation of a competitive event in a single-sex sport may, under some circumstances, create unique demands or imbalances in particular program components. Provided any special demands associated with the activities of sports involving participants of the other sex are met to an equivalent degree, the resulting differences may be found nondiscriminatory. At many schools, for example, certain sports, notably football and men's basketball, traditionally draw large crowds. Since the costs of managing an athletic event increase with crowd size, the overall support made available for event management to men's and women's programs may differ in degree and kind. These differences would not violate Title IX if the recipient does not limit the potential for women's athletic events to rise in spectator appeal and if the levels of event management support available to both programs are based on sex-neutral criteria (e.g. facilities used, projected attendance, and staffing needs).

d. Some aspects of athletic programs may not be equivalent for men and women because institutions are undertaking voluntary affirmative actions to overcome effects of historical conditions that have limited participation in athletics by the members of one sex. This is authorized at 86.3(b) of the regulation.

3. Application of the Policy—General Athletic Program Components

a. Equipment and Supplies (86.41(c)(2)). Equipment and supplies include but are not limited to uniforms, other apparel, sport-specific equipment and supplies, general equipment and supplies, instructional devices, and conditioning and weight training equipment.

Compliance will be assessed by examining, among other factors, the equivalence for men and women of:

(1) The quality of equipment and supplies; (2) The amount of equipment and supplies; (3) The suitability of equipment and supplies; (4) The maintenance and replacement of the equipment and supplies; and (5) The availability of equipment and supplies.

b. Scheduling of Games and Practice Times (86.41(c)(3)). Compliance will be assessed by examining, among other factors, the equivalence for men and women of:

(1) The number of competitive events per sport; (2) The number and length of practice opportunities; (3) The time of day competitive events are scheduled; (4) The time of day practice opportunities are scheduled; and (5) The opportunities to engage in available pre-season and post-season competition.

c. Travel and Per Diem Allowances (86.41(c)(4)). Compliance will be assessed by examining, among other factors, the equivalence for men and women of:

(1) Modes of transportation; (2) Housing furnished during travel; (3) Length of stay before and after competitive events; (4) Per diem allowances; and (5) Dining arrangements.

d. Opportunity to Receive Coaching and Academic Tutoring (86.41(c)(5)). (1) Coaching—Compliance will be assessed by examining, among other factors:

(a) Relative availability of full-time coaches; (b) Relative availability of part-time and assistant coaches; and (c) Relative availability of graduate assistants.

(2) Academic tutoring-Compliance will be assessed by examining, among other factors, the equivalence for men and women of:

(a) The availability of tutoring; and (b) Procedures and criteria for obtaining tutorial assistance.

e. Assignment and Compensation of Coaches and Tutors (86.41(c)(6)). In general, a violation of Section 86.41(c)(6) will be found only where compensation or assignment policies or practices deny male and female athletes coaching of equivalent quality, nature, or availability.

Nondiscriminatory factors can affect the compensation of coaches. In determining whether differences are caused by permissible factors, the range and nature of duties, the experience of individual coaches, the number of participants for particular sports, the number of assistant coaches supervised, and the level of competition will be considered.

Where these or similar factors represent valid differences in skill, effort, responsibility or working conditions they may, in specific circumstances, justify differences in compensation. Similarly, there may be unique situations in which a particular person may possess such an outstanding record of achievement as to justify an abnormally high salary.

(1) Assignment of Coaches—Compliance will be assessed by examining, among other factors, the equivalence for men's and women's coaches of:

(a) Training, experience, and other professional qualifications; (b) Professional standing.

(2) Assignment of Tutors—Compliance will be assessed by examining, among other factors, the equivalence for men's and women's tutors of:

(a) Tutor qualifications; (b) Training, experience, and other qualifications.

(3) Compensation of Coaches—Compliance will be assessed by examining, among other factors, the equivalence for men's and women's coaches of:

(a) Rate of compensation (per sport, per season); (b) Duration of contracts; (c) Conditions relating to contract renewal; (d) Experience; (e) Nature of coaching duties performed; (f) Working conditions; and (g) Other terms and conditions of employment.

(4) Compensation of Tutors—Compliance will be assessed by examining, among other factors, the equivalence for men's and women's tutors of:

(a) Hourly rate of payment by nature subjects tutored; (b) Pupil loads per tutoring season; (c) Tutor qualifications; (d) Experience; (e) Other terms and conditions of employment.

f. Provision of Locker Rooms, Practice and Competitive Facilities (§ 86.41(c)(7)). Compliance will be assessed by examining, among other factors, the equivalence for men and women of:

(1) Quality and availability of the facilities provided for practice and competitive events; (2) Exclusivity of use of facilities provided for practice and competitive events; (3) Availability of locker rooms; (4) Quality of locker rooms; (5) Maintenance of practice and competitive facilities; and (6) Preparation of facilities for practice and competitive events.

g. Provision of Medical and Training Facilities and Services (86.41(c)(8)). Compliance will be assessed by examining, among other factors, the equivalence for men and women of:

(1) Availability of medical personnel and assistance; (2) Health, accident and injury insurance coverage; (3) Availability and quality of weight and training facilities; (4) Availability and quality of conditioning facilities; and (5) Availability and qualifications of athletic trainers.

h. Provision of Housing and Dining Facilities and Services (86.41(c)(9)). Compliance will be assessed by examining, among other factors, the equivalence for men and women of:

(1) Housing provided; (2) Special services as part of housing arrangements (e.g., laundry facilities, parking space, maid service).

i. Publicity (86.41(c)(10)). Compliance will be assessed by examining, among other factors, the equivalence for men and women of:

(1) Availability and quality of sports information personnel; (2) Access to other publicity resources for men's and women's programs; and (3) Quantity and quality of publications and other promotional devices featuring men's and women's programs.

4. Application of the Policy—Other Factors (86.41(c))

a. Recruitment of Student Athletes. The athletic recruitment practices of institutions often affect the overall provision of opportunity to male and female athletes. Accordingly, where equal athletic opportunities are not present for male and female students, compliance will be assessed by examining the recruitment practices of the athletic programs for both sexes to determine whether the provision of equal opportunity will require modification of those practices.

Such examinations will review the following factors:

(1) Whether coaches or other professional athletic personnel in the programs serving male and female athletes are provided with substantially equal opportunities to recruit;

(2) Whether the financial and other resources made available for recruitment in male and female athletic programs are equivalently adequate to meet the needs of each program; and

(3) Whether the differences in benefits, opportunities, and treatment afforded prospective student athletes of each sex have a disproportionately limiting effect upon the recruitment of students of either sex.

b. Provision of Support Services. The administrative and clerical support provided to an athletic program can affect the overall provision of opportunity to male and female athletes, particularly to the extent that the provided services enable coaches to perform better their coaching functions.

In the provision of support services, compliance will be assessed by examining, among other factors, the equivalence of:

(1) The amount of administrative assistance provided to men's and women's programs;

(2) The amount of secretarial and clerical assistance provided to men's and women's programs.

5. <u>Overall Determination of Compliance</u>. The Department will base its compliance determination under 86.41(c) of the regulation upon an examination of the following:

a. Whether the policies of an institution are discriminatory in language or effect; or

b. Whether disparities of a substantial and unjustified nature exist in the benefits, treatment, services, or opportunities afforded male and female athletes in the institution's program as a whole; or

c. Whether disparities in benefits, treatment, services, or opportunities in individual segments of the program are substantial enough in and of themselves to deny equality of athletic opportunity.

C. Effective Accommodation of Student Interests and Abilities

* * *

2. <u>The Policy</u>. The Department will assess compliance with the interests and abilities section of the regulation by examining the following factors:

a. The determination of athletic interests and abilities of students;

b. The selection of sports offered; and

c. The levels of competition available including the opportunity for team competition.

3. <u>Application of the Policy—Determination of Athletic Interests and Abilities</u>.

Institutions may determine the athletic interests and abilities of students by nondiscriminatory methods of their choosing provided:

a. The processes take into account the nationally increasing levels of women's interests and abilities;

b. The methods of determining interest and ability do not disadvantage the members of an underrepresented sex;

c. The methods of determining ability take into account team performance records; and

d. The methods are responsive to the expressed interests of students capable of intercollegiate competition who are members of an underrepresented sex.

4. <u>Application of the Policy—Selection of Sports</u>.

In the selection of sports, the regulation does not require institutions to integrate their teams nor to provide exactly the same choice of sports to men and women. However, where an institution sponsors a team in a particular sport for members of one sex, it may be required either to permit the excluded sex to try out for the team or to sponsor a separate team for the previously excluded sex.

a. Contact Sports—Effective accommodation means that if an institution sponsors a team for members of one sex in a contact sport, it must do so for members of the other sex under the following circumstances:

(1) The opportunities for members of the excluded sex have historically been limited; and

(2) There is sufficient interest and ability among the members of the excluded sex to sustain a viable team and a reasonable expectation of intercollegiate competition for that team.

b. Non–Contact Sports—Effective accommodation means that if an institution sponsors a team for members of one sex in a non-contact sport, it must do so for members of the other sex under the following circumstances:

(1) The opportunities for members of the excluded sex have historically been limited;

(2) There is sufficient interest and ability among the members of the excluded sex to sustain a viable team and a reasonable expectation of intercollegiate competition for that team; and

(3) Members of the excluded sex do not possess sufficient skill to be selected for a single integrated team, or to compete actively on such a team if selected.

5. Application of the Policy—Levels of Competition.

In effectively accommodating the interests and abilities of male and female athletes, institutions must provide both the opportunity for individuals of each sex to participate in intercollegiate competition, and for athletes of each sex to have competitive team schedules which equally reflect their abilities.

a. Compliance will be assessed in any one of the following ways:

(1) Whether intercollegiate level participation opportunities for male and female students are provided in numbers substantially proportionate to their respective enrollments; or

(2) Where the members of one sex have been and are underrepresented among intercollegiate athletes, whether the institution can show a history and continuing practice of program expansion which is demonstrably responsive to the developing interest and abilities of the members of that sex; or

(3) Where the members of one sex are underrepresented among intercollegiate athletes, and the institution cannot show a continuing practice of program expansion such as that cited above, whether it can be demonstrated that the interests and abilities of the members of that sex have been fully and effectively accommodated by the present program.

b. Compliance with this provision of the regulation will also be assessed by examining the following:

(1) Whether the competitive schedules for men's and women's teams, on a program-wide basis, afford proportionally similar numbers of male and female athletes equivalently advanced competitive opportunities; or

(2) Whether the institution can demonstrate a history and continuing practice of upgrading the competitive opportunities available to the historically disadvantaged sex as warranted by developing abilities among the athletes of that sex.

c. Institutions are not required to upgrade teams to intercollegiate status or otherwise develop intercollegiate sports absent a reasonable expectation that intercollegiate competition in that sport will be available within the institution's normal competitive regions. Institutions may be required by the Title IX regulation to actively encourage the development of such competition, however, when overall athletic opportunities within that region have been historically limited for the members of one sex.

6. <u>Overall Determination of Compliance.</u>

The Department will base its compliance determination under 86.41(c) of the regulation upon a determination of the following:

a. Whether the policies of an institution are discriminatory in language or effect; or

b. Whether disparities of a substantial and unjustified nature in the benefits, treatment, services, or opportunities afforded male and female athletes exist in the institution's program as a whole; or

c. Whether disparities in individual segments of the program with respect to benefits, treatment, services, or opportunities are substantial enough in and of themselves to deny equality of athletic opportunity.

* * *

Department of Education, Office of Civil Rights—Clarification of Intercollegiate Athletics Policy Guidance: The Three-Part Test (January 19, 1996)

* * *

The Title IX regulation provides that if an institution sponsors an athletic program it must provide equal athletic opportunities for members of both sexes. Among other factors, the regulation requires that an institution must effectively accommodate the athletic interests and abilities of students of both sexes to the extent necessary to provide equal athletic opportunity.

The 1979 Policy Interpretation provides that as part of this determination OCR will apply the following three-part test to assess whether an institution is providing nondiscriminatory participation opportunities for individuals of both sexes:

1.   Whether intercollegiate level participation opportunities for male and female students are provided in numbers substantially proportionate to their respective enrollments; or

2.   Where the members of one sex have been and are underrepresented among intercollegiate athletes, whether the institution can show a history and continuing practice of program expansion which is demonstrably responsive to the developing interests and abilities of the members of that sex; or

3.   Where the members of one sex are underrepresented among intercollegiate athletes, and the institution cannot show a history and continuing practice of program expansion, as described above, whether it can be demonstrated that the interests and abilities of the members of that sex have been fully and effectively accommodated by the present program.

44 *Fed. Reg.* at 71418.

Thus, the three-part test furnishes an institution with three individual avenues to choose from when determining how it will provide individuals of each sex with nondiscriminatory opportunities to participate in intercollegiate athletics. If an institution has met any part of the three-part test, OCR will determine that the institution is meeting this requirement.

* * *

This Clarification provides specific factors that guide an analysis of each part of the three-part test. In addition, it provides examples to demonstrate, in concrete terms, how these factors will be considered. These examples are intended to be illustrative, and the conclusions drawn in each example are based solely on the facts included in the example.

THREE-PART TEST—Part One: Are Participation Opportunities Substantially Proportionate to Enrollment?

Under part one of the three-part test (part one), where an institution provides intercollegiate level athletic participation opportunities for male and female students in numbers substantially proportionate to their respective full-time undergraduate enrollments, OCR will find that the institution is providing nondiscriminatory participation opportunities for individuals of both sexes.

* * *

[B]ecause in some circumstances it may be unreasonable to expect an institution to achieve exact proportionality—for instance, because of natural fluctuations in enrollment and participation rates or because it would be unreasonable to expect an institution to add athletic opportunities in light of the small number of students that would have to be accommodated to achieve exact proportionality—the Policy Interpretation examines whether participation opportunities are "substantially" proportionate to enrollment rates. Because this determination depends on the institution's specific circumstances and the size of its athletic program, OCR makes this determination on a case-by-case basis, rather than through use of a statistical test.

* * *

OCR would []consider opportunities to be substantially proportionate when the number of opportunities that would be required to achieve proportionality would not be sufficient to sustain a viable team, i.e., a team for which there is a sufficient number of interested and able students and enough available competition to sustain an intercollegiate team. As a frame of reference in assessing this situation, OCR may consider the average size of teams offered for the underrepresented sex, a number which would vary by institution.

For instance, Institution A is a university with a total of 600 athletes. While women make up 52 percent of the university's enrollment, they only represent 47 percent of its athletes. If the university provided women with 52 percent of athletic opportunities, approximately 62 additional women would be able to participate. Because this is a significant number of unaccommodated women, it is likely that a viable sport could be added. If so, Institution A has not met part one.

As another example, at Institution B women also make up 52 percent of the university's enrollment and represent 47 percent of Institution B's athletes. Institution B's athletic program consists of only 60 participants. If the University provided women with 52 percent of athletic opportunities, approximately 6 additional women would be able to participate. Since 6 participants are unlikely to support a viable team, Institution B would meet part one.

THREE-PART TEST—Part Two: Is there a History and Continuing Practice of Program Expansion for the Underrepresented Sex?

Under part two of the three-part test (part two), an institution can show that it has a history and continuing practice of program expansion which is demonstrably responsive to the developing interests and abilities of the underrepresented sex. In effect, part two looks at an institution's past and continuing remedial efforts to provide nondiscriminatory participation opportunities through program expansion.

OCR will review the entire history of the athletic program, focusing on the participation opportunities provided for the underrepresented sex. First, OCR will assess whether past actions of the institution have expanded participation opportunities for the underrepresented sex in a manner that was demonstrably responsive to their developing interests and abilities. Developing interests include interests that already exist at the institution. There are no fixed intervals of time within which an institution must have added participation opportunities. Neither is a particular number of sports dispositive. Rather, the focus is on whether the program expansion was responsive to developing interests and abilities of the underrepresented sex. In addition, the institution must demonstrate a continuing (i.e., present) practice of program expansion as warranted by developing interests and abilities.

* * *

In the event that an institution eliminated any team for the underrepresented sex, OCR would evaluate the circumstances surrounding this action in assessing whether the institution could satisfy part two of the test. However, OCR will not find a history and continuing practice of program expansion where an institution increases the proportional participation opportunities for the underrepresented sex by reducing opportunities for the overrepresented sex alone or by reducing participation opportunities for the overrepresented sex to a proportionately greater degree than for the underrepresented sex. This is because part two considers an institution's good faith remedial efforts through actual program expansion. It is only necessary to examine part two if one sex is overrepresented in the athletic program. Cuts in the program for the underrepresented sex, even when coupled with cuts in the program for the overrepresented sex, cannot be considered remedial because they burden members of the sex already disadvantaged by the present program. However, an institution that has eliminated some participation opportunities for the underrepresented sex can still meet part two if, overall, it can show a history and continuing practice of program expansion for that sex.

In addition, OCR will not find that an institution satisfies part two where it established teams for the underrepresented sex only at the initiation of its program for the underrepresented sex or where it merely promises to expand its program for the underrepresented sex at some time in the future.

The following examples are intended to illustrate the principles discussed above. [Several examples given.] . . .

THREE-PART TEST—Part Three: Is the Institution Fully and Effectively Accommodating the Interests and Abilities of the Underrepresented Sex?

Under part three of the three-part test (part three) OCR determines whether an institution is fully and effectively accommodating the interests and abilities of its students who are members of the underrepresented sex—including students who are admitted to the institution though not yet enrolled. . . .

In making this determination, OCR will consider whether there is (a) unmet interest in a particular sport; (b) sufficient ability to sustain a team in the sport; and (c) a reasonable expectation of competition for the team. If all three conditions are present OCR will find that an institution has not fully and effectively accommodated the interests and abilities of the underrepresented sex.

If an institution has recently eliminated a viable team from the intercollegiate program, OCR will find that there is sufficient interest, ability, and available competition to sustain an intercollegiate team in that sport unless an institution can provide strong evidence that interest, ability, or available competition no longer exists.

a) Is there sufficient unmet interest to support an intercollegiate team?

* * *

An institution may evaluate its athletic program to assess the athletic interest of its students of the underrepresented sex using nondiscriminatory methods of its choosing. Accordingly, institutions have flexibility in choosing a nondiscriminatory method of determining athletic interests and abilities provided they meet certain requirements. See 44 *Fed. Reg.* at 71417. These assessments may use straightforward and inexpensive techniques, such as a student questionnaire or an open forum, to identify students' interests and abilities. Thus, while OCR expects that an institution's assessment should reach a wide audience of students and should be open-ended regarding the sports students can express interest in, OCR does not require elaborate scientific validation of assessments.

An institution's evaluation of interest should be done periodically so that the institution can identify in a timely and responsive manner any developing interests and abilities of the underrepresented sex. The evaluation should also take into account sports played in the high schools and communities from which the institution draws its students both as an indication of possible interest on campus and to permit the institution to plan to meet the interests of admitted students of the underrepresented sex.

b) Is there sufficient ability to sustain an intercollegiate team?

Second, OCR will determine whether there is sufficient ability among interested students of the underrepresented sex to sustain an intercollegiate team. OCR will examine indications of ability such as:

- the athletic experience and accomplishments—in interscholastic, club or intramural competition—of students and admitted students interested in playing the sport;

- opinions of coaches, administrators, and athletes at the institution regarding whether interested students and admitted students have the potential to sustain a varsity team; and

- if the team has previously competed at the club or intramural level, whether the competitive experience of the team indicates that it has the potential to sustain an intercollegiate team.

Neither a poor competitive record nor the inability of interested students or admitted students to play at the same level of competition engaged in by the institution's other athletes is conclusive evidence of lack of ability. It is sufficient that interested students and admitted students have the potential to sustain an intercollegiate team.

c) Is there a reasonable expectation of competition for the team?

Finally, OCR determines whether there is a reasonable expectation of intercollegiate competition for a particular sport in the institution's normal competitive region. In evaluating available competition, OCR will look at available competitive opportunities in the geographic area in which the institution's athletes primarily compete, including:

- competitive opportunities offered by other schools against which the institution competes; and
- competitive opportunities offered by other schools in the institution's geographic area, including those offered by schools against which the institution does not now compete.

Under the Policy Interpretation, the institution may also be required to actively encourage the development of intercollegiate competition for a sport for members of the underrepresented sex when overall athletic opportunities within its competitive region have been historically limited for members of that sex.

* * *

CIVIL RIGHTS ACT OF 1964

Section 201 (42 U.S.C. § 2000a). Prohibition against discrimination or segregation in places of public accommodation

(a) **Equal access.** All Persons shall be entitled to the full and equal enjoyment of the goods, services, facilities, privileges, advantages, and accommodations of any place of public accommodation, as defined in this section, without discrimination or segregation on the ground of race, color, religion, or national origin.

(b) * * * Each of the following establishments which serves the public is a place of public accommodation within the meaning of this subchapter if its operations affect commerce, or if discrimination or segregation by it is supported by State action: * * * (3) any motion picture house, theater, concert hall, sports arena, stadium or other place of exhibition or entertainment; and (4) any establishment (A)(i) which is physically located within the premises of any establishment otherwise covered by this subsection, or (ii) within the premises of which is physically located any such covered establishment, and (B) which holds itself out as serving the patrons of such covered establishment.

* * *

Section 204 (42 U.S.C. § 2000d). Prohibition against exclusion from participation in, denial of benefits of, and discrimination under federally assisted programs on ground of race, color, or national origin

No person in the United States shall, on the ground of race, color, or national origin, be excluded from participation in, be denied the benefits of, or be subjected to discrimination under any program or activity receiving Federal financial assistance.

———

AMERICANS WITH DISABILITIES ACT OF 1990

Section 2 (42 U.S.C. § 12102). Findings and Purposes

The Congress finds that: * * * (5) individuals with disabilities continually encounter various forms of discrimination, including outright intentional exclusion, the discriminatory effects of architectural, transportation, and communication barriers, overprotective rules and policies, failure to make modifications to existing facilities and practices, exclusionary qualification standards and criteria, segregation, and relegation to lesser services, programs, activities, benefits, jobs, or other opportunities.

Section 3 (42 U.S.C. § 12103). Definitions

As used in this Act: * * * (2) Disability. The terms "disability" means with respect to an individual—

(A) a physical or mental impairment that substantially limits one or more of the major life activities of such individual;

(B) a record of such an impairment; or

(C) being regarded as having such an impairment.

TITLE I. EMPLOYMENT

Section 101 (42 U.S.C. § 12111). Definitions

As used in this Title: * * * (6) Illegal use of drugs.

(A) In general. The term "illegal use of drugs" means the use of drugs, the possession or distribution of which is unlawful under the Controlled Substances Act. Such term does not include the use of a drug taken under supervision by a licensed health care professional, or other uses authorized by the Controlled Substances Act or other provisions of Federal law.

(B) Drugs. The term "drug" means a controlled substance, as defined in schedules I through V of section 202 of the Controlled Substances Act.

Section 102 (42 U.S.C. § 12112). Discrimination

(a) General Rule. No covered entity shall discriminate against a qualified individual with a disability because of the disability of such individual in regard to job application procedures, the hiring, advancement, or discharge of employees, employee compensation, job training, and other terms, conditions, and privileges of employment.

Section 103 (42 U.S.C. § 12113). Defenses

(a) In general. It may be a defense to a charge of discrimination under this Act that an alleged application of qualification standards, tests, or selection criteria that screen out or tend to screen out or otherwise deny a job or benefit to an individual with a disability has been shown to be job related and consistent with business necessity, and such performance cannot be accomplished by reasonable accommodation, as required under this Title.

Section 104 (42 U.S.C. § 12114). Illegal Use of Drugs and Alcohol

(a) Qualified individual with a disability. For purposes of this Title, the term "qualified individual with a disability" shall not include any employee or applicant who is currently engaging in the illegal use of drugs, when the covered entity acts on the basis of such use.

(b) Rules of construction. Nothing in subsection (a) of this section shall be construed to exclude as a qualified individual with a disability an individual who—

(1) has successfully completed a supervised drug rehabilitation program and is no longer engaging in the illegal use of drugs, or has otherwise been rehabilitated successfully and is no longer engaging in such use;

(2) is participating in a supervised rehabilitation program and is no longer engaging in such use; or

(3) is erroneously regarded as engaging in such use, but is not engaging in such use; except that it shall not be a violation of this Act for a covered entity to adopt or administer reasonable policies or procedures, including but not limited to drug testing, designed to ensure that an individual described in paragraph (1) or (2) is no longer engaging in the illegal use of drugs.

(c) Authority of covered entity. A covered entity—

(1) may prohibit the illegal use of drugs and the use of alcohol at the workplace by all employees;

(2) may require that the employees shall not be under the influence of alcohol or be engaging in the illegal use of drugs at the workplace;

(3) may require that employees behave in conformance with the requirements established under the Drug–Free Workplace Act of 1988; and

(4) may hold an employee who engages in the illegal use of drugs or who is an alcoholic to the same qualification standards for employment or job performance and behavior that such entity holds other employees, even if any unsatisfactory performance or behavior is related to the drug use or alcoholism of such employee; * * *.

(d) Drug testing.

(1) In general. [A] test to determine the illegal use of drugs shall not be considered a medical examination [prohibited by § 102(d)].

(2) Construction. Nothing in this Title shall be construed to encourage, prohibit, or authorize the conducting of drug testing for the illegal use of drugs by job applicants or employees or making employment decisions based on such test results.

* * *

TITLE III. PUBLIC ACCOMMODATIONS AND SERVICES OPERATED BY PRIVATE ENTITIES

Section 302 (42 U.S.C. § 12182). Prohibition of discrimination by public accommodations

(a) General rule

No individual shall be discriminated against on the basis of disability in the full and equal enjoyment of the goods, services, facilities, privileges, advantages, or accommodations of any place of public accommodation by any person who owns, leases (or leases to), or operates a place of public accommodation.

———

THE TED STEVENS AMATEUR SPORTS ACT OF 1998

(Replacing the Amateur Sports Act of 1978)

Subchapter I—CORPORATION

36 U.S.C.A. § 220501.   Title and Definitions

(b) Definitions.—For purposes of this chapter—

(1) "amateur athlete" means an athlete who meets the eligibility standards established by the national governing body or paralympic sports organization for the sport in which the athlete competes.

(3) "amateur sports organization" means a not-for-profit corporation, association, or other group organized in the United States that sponsors or arranges an amateur athletic competition.

(4) "corporation" means the United States Olympic Committee.

(8) "sanction" means a certificate of approval issued by a national governing body.

36 U.S.C.A. § 220503. Purposes

The purposes of the corporation are—

(1) to establish national goals for amateur athletic activities and encourage the attainment of those goals;

(2) to coordinate and develop amateur athletic activity in the United States, directly related to international amateur athletic competition, to foster productive working relationships among sports-related organizations;

(3) to exercise exclusive jurisdiction, directly or through constituent members of committees, over—(A) all matters pertaining to United States participation in the Olympic Games, the Paralympic Games, and the Pan–American Games, including representation of the United States in the games; and (B) the organization of the Olympic Games, the Paralympic Games, and the Pan–American Games when held in the United States;

(4) to obtain for the United States, directly or by delegation to the appropriate national governing body, the most competent amateur representation possible in each event of the Olympic Games, the Paralympic Games, and Pan-American Games;

(5) to promote and support amateur athletic activities involving the United States and foreign nations; . . . .

36 U.S.C.A. § 220505. Powers

(c) Powers related to amateur athletics and the Olympic Games.— The corporation may—

(1) serve as the coordinating body for amateur athletic activity in the United States directly related to international amateur athletic competition;

(2) represent the United States as its national Olympic committee in relations with the International Olympic Committee and the Pan–American Sports Organization and as its national Paralympic committee in relations with the International Paralympic Committee;

(3) organize, finance, and control the representation of the United States in the competitions and events of the Olympic Games, the Paralympic Games, and the Pan–American Games, and obtain, directly or by delegation to the appropriate national governing body, amateur representation for those games;

(4) recognize eligible amateur sports organizations as national governing bodies for any sport that is included on the program of the Olympic Games or the Pan–American Games, or as paralympic sports organizations for any sport that is included on the program of the Paralympic Games;

(5) facilitate, through orderly and effective administrative procedures, the resolution of conflicts or disputes that involve any of its members and any amateur athlete, coach, trainer, manager, administrator, official, national governing body, or amateur sports organization and that arise in connection with their eligibility for and participation in the Olympic Games, the Paralympic Games, the Pan–American Games, world championship competition, the Pan–American world championship competition, or other protected competition as defined in the constitution and bylaws of the corporation; and

(6) provide financial assistance to any organization or association, except a corporation organized for profit, in furtherance of the purposes of the corporation.

36 U.S.C.A. § 220506.   Exclusive right to name, seals, emblems, and badges

(a) Exclusive right of corporation.—Except as provided in subsection (d) of this section, the corporation has the exclusive right to use—

(1) the name "United States Olympic Committee";

(2) the symbol of the International Olympic Committee, consisting of 5 interlocking rings, the symbol of the International Paralympic Committee, consisting of 3 TaiGeuks, or the symbol of the Pan–American Sports Organization, consisting of a torch surrounded by concentric rings;

(3) the emblem of the corporation, consisting of an escutcheon having a blue chief and vertically extending red and white bars on the base with 5 interlocking rings displayed on the chief; and

(4) the words "Olympic", "Olympiad", "Citius Altius Fortius", "Paralympic", "Paralympiad", "Pan–American", "America Espirito Sport Fraternite", or any combination of those words.

(b) Contributors and suppliers.—The corporation may authorize contributors and suppliers of goods or services to use the trade name of the corporation or any trademark, symbol, insignia, or emblem of the International Olympic Committee, International Paralympic Committee, the Pan–American Sports Organization, or of the corporation to advertise that the contributions, goods, or services were donated or supplied to, or approved, selected, or used by, the corporation, the United States Olympic team, the Paralympic team, the Pan–American team, or team members.

(c) Civil action for unauthorized use.—Except as provided in subsection (d) of this section, the corporation may file a civil action against a person for the remedies provided in the Act of July 5, 1946 (15 U.S.C. § 1051 et seq.) (popularly known as the Trademark Act of 1946) if the person, without the consent of the corporation, uses for the purpose of trade, to induce the sale of any goods or services, or to promote any theatrical exhibition, athletic performance, or competition [any of the symbols, emblems, or words protected by this section, or any mark falsely representing association with any of the Olympic organizations].

(d) Pre-existing and geographic reference rights— . . . (3) Use of the word "Olympic" to identify a business or goods or services is permitted by this section where—(A) such use is not combined with any of the intellectual properties referenced in subsection (a) or (c) of this section; (B) it is evident from the circumstances that such use of the word "Olympic" refers to the naturally occurring mountains or geographical region of the same name that were named prior to February 6, 1998, and not to the corporation or any Olympic activity; and (C) such business, goods, or services are operated, sold, and marketed in the State of Washington west of the Cascade Mountain range and operations, sales, and marketing outside of this area are not substantial.

36 U.S.C.A. § 220509.   Resolution of disputes

(a) General.—The corporation shall establish and maintain provisions in its constitution and bylaws for the swift and equitable resolution of disputes involving any of its members and relating to the opportunity of an amateur athlete, coach, trainer, manager, administrator, or official to participate in the Olympic Games, the Paralympic Games, the Pan–American Games, world championship competition, or other protected competition as defined in the constitution and bylaws of the corporation. In any lawsuit relating to the resolution of a dispute involving the opportunity of an amateur athlete to participate in the Olympic Games, the Paralympic Games, or the Pan–American Games, a court shall not grant injunctive relief against the corporation within 21 days before the beginning of such games if the corporation, after consultation with the chair of the Athletes' Advisory Council, has provided a sworn statement in writing executed by an officer of the corporation to such court that its constitution and bylaws cannot provide for the resolution of such dispute prior to the beginning of such games.

Subchapter II—NATIONAL GOVERNING BODIES

36 U.S.C.A. § 220521.   Recognition of amateur sports organizations as national governing bodies

(a) General authority.—For any sport which is included on the program of the Olympic Games, the Paralympic Games, or the Pan–American Games, the corporation is authorized to recognize as a national governing body (in the case of a sport on the program of the Olympic Games or Pan–American Games) or as a paralympic sports organization (in the case of a sport on the program of the Paralympic Games for which a national governing body has not been designated under section

220522(b)) an amateur sports organization which files an application and is eligible for such recognition in accordance with the provisions of subsection (a) or (b) of section 220522. The corporation may recognize only one national governing body for each sport for which an application is made and approved. . . .

(c) Recommendation to international sports federation.—Within 61 days after recognizing an organization as a national governing body, the corporation shall recommend and support in any appropriate manner the national governing body to the appropriate international sports federation as the representative of the United States for that sport.

(d) Review of recognition.—The corporation may review all matters related to the continued recognition of an organization as a national governing body and may take action it considers appropriate, including placing conditions on the continued recognition.

36 U.S.C.A. § 220523.   Authority of national governing bodies

(a) Authority.—For the sport that it governs, a national governing body may—

(1) represent the United States in the appropriate international sports federation;

(2) establish national goals and encourage the attainment of those goals;

(3) serve as the coordinating body for amateur athletic activity in the United States;

(4) exercise jurisdiction over international amateur athletic activities and sanction international amateur athletic competition held in the United States and sanction the sponsorship of international amateur athletic competition held outside the United States;

(5) conduct amateur athletic competition, including national championships, and international amateur athletic competition in the United States, and establish procedures for determining eligibility standards for participation in competition, except for amateur athletic competition specified in section 220526 of this title;

(6) recommend to the corporation individuals and teams to represent the United States in the Olympic Games, the Paralympic Games, and the Pan–American Games; and

(7) designate individuals and teams to represent the United States in international amateur athletic competition (other than the Olympic Games, the Paralympic Games, and the Pan–American Games) and certify, in accordance with applicable international rules, the amateur eligibility of those individuals and teams.

(b) Replacement of national governing body pursuant to arbitration.—A national governing body may not exercise any authority under subsection (a) of this section for a particular sport after another amateur sports organization has been declared (in accordance with binding arbitration proceedings prescribed by the organic documents of the corporation) entitled to replace that national governing body as the member of the corporation for that sport.

36 U.S.C.A. § 220524. General duties of national governing bodies

For the sport that it governs, a national governing body shall—

(1) develop interest and participation throughout the United States and be responsible to the persons and amateur sports organizations it represents;

(2) minimize, through coordination with other amateur sports organizations, conflicts in the scheduling of all practices and competitions;

(3) keep amateur athletes informed of policy matters and reasonably reflect the views of the athletes in its policy decisions;

(4) disseminate and distribute to amateur athletes, coaches, trainers, managers, administrators, and officials in a timely manner the applicable rules and any changes to such rules of the national governing body, the corporation, the appropriate international sports federation, the International Olympic Committee, the International Paralympic Committee, and the Pan–American Sports Organization;

(5) allow an amateur athlete to compete in any international amateur athletic competition conducted by any amateur sports organization or person, unless the national governing body establishes that its denial is based on evidence that the organization or person conducting the competition does not meet the requirements stated in section 220525 of this title;

(6) provide equitable support and encouragement for participation by women where separate programs for male and female athletes are conducted on a national basis;

(7) encourage and support amateur athletic sports programs for individuals with disabilities and the participation of individuals with disabilities in amateur athletic activity, including, where feasible, the expansion of opportunities for meaningful participation by individuals with disabilities in programs of athletic competition for able-bodied individuals;

(8) provide and coordinate technical information on physical training, equipment design, coaching, and performance analysis; and

(9) encourage and support research, development, and dissemination of information in the areas of sports medicine and sports safety.

36 U.S.C.A. § 220525. Granting sanctions for amateur athletic competitions

(a) Prompt review and decision.—For the sport that it governs, a national governing body promptly shall—

(1) review a request by an amateur sports organization or person for a sanction to hold an international amateur athletic competition in the United States or to sponsor United States amateur athletes to compete in international amateur athletic competition outside the United States; and

(2) grant the sanction if—(A) the national governing body does not decide by clear and convincing evidence that holding or sponsoring an international amateur athletic competition would be detrimental to the best interest of the sport; and (B) the requirements of subsection (b) of this section are met.

(b) Requirements.—An amateur sports organization or person may be granted a sanction under this section only if the organization or person meets the following requirements: [lengthy list of requirements designed to assure that the event is financially solvent, the interests and safety of the athletes are protected, and the event is operated in a competent manner].

36 U.S.C.A. § 220527. Complaints against national governing bodies

(a) General.—(1) An amateur sports organization or person that belongs to or is eligible to belong to a national governing body may seek to compel the national governing body to comply with sections 220522, 220524, and 220525 of this title by filing a written complaint with the corporation. A copy of the complaint shall be served on the national governing body. (2) The corporation shall establish procedures for the filing and disposition of complaints under this section.

(d) Disposition of complaint.—

(1) If the corporation decides, as a result of the hearing, that the national governing body is complying ..., it shall so notify the complainant and the national governing body.

(2) If the corporation decides, as a result of the hearing, that the national governing body is not complying ..., it shall—(A) place the national governing body on probation for a specified period of time, not to exceed 180 days, which the corporation considers necessary to enable the national governing body to comply with those sections; or (B) revoke the recognition of the national governing body.

(3) If the corporation places a national governing body on probation under paragraph (2) of this subsection, it may extend the probationary period if the national governing body has proven by clear and convincing evidence that, through no fault of its own, it needs additional time to comply.... If, at the end of the period allowed by the corporation, the national governing body has not complied with those sections, the corporation shall revoke the recognition of the national governing body.

36 U.S.C.A. § 220528. Applications to replace an incumbent national governing body

(a) General.—An amateur sports organization may seek to replace an incumbent as the national governing body for a particular sport by filing a written application for recognition with the corporation.

(b) Establishment of procedures.—The corporation shall establish procedures for the filing and disposition of applications under this section. If 2 or more organizations file applications for the same sport, the applications shall be considered in a single proceeding.

(e) Standards for granting applications.—In the hearing, the applicant must establish by a preponderance of the evidence that—

(1) it meets the criteria for recognition as a national governing body under section 220522 of this title; and

(2)(A) the national governing body does not meet the criteria of section 220522, 220524, or 220525 of this title; or (B) the applicant more adequately meets the criteria of section 220522 of this title, is capable of more adequately meeting the criteria of sections 220524 and 220525 of this title, and provides or is capable of providing a more effective national program of competition than the national governing body in the sport for which it seeks recognition.

(f) Disposition of applications.—Within 30 days after the close of the hearing required by this section, the corporation shall—

(1) uphold the right of the national governing body to continue as the national governing body for its sport;

(2) revoke the recognition of the national governing body and declare a vacancy in the national governing body for that sport;

(3) revoke the recognition of the national governing body and recognize the applicant as the national governing body; or

(4) place the national governing body on probation for a period not exceeding 180 days, pending the compliance of the national governing body. . . .

36 U.S.C.A. § 220529. Arbitration of corporation determinations

(a) Right to review.—A party aggrieved by a determination of the corporation under section 220527 or 220528 of this title may obtain review by any regional office of the American Arbitration Association.

(d) Binding nature of decision.—Final decision of the arbitrators is binding on the parties if the award is not inconsistent with the constitution and bylaws of the corporation.

———

PROFESSIONAL BOXING SAFETY ACT OF 1996

(as amended by the Muhammad Ali Boxing Reform Act of 2000)

15 U.S.C. § 6302.   Purposes

The purposes of this chapter are—

(1) to improve and expand the system of safety precautions that protects the welfare of professional boxers; and

(2) to assist State boxing commissions to provide proper oversight for the professional boxing industry in the United States.

15 U.S.C. § 6303.   Boxing matches in States without boxing commissions

(a) No person may arrange, promote, organize, produce, or fight in a professional boxing match held in a State that does not have a boxing commission unless the match is supervised by a boxing commission from another State and subject to the most recent version of the recommended regulatory guidelines certified and published by the Association of Boxing Commissions as well as any additional relevant professional boxing regulations and requirements of such other State.

15 U.S.C. § 6304.   Safety standards

No person may arrange, promote, organize, produce, or fight in a professional boxing match without meeting each of the following requirements or an alternative requirement in effect under regulations of a boxing commission that provides equivalent protection of the health and safety of boxers:

(1) A physical examination of each boxer by a physician certifying whether or not the boxer is physically fit to safety compete, copies of which must be provided to the boxing commission.

(2) Except as otherwise expressly provided under regulation of a boxing commission promulgated subsequent to the enactment of this Act, an ambulance or medical personnel with appropriate resuscitation equipment continuously present on site.

(3) A physician continuously present at ringside.

(4) Health insurance for each boxer to provide medical coverage for any injuries sustained in the match.

15 U.S.C. § 6305.   Registration

(a) Requirements

Each boxer shall register with—

(1) the boxing commission of the State in which such boxer resides; or

(2) in the case of a boxer who is a resident of a foreign country, or a State in which there is no boxing commission, the boxing commission of any State that has such a commission.

(b) Identification card

(1) Issuance

A boxing commission shall issue to each professional boxer who registers in accordance with subsection (a) of this section, an identification card that contains each of the following:

(A) A recent photograph of the boxer.

(B) The social security number of the boxer (or, in the case of a foreign boxer, any similar citizen identification number or professional boxer number from the country of residence of the boxer).

(C) A personal identification number assigned to the boxer by a boxing registry.

(2) Renewal

Each professional boxer shall renew his or her identification card at least once every 2 years.

(3) Presentation

Each professional boxer shall present his or her identification card to the appropriate boxing commission not later than the time of the weigh-in for a professional boxing match.

(c) Health and safety concerns

It is the sense of Congress that a boxing commission should, upon issuing an identification card . . ., make a health and safety disclosure to that boxer as that commission considers appropriate. The health and safety disclosure should include the health and safety risks associated with boxing, and, in particular, the risk and frequency of brain injury and the advisability that a boxer periodically undergo medical procedures designed to detect brain injury.

15 U.S.C. § 6306.   Review

(a) Procedures

Each boxing commission shall establish each of the following procedures:

(1) Procedures to evaluate the professional records and physician's certification of each boxer participating in a professional boxing match in the State, and to deny authorization for a boxer to fight where appropriate.

(2) Procedures to ensure that, except as provided in subsection (b) of this section, no boxer is permitted to box while under suspension from any boxing commission due to—

(A) a recent knockout or series of consecutive losses;

(B) an injury, requirement for a medical procedure, or physician denial of certification;

(C) failure of a drug test;

(D) the use of false aliases, or falsifying, or attempting to falsify, official identification cards or documents; or

(E) unsportsmanlike conduct or other inappropriate behavior inconsistent with generally accepted methods of competition in a professional boxing match.

(3) Procedures to review a suspension where appealed by a boxer, licensee, manager, matchmaker, promoter, or other boxing service provider, including an opportunity for [the appellant] to present contradictory evidence.

(4) Procedures to revoke a suspension where a boxer—

(A) was suspended under subparagraph (A) or (B) of paragraph (2) of this subsection, and has furnished further proof of a sufficiently improved medical or physical condition; or

(B) furnishes proof under subparagraph (C) or (D) of paragraph (2) that a suspension was not, or is no longer, merited by the facts.

(b) Suspension in another State

A boxing commission may allow a boxer who is under suspension in any State to participate in a professional boxing match—

(1) for any reason other than those listed in subsection (a) of this section if such commission notifies in writing and consults with the designated official of the suspending State's boxing commission prior to the grant of approval for such individual to participate in that professional boxing match; or

(2) if the boxer appeals to the Association of Boxing Commissions, and the Association of Boxing Commissions determines that the suspension of such boxer was without sufficient grounds, for an improper purpose, or not related to the health and safety of the boxer or the purposes of this chapter.

15 U.S.C. § 6307.   Reporting

Not later than 48 business hours after the conclusion of a professional boxing match, the supervising boxing commission shall report the results of such boxing match and any related suspensions to each boxer registry.

15 U.S.C. § 6307a.   Contract requirements

Within 2 years after May 26, 2000, the Association of Boxing Commissions (ABC) shall develop and shall approve by a vote of no less than a majority of its member State boxing commissioners, guidelines for minimum contractual provisions that should be included in bout agreements and boxing contracts. It is the sense of the Congress that State boxing commissions should follow these ABC guidelines.

15 U.S.C. § 6307b. Protection from coercive contracts

(a) General rule

(1)(A) A contract provision shall be considered to be in restraint of trade, contrary to public policy, and unenforceable against any boxer to the extent that it—

(i) is a coercive provision described in subparagraph (B) and is for a period greater than 12 months; or

(ii) is a coercive provision described in subparagraph (B) and the other boxer under contract to the promoter came under that contract pursuant to a coercive provision described in subparagraph (B).

(B) A coercive provision described in this subparagraph is a contract provision that grants any rights between a boxer and a promoter, or between promoters with respect to a boxer, if the boxer is required to grant such rights, or a boxer's promoter is required to grant such rights with respect to a boxer to another promoter, as a condition precedent to the boxer's participation in a professional boxing match against another boxer who is under contract to the promoter.

(2) This subsection shall only apply to contracts entered into after May 26, 2000.

(3) No subsequent contract provision extending any rights or compensation covered in paragraph (1) shall be enforceable against a boxer if the effective date of the contract containing such provision is earlier than 3 months before the expiration of the relevant time period set forth in paragraph (1).

(b) Promotional rights under mandatory bout contracts.

No boxing service provider may require a boxer to grant any future promotional rights as a requirement of competing in a professional boxing match that is a mandatory bout under the rules of a sanctioning organization.

(c) Protection from coercive contracts with broadcasters.

Subsection (a) of this section applies to any contract between a commercial broadcaster and a boxer, or granting any rights with respect to that boxer, involving a broadcast in or affecting interstate commerce, regardless of the broadcast medium. For the purpose of this subsection, any reference in subsection (a)(1)(B) of this section to ''promoter'' shall be considered a reference to ''commercial broadcaster''.

15 U.S.C. § 6307c. Sanctioning Organizations

(a) Objective criteria. Within 2 years after May 26, 2000, the Association of Boxing Commissions shall develop and shall approve by a vote of no less than a majority of its member State boxing commissioners, guidelines for objective and consistent written criteria for the ratings of professional boxers. It is the sense of Congress that sanctioning bodies and State boxing commissions should follow these ABC guidelines.

(c) Notification of change in rating. A sanctioning organization shall not be entitled to receive any compensation, directly or indirectly, in connection with a boxing match, until, with respect to a change in the rating of a boxer previously rated by such organization in the top 10 boxers, the organization—(1) posts a copy, within 7 days of such change, on its Internet website or home page, if any, including an explanation of such change, for a period of not less than 30 days; and (2) provides a copy of the rating change and explanation to an association to which at least a majority of the State boxing commissions belong.

(d) Public disclosure

1.   Federal Trade Commission filing. A sanctioning organization shall not be entitled to receive any compensation, directly or indirectly, in connection with a boxing match unless, not later than January 31 of each year, it submits to the Federal Trade Commission and to the ABC—(A) a complete description of the organization's ratings criteria, policies, and general sanctioning fee schedule; (B) the bylaws of the organization; (C) the appeals procedure of the organization for a boxer's rating; and (D) a list and business address of the organization's officials who vote on the ratings of boxers.

15 U.S.C. § 6307d.   Required disclosures to state boxing commissions by sanctioning organizations

A sanctioning organization shall not be entitled to receive any compensation, directly or indirectly, in connection with a boxing match until it provides to the boxing commission responsible for regulating the match in a State a statement of—(1) all charges, fees, and costs the organization will assess any boxer participating in that match; (2) all payments, benefits, complimentary benefits, and fees the organization will receive for its affiliation with the event, from the promoter, host of the event, and all other sources; and (3) such additional information as the commission may require.

15 U.S.C. § 6307e.   Required disclosures for promoters

(a) Disclosures to the boxing commissions

A promoter shall not be entitled to receive any compensation directly or indirectly in connection with a boxing match until it provides to the boxing commission responsible for regulating the match in a State a statement of—

(1) a copy of any agreement in writing to which the promoter is a party with any boxer participating in the match;

(2) a statement made under penalty of perjury that there are no other agreements, written or oral, between the promoter and the boxer with respect to that match; and

(3)(A) all fees, charges, and expenses that will be assessed by or through the promoter on the boxer pertaining to the event, including any portion of the boxer's purse that the promoter will receive, and training expenses;

(B) all payments, gifts, or benefits the promoter is providing to any sanctioning organization affiliated with the event; and

(C) any reduction in a boxer's purse contrary to a previous agreement between the promoter and the boxer or a purse bid held for the event.

(b) Disclosures to the boxer

A promoter shall not be entitled to receive any compensation directly or indirectly in connection with a boxing match until it provides to the boxer it promotes—(1) the amounts of any compensation or consideration that a promoter has contracted to receive from such match; (2) all fees, charges, and expenses that will be assessed by or through the promoter on the boxer pertaining to the event, including any portion of the boxer's purse that the promoter will receive, and training expenses; and (3) any reduction in a boxer's purse contrary to a previous agreement between the promoter and the boxer or a purse bid held for the event.

(c) Information to be available to State Attorney General

A promoter shall make information required to be disclosed under this section available to the chief law enforcement officer of the State in which the match is to be held upon request of such officer.

15 U.S.C. § 6307f.   Required disclosures for judges and referees

A judge or referee shall not be entitled to receive any compensation, directly or indirectly, in connection with a boxing match until it provides to the boxing commission responsible for regulating the match in a State a statement of all consideration, including reimbursement for expenses, that will be received from any source for participation in the match.

15 U.S.C. § 6308.   Conflicts of interest

(a) Regulatory personnel. No member or employee of a boxing commission, no person who administers or enforces State boxing laws, and no member of the Association of Boxing Commissions may belong to, contract with, or receive any compensation from, any person who sanctions, arranges, or promotes professional boxing matches or who otherwise has a financial interest in an active boxer currently registered with a boxer registry. For purposes of this section, the term "compensation" does not include funds held in escrow for payment to another person in connection with a professional boxing match. The prohibition set forth in this section shall not apply to any contract entered into, or any reasonable compensation received, by a boxing commission to supervise a professional boxing match in another State as described in section 6303 of title.

(b) Firewall between promoters and managers.

(1) In general—It is unlawful for—(A) a promoter to have a direct or indirect financial interest in the promotion of a boxer; or (B) a manager—(i) to have a direct or indirect financial interest in the promotion of a boxer; or (ii) to be employed by or receive compensation or other benefits from a promoter, except for amounts received as compensation under the manager's contract with the boxer.

(c) Sanctioning organization.

(1) Prohibition on receipts— ... [N]o officer or employee of a sanctioning organization may receive any compensation, gift, or benefit, directly or indirectly, form a promoter, boxer, or manager.

15 U.S.C. § 6309.   Enforcement

(a) Injunctions

Whenever the Attorney General of the United States has reasonable cause to believe that a person is engaged in a violation of this chapter, the Attorney General may bring a civil action in the appropriate district court of the United States requesting such relief, including a permanent or temporary injunction, restraining order, or other order, against the person, as the Attorney General determines to be necessary to restrain the person from continuing to engage in, sanction, promote, or otherwise participate in a professional boxing match in violation of this chapter.

(b) Criminal penalties

(1) **Managers, promoters, matchmakers, and licensees—** Any manager, promoter, matchmaker, and licensee who knowingly violates, or coerces or causes any other person to violate, any provision of this chapter, other than sections 6307a–h of this title, shall, upon conviction, be imprisoned for not more than 1 year or fined not more than $20,000, or both.

(2) **Violation of antiexploitation, sanctioning organization, or disclosure provisions**—Any person who knowingly violates any provision of sections 6307a–h of this title shall, upon conviction, be imprisoned for not more than 1 year or fined not more than—(A) $100,000; and (B) if a violation occurs in connection with a professional boxing match the gross revenues for which exceed $2,000,000, an additional amount which bears the same ratio to $100,000 as the amount such revenues compared to $2,000,000, or both.

(3) **Conflict of interest**—Any member or employee of a boxing commission, any person who administers or enforces State

boxing laws, and any member of the Association of Boxing Commissions who knowingly violates section 6308 of this title shall, upon conviction, be imprisoned for not more than 1 year or fined not more than $20,000, or both.

(4) Boxers—Any boxer who knowingly violates any provision of this chapter shall, upon conviction, be fined not more than $1,000.

(c) Actions by States—Whenever the chief law enforcement officer of any State has reason to believe that a person or organization is engaging in practices which violate any requirement of this chapter, the State, as parens patriae, may bring a civil action on behalf of its residents in an appropriate district court of the United States—(1) to enjoin the holding of any professional boxing match which the practice involves; (2) to enforce compliance with this chapter; (3) to obtain the fines provided under subsection (b) of this section or appropriate restitution; or (4) to obtain such other relief as the court may deem appropriate.

(d) Private right of action—Any boxer who suffers economic injury as a result of a violation of any provisions of this chapter may bring an action in the appropriate Federal or State court and recover the damages suffered, court costs, and reasonable attorneys fees and expenses.

15 U.S.C. § 6310. Notification of supervising boxing commission

Each promoter who intends to hold a professional boxing match in a State that does not have a boxing commission shall, not later than 14 days before the intended date of that match, provide written notification to the supervising boxing commission designated under section 6303 of this title. Such notification shall contain each of the following:

(1) Assurances that, with respect to that professional boxing match, all applicable requirements of this chapter will be met.

(2) The name of any person who, at the time of the submission of the notification—

(A) is under suspension from a boxing commission; and

(B) will be involved in organizing or participating in the event.

(3) For any individual listed under paragraph (2), the identify of the boxing commission that issued the suspension described in paragraph (2)(A).

15 U.S.C. § 6313. Relationship with State law

Nothing in this chapter shall prohibit a State from adopting or enforcing supplemental or more stringent laws or regulations not inconsistent with this chapter, or criminal, civil, or administrative fines for violations of such laws or regulations.

B. LEAGUE CONSTITUTIONS

MAJOR LEAGUE BASEBALL CONSTITUTION

(adopted in 2000, replacing and modeled on the Major League Agreement in effect from 1921 to 2000)

Article II—THE COMMISSIONER

Sec. 2. The functions of the Commissioner shall include:

(a) To serve as Chief Executive Officer of Major League Baseball. The Commissioner shall also have executive responsibility for labor relations and serve as Chairman, or shall designate a Chairman, of such committees as the Commissioner shall name or the Major League Clubs shall from time to time determine by resolution.

(b) To investigate, either upon complaint or upon the Commissioner's own initiative, any act, transaction or practice charged, alleged or suspected to be not in the best interests of the national game of Baseball, with authority to summon persons and to order the production of documents, and, in case of refusal to appear or produce, to impose such penalties as are hereinafter provided.

(c) To Determine, after investigation, what preventive, remedial or punitive action is appropriate in the premises, and to take such action either against Major Leagues, Major League Clubs or individuals, as the case may be.

(d) From time to time, to formulate and to announce the rules of procedure to be observed by the Commissioner and all other parties in connection with the discharge of the Commissioner's duties. Such rules shall always recognize the right of any party in interest to appear before the Commissioner and to be heard.

(e) To appoint a President of each League to perform such duties as the Commissioner may direct.

(f) To make decisions, or to designate an officer of the Commissioner's Office to make decisions, regarding on-field discipline, playing rule interpretations, game protests and any other matter within the responsibility of the League Presidents prior to 2000.

Sec. 3. In the case of conduct by Major League Clubs, owners, officers, employees or players that is deemed by the Commissioner not to be in the best interests of Baseball, punitive action by the Commissioner for each offense may include any one or more of the following: (a) a reprimand; (b) deprivation of a Major League Club of representation in Major League Meetings; (c) suspension or removal of any owner, officer or employee of a Major League Club; (d) temporary or permanent ineligibility of a player; and (e) a fine, not to exceed $2,000,000 in the case of a Major League Club, not to exceed $500,000 in the case of an owner, officer or employee, and not to exceed $500 in the case of a player; (f) loss of the benefit of any or all of the Major League Rules, including but not limited to the denial or transfer of player selection rights provided by Major League Rules 4 and 5; and (g) such other actions as the Commissioner may deem appropriate.

Sec. 4 Notwithstanding the provisions of Section 2, above, the Commissioner shall take no action in the best interests of Baseball that requires the Clubs to take, or refrain from taking, action (by vote, agreement or otherwise) on any of the matters requiring a vote of the Clubs at a Major League Meeting that are set forth in Article II, Section 9 or in Article V, Section 2(a) or (b); provided, however, that nothing in this Section 4 shall limit the Commissioner's authority to act on any matter that involves the integrity of, or public confidence in, the national game of Baseball. Integrity shall include without limitation, as determined by the Commissioner, the ability of, and the public perception that, players and Clubs perform and compete at all times to the best of their abilities. Public confidence shall include without limitation the public perception, as determined by the Commissioner, that there is an appropriate level of long-term competitive balance among Clubs.

Sec. 5. Notwithstanding the provisions of Section 2 and 4, above, the powers of the Commissioner to act in the best interests of Baseball shall be inapplicable to any matter relating to the process of collective bargaining between the Clubs and the Major League Baseball Players Association.

Sec. 6. In the case of conduct by organizations not parties to this Constitution, or by individuals not connected with any of the parties hereto, that is deemed by the Commissioner not to be in the best interests of Baseball, the Commissioner may pursue appropriate legal remedies, advocate remedial legislation and take such other steps as the Commissioner may deem necessary and proper in the interests of the morale of the players and the honor of the game.

* * *

Sec. 8. (a) The Commissioner shall hold office for a minimum term of three years or for such longer term as shall be established by the Major League Clubs at the time of the Commissioner's election. The Commissioner shall be eligible to succeed himself or herself.

(b) Any re-election shall be considered at a Major League Meeting held not less than six months nor more than 15 months prior to the expiration of any term. The Commissioner's compensation shall be fixed at the time of his election.

(c) No diminution of the compensation or powers of the present or any succeeding Commissioner shall be made during the Commissioner's term of office.

Sec. 9. The election of a Commissioner hereunder shall be at a Major League Meeting; * * * [election] shall require the affirmative vote of not less than three-fourths of all Major League Clubs. The re-election of a Commissioner to succeed himself or herself * * * shall require the affirmative vote of not less than a majority of all Major League Clubs. During any period of incapacity of the Commissioner, as determined by a majority of the Executive Council or by the Commissioner, all the powers and duties of the Commissioner shall be conferred upon and exercised by the Executive Council. During any vacancy in the Office of Commissioner, all the powers and duties of the Commissioner shall be conferred upon and thenceforth exercised by the Executive Council, until a Commissioner of Baseball has been elected as herein set forth. . . .

Article VI—ARBITRATION

Sec. 1. All disputes and controversies related in any way to professional baseball between Clubs or between a Club(s) and any Major League Baseball entity(ies) (including in each case, without limitation, their owners, officers, directors, employees and players), other than those whose resolution is expressly provided for by another means in this Constitution, the Major League Rules, the Basic Agreement between the Major Leagues and the Major League Baseball Players Association, or the collective bargaining agreement with any representative of the Major League umpires, shall be submitted to the Commissioner, as arbitrator, who, after hearing, shall have the sole and exclusive right to decide such disputes and controversies. The procedure set forth in this Section is separate from and shall not alter or affect the procedure set forth in Article V governing the role of the Commissioner at Major League Meetings, or the Commissioner's powers to act in the best interests of Baseball under Article II.

Sec. 2. The Major Leagues Clubs recognize that it is in the best interests of Baseball that all actions taken by the Commissioner under the authority of this Constitution, including, without limitation, Article II and this Article VI, be accepted and complied with by the Clubs, and that the Clubs not otherwise engaged in any form of litigation between or among themselves or with any Major League Baseball entity, but resolve their differences pursuant to the provisions of this Constitution. In furtherance thereof, the Clubs (on their own behalf and including, without limitation, on behalf of their owners, officers, directors and employees) severally agree to be finally and unappealably bound by actions of the Commissioner and all other actions, decisions or interpretations taken or reached pursuant to the provisions of this Constitution and severally waive such right of recourse to the courts as would otherwise have existed in their favor. * * *

Sec. 3. The form of player's contract to be used by the Major League Clubs, and all contracts between Major League Clubs and their officers and employees, shall contain a clause by which the parties agree to submit themselves to the jurisdiction of the Commissioner, and to accept the Commissioner's decisions rendered in accordance with this Constitution.

Article VIII—CLUBS AND TERRITORIES

Sec. 1. Clubs. There shall be 30 Major League Clubs, which agree hereby to act at all times in the best interests of Baseball. The Clubs shall be organized into two Leagues, the American League and the National League, with three divisions in each League, as follows: [list of divisions and teams in each division omitted].

Sec. 2. Expansion, Contraction, Realignment, Divisions. Any increase or decrease in the number of or any realignment of the Major League Clubs or any change from the present form of three-division play shall be governed by the voting provisions in Article V, Section 2(b) [to wit, a three-fourths vote of all the Clubs].

Sec. 4. Involuntary Termination. The rights, privileges and other property rights of a Major League Club hereunder and any other Baseball-related agreement may be terminated (i) in the event of contraction . . . or (ii) involuntarily, with the approval of three-fourths of all Major League Clubs, if the Club in question shall do or suffer any of the following: [list of 12 categories of misconduct or circumstances omitted].

Sec. 8. Operating Territories. The Major League Clubs shall have assigned operating territories within which they have the right and obligation to play baseball games as the home club. [Detailed specific description of each club's home territory omitted.]

Sec. 9. Home Television Territories. The definitions of the home television territories of the Major League Clubs shall be maintained in the Commissioner's Office. Amendments to such territories shall be made only with the approval of the Executive Council.

Article X—MAJOR LEAGUE CENTRAL FUND

Sec. 1. Maintenance of Major League Central Fund. There shall be maintained for the Major League Clubs in the Office of the Commissioner a separate account to be known as the "Major League Central Fund" and to be administered by the Executive Council. All sums received for the account of the parties hereto under this Constitution shall be deposited in the Major League Central Fund. The Commissioner is hereby appointed the fiscal agent of the Major League Central Fund.

Sec. 3. Major League Club Broadcasts. Major League Club practices with regard to the telecasting and radio broadcasting of games are governed as follows:

(a) The Clubs hereby agree that each Club shall have, with respect to each game in which it participates, the right to authorize the telecast of such game only by means of over-the-air, cable and satellite technology, and only within its home television territory.

(c) Each Club shall provide in its ballpark to the visiting Club suitable space to be used for the purposes described in [(a)] above. . . .

MAJOR LEAGUE (BASEBALL) RULES

Rule 2—PLAYER LIMITS AND RESERVE LISTS

(a) RESERVE LISTS

(1) Filing of Reserve Lists. On a date designated by the Commissioner (which shall be no later than November 20), each Major League Club shall file Major League and Minor League Reserve Lists with the Commissioner and/or the Commissioner's designee. A Major League Club shall include on its Major League Reserve List all players, player-managers and player-coaches who are currently under Major League Uniform Player's Contracts (unless they have been assigned outright to a Minor League Club) or who have been promoted to Major League status and must be tendered a Major League Uniform Player's Contract for the following championship season by December 20.

A Major League Club also must file a separate Minor League Reserve List for each Minor League classification in which it desires to reserve Minor League players. A Major League Club, however, may reserve players only in classifications in which it owned or had a PDC with a Minor League Club during the previous season.... All players on one of the Minor League Reserve Lists filed by a Major League Club shall be reserved only to the Major League Club, which shall have the exclusive contractual right to the services of the players on such a list.

(3) Effect of Placement on Reserve List. No player on a Reserve List filed by a Major League or Minor League Club shall be eligible to play or negotiate with any other Major League or Minor League Club until the player is removed from the Reserve List because the player's contract has been terminated or assigned.

(b) MAXIMUM NUMBER OF RESERVED PLAYERS

(1) Major League Club Limits. A Major League Club may place a maximum number of

(A) 40 players on its Major League Reserve List;

(B) 38 players on its Class AAA Reserve List for each Class AAA Club that it owned or with which it had a PDC during the previous season;

(C) 37 players on its Class AA Reserve List for each Class AA Club that it owned or with which it had a PDC during the previous season;

(D) 35 players on its Class A Reserve List for each Class A or Short–Season A Club that it owned or with which it had a PDC during the previous season; and

(E) 35 players on its Rookie Reserve List for each Rookie classification Club that it owned or with which it had a PDC during the previous season.

(c) ACTIVE LISTS

(1) Filing and Maintenance. Each Major League Club must file and maintain an Active List with the Commissioner and/or the Commissioner's designee for the Major League Club itself and for all Minor League Clubs that it owns or with which it has a PDC....

An Active List must include all players who are currently eligible to play in a championship season game for the Major League or the Minor League Club for which the list was filed....

(2) Numerical Limits.

(A) The maximum number of players who may be placed on an Active List for a Major League Club shall be 25 from opening day until midnight on August 31 of the same championship season, at which time the number of players on the Active List of a Major League Club may be increased to 40.

* * *

(d) VOLUNTARILY RETIRED, RESTRICTED, DISQUALI-FIED AND INELIGIBLE LISTS.
Players on the Voluntarily Retired, Restricted, Disqualified or Ineligible Lists shall not count against either the Reserve List or Active List limits. A player under a Major League Uniform Player's Contract or Minor League Uniform Player Contract who has been reserved for two consecutive years on the Voluntarily Retired, Restricted, Disqualified or Ineligible Lists shall be omitted from further Reserve Lists and shall not be eligible to play until the player is first reinstated in accordance with Rule 16 (Reinstatement of Players). Upon reinstatement, the Major League or Minor League Club to which the player is reserved shall restore the player to the same status that the player had at the time when the player retired or became ineligible.

* * *

(g) MAJOR LEAGUE DISABLED LIST.
Upon written application to the Commissioner and/or the Commissioner's designee, a Major League Club may request that a player on its Major League Active List, who is unable to render services because of a specific injury or ailment, be placed on one of the Disabled Lists set forth in this Rule 2(g)....

Rule 3—ELIGIBILITY TO SIGN CONTRACT, CONTRACT TERMS, AND CONTRACT TENDERS

(a) ELIGIBILITY TO SIGN PROFESSIONAL BASEBALL CONTRACTS.

(1) General Rules. Subject to the High School, College, and Junior College Rules listed in this Rule 3(a), a Major or Minor League Club may contract with a player under the conditions and restrictions set forth in this Rule 3....

(A) A player who has not previously contracted with a Major or Minor League Club, and who is a resident of the United States or Canada, may be signed to a contract only after having been eligible for selection in the Rule 4 draft. A player shall be considered a "resident of the United States" if the player enrolls in a United States high school or college or establishes a legal residence in the United States on the date of the player's contract or within one year prior to that date.

(B) A player who has not previously contracted with a Major or Minor League Club, who is not a resident of the United States or Canada, and who is not subject to the High School, College, Junior College or American Legion Rules, may be signed to a contract if the player: (i) is at least 17 years old at the time of signing, or (ii) is 16 at the time of signing, but will attain age 17 prior to either the end of the effective season for which the player has signed or September 1 of such effective season, whichever is later.

* * *

(2) High School Rules.

(A) United States and Canada. Except as noted in this Rule 3(a)(2), no high school student in the United States or Canada shall be signed to a contract by a Major or Minor League Club during any period the student is eligible for participation in high school athletics. . . .

(3) College Players.

(B) Except as set forth in Rule 3(a)(3)(E) (Exceptions), a player who is a member (or, if a freshman, a prospective member) of a baseball team that represents a college in intercollegiate competition may not be signed by a Major or Minor League Club during the period beginning with the date the player attends the first class in the player's freshman year and ending with the graduation of the class with which the player originally entered college.

(E) Exceptions. Rule 3(a)(3)(B) shall not apply to any player: (i) who is at least 21 years old and is currently between school years; (ii) who has completed junior year and is currently between school years; (iii) who has completed the full period of eligibility for intercollegiate baseball; (iv) whose association with the player's college has been terminated by reasons of scholastic deficiency; or (v) who withdraws from college and remains out for at least 120 days (including the date of withdrawal).

Rule 13—SUSPENDED PLAYERS

(a) MISCONDUCT OR INSUBORDINATION. A Major or Minor League Club may suspend a player that it has under a Major League Uniform Player's Contract or Minor League Uniform Player Contract for insubordination or other misconduct or for violation by the player of any regulation or other provision of the player's contract. At its discretion, the Major or Minor League Club with which the player is under contract may impose a reasonable fine and deduct the amount of the fine from the player's salary or may suspend the player without salary for a period not exceeding 30 days, or both. Written notice of the fine, or suspension, or both, and of the reason for the fine and/or suspension shall in every case be given to the player. During the period of suspension the player shall be ineligible to play with any other Major or Minor League Club.

(b) PLAYER NOT IN CONDITION. A player under a Major League Uniform Player's Contract or Minor League Uniform Player Contract who fails to get into playing condition within 60 days after the commencement of the training season of the player's Club may be suspended without pay until the player is in condition to play.

(c) APPEAL. A player suspended by a Major or Minor League Club or a Major or Minor League for a term longer than 10 days shall have the right to appeal to the Commissioner and/or the Commissioner's designee. . . .

Rule 21—MISCONDUCT

(a) MISCONDUCT IN PLAYING BASEBALL. Any player or person connected with a Club who shall promise or agree to lose, or to attempt to lose, or to fail to give his best efforts towards the winning of any baseball game with which he is or may be in any way concerned, or who shall intentionally lose or attempt to lose, or intentionally fail to give his best efforts towards the winning of any such baseball game, or who shall solicit or attempt to induce any player or person connected with a Club to lose or attempt to lose, or to fail to give his best efforts towards the winning of any baseball game with which such other player or person is or may be in any way concerned, or who, being solicited by any person, shall fail to inform his Major League President and the Commissioner (in the case of a player or person associated with a Major League Club) or the President of the Minor League Association (in the case of a player or person associated with an independent Minor League Club) immediately of such solicitation, and of all facts and circumstances connected therewith, shall be declared permanently ineligible.

(d) BETTING ON BALL GAMES.

(1) Any player, umpire, or Club or League official or employee, who shall bet any sum whatsoever upon any baseball game in connection with which the bettor has no duty to perform, shall be declared ineligible for one year.

(2) Any player, umpire, or Club or League official or employee, who shall bet any sum whatsoever upon any baseball game in connection with which the bettor has a duty to perform, shall be declared permanently ineligible.

(f) OTHER MISCONDUCT. Nothing herein contained shall be construed as exclusively defining or otherwise limiting acts, transactions, practices or conduct not to be in the best interests of Baseball; and any and all other acts, transactions, practices or conduct not to be in the best interests of Baseball are prohibited and shall be subject to such penalties, including permanent ineligibility, as the facts in the particular case may warrant.

———

NATIONAL FOOTBALL LEAGUE CONSTITUTION AND BY–LAWS

Article II—PURPOSES AND OBJECTS

2.1 The purpose and objects for which the League is organized are:

(A) To promote and foster the primary business of League members, each member being an owner of a professional football club located in the United States.

(B) To do and perform such other functions as may be necessary to carry out the purpose and objects of the League.

2.2 The League is not organized nor to be operated for profit.

Article III—MEMBERSHIP

Members

3.1 (A) Membership in the League shall be limited to the thirty-two (32) member clubs specified in Section 4.4 hereof and such new members as may be thereafter duly elected.

(B) The admission of a new member club, either within or outside the home territory of an existing member club, shall require the affirmative vote of three-fourths of the existing member clubs of the League.

Eligibility of New Members

3.2 Any person, association, partnership, corporation, or other entity of good repute organized for the purpose of operating a professional football club shall be eligible for membership except:

(A) No corporation, association, partnership or other entity not operated for profit nor any charitable organization or entity not presently a member of the League shall be eligible for membership.

(B) If any privately held corporation, partnership, trust, or other entity owns or operates, directly or indirectly, any substantial non-football business or assets and owns, directly or indirectly, an interest in or otherwise operates a member club, then:

(1) The member club shall be held in a separate corporation, partnership, or trust (the "Football Company"), the primary purpose of which shall at all times be and remain the operation of a professional football team as a member club of the League, which such primary purpose shall not be changed, and the only material asset of which shall be the member club;

(2) The ownership interest in the Football Company shall be held directly by a holding company that shall have no operating business or material assets but only ownership interests in other entities, and the ownership interests in the holding company shall be owned directly by individuals (or certain trusts or partnerships approved by the Commissioner's office); . . . .

[EXCERPT OF NFL RESOLUTION FC–3, not in the Constitution, adopted in 1997:

Be it *Resolved*, As follows: That the controlling owner of an NFL club may acquire an interest in a major league baseball, basketball or hockey ("other major sports league") franchise (subject to prior notice to the Commissioner and to such covenants and safeguards as the Commissioner and Finance Committee may determine are appropriate to address actual or perceived conflicts of interest that may arise in the particular situation), but only if such other franchise is located (1) within the home territory of the owner's NFL club, or (2) within a neutral area, i.e., any area that is not within the home territory of any NFL club. . . .]

Transfer of Membership

3.5   No membership, or any interest therein, may be sold, assigned, or otherwise transferred in whole or in part except in accordance with and subject to the following provisions: [*application procedures omitted*]

(B)   . . . [T]he Commissioner shall conduct such investigation as he deems appropriate. Upon completion thereof, the Commissioner shall submit the proposed transfer to the members for approval, together with his recommendation thereon, and all information in respect thereto that the Commissioner deems pertinent. All sales, transfers or assignments except a transfer referred to in Section 3.5 (C) hereof, shall only become effective if approved by the affirmative vote of not less than three-fourths or 20, whichever is greater, of the members of the League.

Effect of Termination

3.8   (A) Upon the expulsion of a member or upon any other involuntary termination of membership, the following shall occur:

(1) The lease of its playing field or interest of the member therein, if and to the extent the lease or interest is assignable, shall, upon demand of the League, be assigned to the League or its nominee, provided, however, that the assignment of said lease to the League shall first be approved by the affirmative vote or written

consent of no less than three-fourths or 20, whichever is greater, of the members of the League....

(2) Title to all players contracts of the terminated member and title to all players on the Reserve or Selection List of such terminated member and any interest or right to such players and contracts shall, if demanded by the League, be assigned to the League or its nominee, provided that such assignments are first approved by the affirmative vote or written consent of not less than three-fourths or 20, whichever is greater, of the remaining League members....

(3) All interest of the terminated member in and to any funds or property of the League, or any right or interest therein, shall cease.

Article IV—TERRITORIAL RIGHTS

Home Territory Defined

4.1 "Home Territory" with respect to any club means the city in which such club is located and for which it holds a franchise and plays its home games and includes the surrounding territory to the extent of 75 miles in every direction from the exterior corporate limits of such city except as follows:

(A) Whenever any two member clubs * * * are located and hold franchises for different cities within 100 miles of each other measured from the exterior corporate limits of such city, then the territorial rights of each of such clubs shall only extend to and include an area of one-half the distance between such cities.

(B) The "home territory" of the Green Bay Packers shall extend to and include all of Milwaukee County, Wisconsin, despite the fact that portions of such County are outside the 75 mile limits from the exterior corporate limits of the City of Green Bay.

Rights Within Home Territory

4.2 Each member shall have the exclusive right within its home territory to exhibit professional football games played by teams of the League except that:

(A) Whenever two club franchises in the League are located in the same city, then the owners of each of such franchises shall have equal rights within the home territory of such city.

(C) ... [N]o club in the League shall be permitted to play games within the home territory of any other club unless a home club is a participant.

League Control of Games

4.3 The League shall have exclusive control of the exhibition of football games by member clubs within the home territory of each member. No member club shall have the right to transfer its franchise or playing site to a different city, either within or outside its home territory, without prior approval by the affirmative vote of three-fourths of the existing member clubs of the League.

Article VIII—COMMISSIONER

Employment

8.1   The League shall select and employ a person of unquestioned integrity to serve as Commissioner of the League, and shall determine the period and fix the compensation of his employment. . . .

Jurisdiction to Resolve Disputes

8.3   The Commissioner shall have full, complete, and final jurisdiction and authority to arbitrate:

(A) Any dispute involving two or more members of the League, or involving two or more holders of an ownership interest in a member club of the League, certified to him by any of the disputants;

(B) Any dispute between any player, coach, and/or other employee of any member of the League (or any combination thereof) and any member club or clubs;

(C) Any dispute between or among players, coaches, and/or other employees of any member club or clubs of the League, other than disputes unrelated to and outside the course and scope of the employment of such disputants within the League;

(D) Any dispute between a player and any official of the League;

(E) Any dispute involving a member or members in the League or any players or employees of the members of the League or any combination thereof that in the opinion of the Commissioner constitutes conduct detrimental to the best interests of the League or professional football.

Disciplinary Powers of Commissioner

8.13   (A) Whenever the Commissioner, after notice and hearing, decides that an owner, shareholder, partner or holder of an interest in a member club, or any player, coach, officer, director or employee thereof, or an officer, employee or official of the League has either violated the Constitution and Bylaws of the League, or has been or is guilty of conduct detrimental to the welfare of the League or professional football, then the Commissioner shall have complete authority to:

(1) Suspend and/or fine such person in an amount not in excess of five hundred thousand dollars ($500,000), . . .; and/or

(2) Cancel any contract or agreement of such person with the League or with any member thereof;

(3) In cases involving a violation of the prohibitions against tampering ..., award or transfer selection choices and/or deprive the offending club of a selection choice or choices; and

(4) In cases involving a violation affecting the competitive aspects of the game, award selection choices and/or deprive the offending club of a selection choice or choices and/or cancel any contract or agreement of such person with the League or with any member thereof and/or fine the offending club in an amount not in excess of five hundred thousand dollars ($500,000)....

(C) Whenever the Commissioner, after notice and hearing, determines that a person employed by or connected with the League or any member club thereof has bet money or any other thing of value on the outcome or score of any game or games played in the League or has had knowledge of or has received an offer, directly or indirectly, to control, fix or bet money or other consideration on the outcome or score of a professional football game and has failed to report the same in the manner hereinafter prescribed, then such Commissioner shall have complete and unrestricted authority to enforce any or all of the following penalties:

(1) Suspend such person indefinitely or for a prescribed period of time;

(2) Bar such person from the League for life;

(3) Cancel or terminate the contract of such person in the League or any member club thereof;

(4) Require the sale of any stock, or other interest of such offending person in any member club by the method and under the procedure specified in Section 3.8 (B) hereof;

(5) Fine such person in an amount not in excess of five hundred thousand dollars ($500,000);

(6) Cancel or declare to be forfeited any interest in a member club, or in the franchise thereof, owned by any person so involved....;

(7) Assign to another club or a member of the League the lease on any stadium or playing field held for or owned by the offending club or by any person owning any interest therein;

(8) Assign to one or more other clubs players on the Selection or Reserve Lists of the offending club;

(9) Impose such other or additional punishment or discipline as the Commissioner may decide.

* * *

Miscellaneous Power of the Commissioner

8.14   (A) The Commissioner shall have the power, without a hearing, to disapprove contracts between a player and a club, if such a contract has been executed in violation of or contrary to the Constitution and By–Laws of the League, or, if either or both of the parties to such contracts have been or are guilty of an act or conduct which is or may be detrimental to the League or to the sport of professional football. . . .

(B) The Commissioner shall have the power to hear and determine disputes between clubs in respect to any matter certified to by him by either or both of the clubs. He shall also have the power to settle and determine any controversy between two clubs which, in the opinion of the Commissioner involves or affects League policy.

Article IX—PROHIBITED CONDUCT

Conflicting Interests and Prohibited Conduct

9.1   (A) The violation of any of the provisions of this Article IX shall constitute conduct detrimental to the League and professional football.

(B) No member, or stockholder, officer, director, partner or employee thereof, and no officer or employee of the League, including a game official shall:

(1) Own or have any financial interest directly or indirectly, in any other member club the League.

(2) Directly or indirectly loan money to or become surety or guarantor for any other member club or any player, coach, or employee thereof. . . .

(4) Act as the contracting agent or representative for any player or share or be financially interested in the compensation of any player in the League. . . .

(C) No member, nor any stockholder, director, officer, partner, or employee thereof, or person holding an interest therein, nor any office or employee of the League shall:

(7) Own, directly or indirectly, any interest whatsoever in a professional football organization, league, club or team not a member of the League, except that these prohibitions shall not apply to the direct or indirect ownership by NFL owners of interests in clubs in the Arena Football League playing in the home territory of the owner's NFL club. . . . ;

(10) Tamper with players of college teams who are not eligible for play in the League under the eligibility rules thereof;

(11) Tamper with a player or coaches or other employee under contract to or the property of another member club;

(12) Offer, agree, conspire, or attempt to illegally influence the outcome of the member or fail to suspend immediately any officer or player or other employee of the member who shall be proven guilty of offering, agreeing, conspiring, or attempting to influence the outcome of any game or be interested in any pool or wager of any game in which a member club participates.

Article X—BROADCASTING AND TELEVISION

Contract Conditions

10.1 Any contract entered into by any club for telecasting or broadcasting its games, and the sponsor or sponsors of each game telecast or broadcast pursuant to such a contract, must be approved in writing by the Commissioner in advance of such telecast or broadcast.

Television Restrictions

10.2 Subject to the limitations and exceptions set forth in this Article, member clubs participating in any game are authorized to telecast and broadcast such game anywhere except as follows:

(A) No club shall cause or permit a game in which it is engaged to be telecast into any area included within the home territory of any other club on the day that such other club is engaged in playing a game at home;

(B) No telecast of a home game within the home territory of a club shall be caused or permitted, except by agreement between the participating clubs;

(C) Each home club grants to the visiting club the exclusive right to permit or license the telecast of the game being played between them back to the home territory of the visiting club.

Television Income

10.3 All regular season (and pre-season network) television income will be divided equally among all member clubs of the League regardless of the source of such income, except that the member clubs may, by unanimous agreement, provide otherwise in a specific television contract or contracts.

Article XII—ELIGIBILITY OF PLAYERS

General Rules of Eligibility

12.1 (A) No person shall be eligible to play or be selected as a player unless (1) all college football eligibility of such player has expired, or (2) at least five (5) years shall have elapsed since the player first entered or attended a recognized junior college, college, or university, or (3) such player receives a diploma from a recognized college or university prior to September 1st of the next football season of the League....

Any player who does not attend college is automatically eligible for selection in the next principal draft that is conducted after four football seasons have elapsed since the player discontinued high school ...

[**SPECIAL DRAFT ELIGIBILITY POLICY AND PROCEDURE**, not in the Constitution, announced February 16, 1990:

1. Applications for special eligibility for the [] draft will be accepted only from college players as to whom three full college seasons have elapsed since their high school graduations,

3. To be declared eligible for the [] draft, a player filing for special eligibility must include in his application an irrevocable renunciation of any further college football eligibility.]

———

(J) SUPPLEMENTAL DRAFT. Whenever a player or players become eligible for the League subsequent to the principal selection meeting, a supplemental draft will be conducted to admit such players.

Article XIV—SELECTION MEETING

14.1 [An annual] A Selection Meeting of the League shall be held on the second Tuesday following the playing of the last post-season game; * * *.

14.3 (A) At each Selection Meeting each club participating therein shall select players of its own choice; selection shall be made by the clubs in each round in the reverse order of their standing.

Reserve List—Selectees

14.5 The selecting club shall have the exclusive right to negotiate for the services of each player selected by it in the Selection Meeting. Selected players shall be placed on the Reserve List of that club.

Article XVII—PLAYER LIMITS AND ELIGIBILITY

Reserve List

17.6 The Reserve List of each club may consist of players in the following categories: (A) Retired; (B) Did not report; (C) Left squad (quit team); (D) Injured; (E) Physically unable to perform (At the time of the training camp physical); (F) N–F/I (Non-football injury or illness); (G) In military; (H) Selected in Selection Meeting by the club, but never under contract; (I) Suspended or declared ineligible, or expelled from the League for violation of the contract between the player and the club, or for other reasons permitted by this Constitution and By–Laws....

A player on a club's Reserve List shall not be eligible to contract with any other club unless and until the player is released or his contract assigned as provided in this Constitution and By–Laws.

Article XVIII—WAIVERS

When Required

18.1 (A) Clubs desiring to release players must first give written notice to the Commissioner of such intention. At 4:00 p.m., New York Time, during each day, exclusive of Sundays, the Commissioner shall notify each club of such waiver request and any club desiring the services of said player may claim him. Regardless of the time when the League receives a request for waiver, the Commissioner shall not give the notice thereof to the clubs until 4:00 p.m., New York Time, on the same or succeeding day.

———

NATIONAL BASKETBALL ASSOCIATION CONSTITUTION AND BY–LAWS

OBJECTS

2. This Association is organized to operate a league consisting of professional basketball teams, each of which shall be operated by a Member of the Association. The Association shall not be operated for profit.

All sales, transfers or assignments shall only become effective if approved by the affirmative vote of not less than three-fourths (3/4) of all its Members at a meeting duly warned for such purpose.

TRANSFER OF MEMBERSHIP

7. No membership, or any interest therein, may be sold, assigned or otherwise transferred in whole or in part, directly or indirectly, except in accordance with and subject to the following provisions:

(b) .... All sales, transfers or assignments shall only become effective if approved by the affirmative vote of not less than three-fourths (3/4) of all its members at a meeting duly warned for such purpose.

FRANCHISE RELOCATION

9A. A Member may transfer its franchise, city of operation, or playing site of any or all of its home games, to a different location, within or outside its existing Territory, as defined in Article 10, only in accordance with and subject to the following provisions:....

(b) No application to relocate may be made after the first day of March preceding the season in which the proposed relocation is to take effect. Within ten (10) days of the receipt of an application to relocate, the Commissioner shall refer the application to a Committee to investigate the application. The Committee shall be appointed by the Commissioner and shall consist of no fewer than five Governors or Alternate Governors.... The recommendation of the Committee shall be based solely and exclusively upon the following factors:

(i) Whether the proposed new location can support a franchise in the Association or, if the proposed new location is within the existing Territory of a Member, whether the proposed new location can support another franchise. In evaluating this factor, the Committee shall consider: existing and projected population, income levels and age distribution; existing and projected markets for radio, broadcast television, cable television, and other forms of audio-visual transmission of Association games; the size, quality and location of the arena in which the Member proposes to play its home games; and the presence, history and popularity in the proposed new location of other professional sports teams and major college basketball teams.

(ii) Whether the applicant has demonstrated that it will be able successfully to operate an Association team in the proposed new location. In evaluating this factor, the Committee shall consider the applicant's present and projected financial condition and resources and its past performance in operating a team in the Association.

(iii) Whether the proposed relocation is likely to have an adverse effect upon the Association's ability to market and promote Association basketball on a nationwide basis in a diverse group of geographic markets.

(iv) Whether the proposed new location presents particular disadvantages for the operation of the Association, such as by creating significant traveling or scheduling difficulties or because of adverse state or local laws or regulations.

(v) Whether other Association Members, in addition to the applicant, are interested in transferring their franchises to the proposed new location, or whether there are persons or entities interested in obtaining an expansion franchise in the proposed new location. . . .

(d) The report and recommendation of the Committee shall be delivered to each Member of the Board of Governors. . . . The question whether to approve the proposed relocation shall be decided by a majority vote of all of the members, and no vote by proxy shall be permitted. The vote of each Governor on the proposed relocation shall be based solely and exclusively upon the factors listed in subparagraph (b)(i through v) of this Article 1.

TERRITORY

10. (a) Except as provided in Paragraphs (b) and (c) of this Article 10, the Territory of a Member shall be the territory incorporated within an area of seventy-five (75) air miles of the corporate limits of the city of operation, except that when the line circumscribing the Territory of a Member intersects with the line circumscribing the Territory of another Member, the respective Territories shall be evenly divided by a line between the two (2) points of intersection.

(c) A Team operated by a Member shall have no right to play in the Territory of another Member without the consent of the resident Member.

AUTHORITY AND DUTIES OF THE COMMISSIONER

24. (a) A Commissioner shall be elected by the affirmative vote of three-fourth (3/4) of all the Governors. His term of office may be

terminated by a vote of three-fourths (3/4) of the Governors at a meeting duly called for such purpose.

(b) The Commissioner shall have no financial interest, direct or indirect, in any professional sport.

(c) The Commissioner shall have full, complete and final jurisdiction of any dispute involving two (2) or more Members of the Association.

(e) The Commissioner shall ... interpret and from time to time establish policy and procedure in respect to the provisions of the Constitution, Bylaws and playing rules and any enforcement thereof and any decision emanating therefrom shall be final and unappealable.

(f)(i) The Commissioner shall have the power to suspend for a definite or indefinite period and to impose such fines as are authorized.... he shall have the power to declare null and void any Player transaction made by and between Members of the Association or by and between Members of the Association and any organization outside of the Association.

(j) The Commissioner shall, wherever there is a rule for which no penalty is specifically fixed for violation thereof, have the authority to fix such penalty as in his judgment shall be in the best interest of the Association. Where a situation arises which is not covered in the Constitution and Bylaws, he shall have the authority to make such decision as in his judgment shall be in the best interest of the Association. No monetary penalty fixed under this provision shall exceed $250,000.

(k) All actions duly taken by the Commissioner pursuant to ... the Constitution, which are not specifically referable to the Board of Governors, shall be final, binding and conclusive, as an award in arbitration, and enforceable in a court of competent jurisdiction in accordance with the laws of the State of New York.

MISCONDUCT

35.   The provisions of this Article 35 shall govern all Players in the Association, hereinafter referred to as "Players."

(a) Each Member shall provide and require in every contract with any of its Players that they shall be bound and governed by the provisions of this Article. Each Member, at the direction of the Board of Governors or the Commissioner, as the case may be, shall take such action as the Board or the Commissioner may direct in order to effectuate the purposes of this Article.

(b) The Commissioner shall direct the dismissal and perpetual disqualification from any further association with the Association or any of its Members, of any Player found by the Commissioner after a hearing to have been guilty of offering, agreeing, conspiring, aiding or attempting to cause any game of basketball to result otherwise than on its merit.

(c) Any Player who gives, makes, issues, authorizes or endorses any statement having, or designed to have, an effect prejudicial or detrimental to the best interests of basketball or of the Association or of a Member or its Team, shall be liable to a fine not exceeding $2,000, to be imposed by the Board of Governors....

(d) If in the opinion of the Commissioner any other act or conduct of a Player at or during a Pre–Season, Regular Season, Playoff or Exhibition Game has been prejudicial to or against the best interests of the Association or the game of basketball, the Commissioner shall impose upon such Player a fine not exceeding $20,000, or may order for a time the suspension of any such Player from any connection or duties with Pre–Season, Regular Season, Playoff or Exhibition Games, or he may order both such fine and suspension.

(e) The Commissioner shall have the power to suspend for a definite or indefinite period, or to impose a fine not exceeding $2,000, or inflict both such suspension and fine upon any Player who, in his opinion, shall have been guilty of conduct prejudicial or detrimental to the Association.

(g) Any Player who, directly or indirectly, wagers money or anything of value on the outcome of any game played by a Team in the league operated by the Association shall, on being charged with such wagering, be given an opportunity to answer such charges after due notice, and the decision of the Commissioner shall be final, binding and conclusive and unappealable. The penalty for such offense shall be within the absolute and sole discretion of the Commissioner and may include a fine, suspension, expulsion and/or perpetual disqualification from further association with the Association or any of its Members.

(h) Except for a penalty imposed under Paragraph (g) of this Article 35, the decisions and acts of the Commissioner pursuant to Article 35 shall be appealable to the Board of Governors, which shall determine such appeals in accordance with such rules and regulations as may be adopted by the Board in its absolute and sole discretion.

NBA BY–LAWS
ARTICLE II

Eligibility of Players

2.01. Good Character. All Players shall be of good moral character and possess qualities which will make them proper members of their respective Teams. The Commissioner shall have the right to disqualify a Player if the Commissioner finds that the Player does not possess the requisite qualities of character and morality. Such disqualification may be made by the Commissioner only after a hearing before the Commissioner, at which hearing the Player shall be afforded the right to call witnesses, to submit written evidence and to be represented by counsel. The decision of the Commissioner shall be appealable to the Board of Governors....

2.04. Age. A person who is not at least seventeen (17) years old shall not be eligible to be drafted or to be a Player, may not be signed by a Member to any agreement, nor may his future services in any way be negotiated for, contracted for or otherwise reserved.

2.05.   Undergraduate Eligibility. (a) A person who has not completed high school or who has completed high school but has not entered college, shall not be eligible to be drafted or to be a Player until four (4) years after he has been graduated or four (4) years after his original high school class has been graduated, as the case may be, nor may the future services of any such person be negotiated or contracted for, other wise reserved. Similarly, a person who has entered college but is no longer enrolled shall not be eligible to be drafted or to be a Player until the time when he would have first become eligible had he remained in college. Any negotiations or agreements with any such person during such period shall be null and void and shall confer no rights whatsoever. No Member violating the provisions of this Subsection shall be permitted to acquire the rights to the services of such person at any time thereafter.

(b) Notwithstanding the provisions of Subsection (a) above, a person who has been graduated from high school or whose high school class has been graduated shall become eligible to be drafted if he renounces his intercollegiate basketball eligibility by written notice to the Association at least forty-five (45) days prior to the annual College Draft for which the person desires to be eligible.

NATIONAL HOCKEY LEAGUE CONSTITUTION & BY-LAWS

3.3   *Admission of New Members.* Each applicant for membership shall make a written application to the League. . . . A favorable vote of three-fourths of the members of the League shall be required for election to membership. The Board of Governors by majority vote shall determine from time to time the amount that shall be paid for a membership in the National Hockey League. . . .

3.5   *Transfer of Membership or Ownership Interest in a Member Club.* No membership or ownership interest in a Member Club may be sold, assigned or otherwise transferred except (a) with the consent of three-fourths of the members of the League, ...

4.1   *Definitions.* For the purposes of this Article:

(c) "Home territory" with respect to any member, means: Each Member Club shall have exclusive territorial rights in the city in which it is located and within 50 miles of that city's corporate limits

4.2   *Territorial Rights of League.* The League shall have exclusive control of the playing of hockey by Member Clubs in the home territory of each member, subject to the rights hereinafter granted to members. The members shall have the right to and agree to operate professional hockey clubs and play the League schedule in their respective cities or boroughs as indicated opposite their signatures hereto. No member shall transfer its club and franchise to a different city or borough. No additional cities or boroughs shall be added to the League circuit without the consent of three-fourths of all members of the League. Any admission of new members with the franchises to operate in additional cities or boroughs shall be subject to the provisions of Section 4.3.

4.3 *Territorial Rights of the Members.* Each member shall have exclusive control of the playing of hockey games within its home territory including, but not being limited to, the playing in such home territory of hockey games by any teams owned or controlled by such member or by other members of the League. Subject only to the exclusive rights of other members with respect to their respective home territories as herein above set forth, nothing herein contained shall be construed to limit the right of any Member Club to acquire any interest in any hockey team, whether professional or amateur, in any league which recognizes and honors the territorial rights, contracts, and reserve lists of the National Hockey League, except as limited by Section 8.1(a) of this Constitution. No other member of the League shall be permitted to play games (except regularly scheduled League games with the home club) in the home territory of a member without the latter member's consent. No franchise shall be granted for a home territory within the home territory of a member, without the written consent of such member.

4.4 *Property Rights of Home Club.* Each member hereby irrevocably conveys, grants and assigns forever all the right, title and interest which it has or may have in and to each hockey game played by its team as a visiting club and in the news of said game . . . , to the member in whose home territory said game is played.

Officers

6.3 (a) The Commissioner shall be the Chief Executive Officer of the League. He shall be charged with the operation, general supervision and direction of all the business and affairs of the League and shall discharge all duties imposed on him by the Constitution and By–Laws and as may be required by the Board of Governors from time to time.

(b) He shall act as arbitrator in any dispute between Member Clubs over the contracts or for the services of players; provided, however, that if any Member Club which is a party to any such dispute shall so elect, such dispute shall be determined by arbitrators selected as hereinafter provided. . . . The decision of the Commissioner, or of the arbitrators, as the case may be, shall be final. . . .

NATIONAL HOCKEY LEAGUE BY–LAWS

Section 2—Agreements With Players

2.8 A player who will not have attained his eighteenth birthday by midnight September 15th of the year of his signing may not be signed to any agreement by a Member Club, nor may his services in any way be negotiated for or contracted for, nor may his name be placed on a Reserve List, nor may he be permitted to attend any training camp. Any such negotiations or any agreement signed as a result thereof shall be null and void and confer no rights whatsoever.

Section 4—League Player Lists

4.1 The Commissioner shall keep with respect to each Member Club the following player lists:

   (a) Reserve List—players
       Reserve List—goalkeeper
       Reserve List—unsigned draft choices
   (b) Voluntary Retired List
   (c) Inactive List
   (d) Protected List
   (e) Play-off Eligibility List
   (f) Free Agent List

Section 5—Reserve Lists

5. A Member Club may have on its Reserve List, at any one time, not more than 90 players, which shall include the following:

   (a) Not more than 50 players signed to a Standard Player's Contract and not less than 24 players and 3 goalkeepers under contract. Age 18 and age 19 players who were returned to Canadian Major Junior Hockey clubs, and who have not played 11 games in the NHL in one season, shall be exempt from inclusion in the 50 player limit. . . .

Section 12—Eligibility of Players

12.6 A player with only one eye, or one whose eyes has a vision of only three-sixtieths (3/60ths) or under, shall not be eligible to play for a Member Club.

Section 17—Fines, Suspensions, and Expulsions

17.1 A player suspended or expelled by any organization or body, amateur or professional, shall at the request of that organization and with the approval of the Commissioner, be deemed to be suspended by the League until such suspension has been lifted or such expulsion has been revoked by the body imposing the same, or until the Commissioner declares that such suspension or expulsion will not be observed by the League.

17.2 Any player or person connected with a Member Club who undertakes to contribute in any way, or does intentionally contribute in any way to the losing or attempting to lose a game of hockey by the team of that Member Club, or who solicits or attempts to induce any player or person connected with a Member Club to lose or contribute to losing any hockey game in which that player is or may be concerned, or upon being solicited to do so fails to inform the Commissioner immediately, shall, in the discretion and by the ruling of the Commissioner, be expelled.

17.3 (a) If, in the opinion of the Commissioner, based upon such information and reports as he may deem sufficient, any act of the conduct of any official of a Member Club or player or employee whether during or outside the playing season, has been dishonorable, prejudicial to or against the welfare of the League or the game of hockey, he may expel or suspend such person or impose on such a person and/or Member Club a fine not exceeding One Hundred Thousand ($100,000) Dollars in the case of an official of a Member Club, or Five Hundred ($500) Dollars in the case of a player or employee, or he may order and impose both a suspension and a fine. . . .

NOTE: A player betting or being interested in any pool or wager on the outcome of any NHL Championship or Playoff game, whether or not the player has any connection with such game; or a physical attack or other violence upon a League Official . . . will be deemed to come under this Section. These instances are only given as examples and are not to be regarded as the only acts or conduct subjecting the offender to the above penalties. . . .

17.4 (a) Any official, player or employee of a Member Club who gives, makes, issues, authorizes or endorses any statement having or designed to have, in the opinion of the Commissioner, an effect prejudicial to the welfare of the League of the game of hockey or of a Member Club; or who makes any public statement that is critical of the League Officiating Staff shall be liable for a fine not exceeding $25,000 in the case of officers and employees of Member Clubs, and $10,000 in the case of players, to be imposed by the Commissioner. In addition in lieu of the above, in the case of officers and employees, the Commissioner in his discretion may also impose a fine upon the Member Club whose officer or employee violates this By–Law. Said fine shall not exceed $25,-000. . . .

17.11 (a) In the case of a suspension or expulsion, or a fine in excess of $500 ordered by the Commissioner, there shall be a right of appeal to the Board of Governors upon written request filed with the Commissioner within ten days from the date of the order of the suspension, expulsion or fine. . . . The Governors not directly affected by the order shall review the evidence by which the Commissioner arrived at his decision to determine whether in their opinion the Commissioner reasonably exercised the powers vested in him by the Constitution and By–Laws, and shall confirm, amend or quash the order made, and confirm or mitigate the penalty imposed. The decision of the Governors shall be final and conclusive. However, when such suspension, expulsion or fine is ordered for betting on a championship or playoff game no such right of appeal or review will be available.

Section 18—Undesirable Employees

18. If, in the opinion of the Commissioner, the employment of any person by a Member Club would be prejudicial to or against the welfare of the League he may prohibit the employment or continuation of

employment of such person by any Member Club in any capacity whatsoever.

Section 36—Transfer of Franchise Application

36.1 *Application*

(a) Any Member Club seeking consent to a transfer of its franchise and club to a different city or borough in accordance with section 4.2 of the Constitution, shall file a written application for such consent with the Commissioner of the League.

36.4 *Vote*

(a) Following such presentation(s) to the Board, there shall be a vote of the members as to whether to consent to the proposed transfer of location, . . . and if applicable, as to whether to consent to any proposed sale, assignment, or transfer of a membership or ownership interest in a Member Club. . . .

(c) A proposed transfer of location receiving the affirmative votes of a majority of the Member Clubs present and voting shall be deemed to have been consented to by the League in the event that the prohibition on transfers recited in Section 4.2 of the Constitution is determined by counsel to the League specially retained for this purpose, based on all relevant factors, to be unlawful with respect to that proposed transfer.

36.5 In determining whether to consent to the transfer of a Member Club's franchise to a different city or borough pursuant to Section 4.2 of the Constitution, each Member Club shall be guided by the following considerations:

(a) Whether the club in question is financially viable in its present location and, if not, whether there is a reasonable prospect . . . that it could become financially viable there, either under its present ownership or under new ownership.

(b) The extent to which the fans have historically supported the franchise in its current location.

(c) The extent to which the club has historically operated profitably or at a loss at its present location.

(d) Whether the present owner of the club has made a good faith effort to find prospective purchasers who are prepared to continue operating the club in its present location and/or has engaged in good faith negotiations with such prospective purchasers.

(e) Whether there is any prospective purchaser of the club and franchise who is prepared to continue operating the club in its present location and, if so, whether any such prospective purchaser is willing and able, if necessary, to sustain losses during at least the initial years of its operation there.

(f) The extent to which the club might be operated in its present location in a more prudent, efficient and/or cost-effective manner than it has been in the past.

(g) The extent to which there is a reasonable prospect that significant additional revenues may become available to the club within a reasonable time in its present location, either from the sale of media rights or from other sources.

(h) The extent to which the local government authorities in the present location are prepared to reduce the operating costs of the club, either by granting tax relief or otherwise.

(i) The extent to which the operating costs of the club in its present location might be reduced through the willingness of the applicable arena authority to reduce the rent charged to the club or otherwise reduce the club's costs or increase its revenues, and/or through the willingness of other suppliers to reduce their charges for goods or services provided to the club.

(j) The adequacy of the arena in which the club plays its home games and the willingness of the applicable arena authority to remedy any deficiencies in the arena.

(k) Whether there will be a suitable arena available in which the club can play its home games in the proposed new location.

(*l*) The extent to which it appears likely, based on the population, demographics and interest in hockey in the area of the proposed new location, or based on any other relevant facts, that support for a franchise there will be sufficient to make the franchise financially viable in the proposed new location on a continuing basis.

(m) The extent to which the owners of the club are willing and able, if necessary, to sustain losses during at least the initial years of its operation in the proposed new location.

(n) The extent to which consent to proposed transfer is likely to damage the image of the League as a major sports league, be a disincentive to participation in the League, or otherwise to have an adverse effect on the League's ability to market and promote League hockey in the United States and/or Canada.

(*o*) The extent to which the proposed transfer would adversely affect traditional rivalries that have been established between the club in its present location and other Member Clubs.

(p) The extent to which consent to the proposed transfer would result in the absence of a League franchise in a major market.

(q) The extent to which it appears likely that, if the proposed transfer is approved, the club would draw more or fewer fans when playing as the visiting team in the home arenas of other Member Clubs.

(r) The extent to which the proposed transfer would present particular disadvantages for the operation of the League, such as travel or scheduling difficulties or a need for a divisional realignment.

(s) The extent to which the club has, directly or indirectly, received public financial support in its present location by virtue of any publicly financed arena, special tax treatment, or any other form of public financial support.

(t) The extent to which the proposed transfer, if approved, would affect any contract or agreement in effect between the club and any public or private party.

(u) The extent to which League consent to the proposed transfer might expose the League to liability to any third party for breach of contract, interference with contractual relations, or for any other cause.

(v) The extent to which the ownership or management of the club has contributed to any circumstance which might otherwise demonstrate a need to transfer the club to a new location.

(w) The extent to which the club has engaged in good faith negotiations with representatives from the community in which it is presently located concerning terms and conditions under which the club would continue to operate in that location.

(x) Any other considerations relevant to whether it would be in the best interest of the League to consent to the proposed transfer.

Section 37—Admission of New Members

37. . . . . In determining whether to grant a franchise pursuant to Section 3.3 of the Constitution, each member of the League shall cast its vote based upon its own conclusion as to whether admission of the applicant would be in the best interest of the League. In addition to any admission fee determined by the League, the League may impose an indemnification fee (or fees) in like manner as provided for transfer in By–Law Section 36.6.

C. COLLECTIVE BARGAINING AGREEMENTS

BASIC AGREEMENT BETWEEN MAJOR LEAGUE BASEBALL AND MAJOR LEAGUE BASEBALL PLAYERS ASSOCIATION

(2002–2006)

ARTICLE VI—Salaries

Individual Player salaries shall be those as agreed upon between a Player and a Club, as evidenced by the execution of a Uniform Player's Contract, subject to the following: . . . .

B. Minimum Salary

(1) The minimum rate of payment to a Player for each day of service on a Major League Club shall be as follows:

2003—at the rate per season of $300,000;

2004—at the rate per season of $300,000;

2005—at the rate per season of $300,000 plus a cost of living adjustment, rounded to the nearest $500, provided that the . . . adjustment shall not reduce the minimum salary below $300,000;

2006—at the 2005 rate per season plus a cost of living adjustment rounded to the nearest $500, provided that the . . . adjustment shall not reduce the minimum salary below the 2005 rate per season.

D. Maximum Salary Reduction

(1) No Player's contract shall be renewed pursuant to paragraph 10(a) of the Uniform Player's Contract in any year for a salary which constitutes a reduction in excess of 20% of his previous year's salary or in excess of 30% of his salary two years previous. For the purposes of this section, the "salary" of a Player with a salary stipulated in paragraph 2 of his Major League contract of less than the then applicable Major League minimum salary shall be deemed to be the greater of either (a) the total amount of his actual baseball salary earnings from Major League Clubs (and from Minor League clubs if any) in that season or (b) the amount stipulated in paragraph 2 of his Major League contract for that season. . . .

F. Salary Arbitration

The following salary arbitration procedure shall be applicable:

(1) *Eligibility.* The issue of a Player's salary may be submitted to final and binding arbitration by any Player or his Club, provided the other party to the arbitration consents thereto. Any Club, or any Player with a total of three or more years of Major League service, however accumulated, but with less than six years of Major League service, may submit the issue of the Player's salary to final and binding arbitration without the consent of the other party, subject to the provisions of paragraph (4) below.

In addition, a Player with at least two but less than three years of Major League service shall be eligible for salary arbitration if: (a) he has accumulated at least 86 days of service during the immediately preceding season; and (b) he ranks in the top seventeen percent (17%) (rounded to the nearest whole number) in total service in the class of Players who have at least two but less than three years of Major League service, however accumulated, but with at least 86 days of service accumulated during the immediately preceding season. If two or more Players are tied in ranking, ties shall be broken consecutively based on the number of days of service accumulated in each of the immediately preceding seasons. If the Players remain tied, the final tie breaker will be by lot.

(3) *Notice of Submission*

(a) *Player Submission....* Within three days after the notice of submission has been given, the Association and the LRD [MLB's Labor Relations Department] shall exchange salary figures. It shall be the responsibility of the Association during this three-day period to obtain the salary figure from the Player, and the LRD shall have a similar responsibility to obtain the Club's figure.

* * *

(4) *Withdrawal from Arbitration.* In the event the Club submits the matter to arbitration, the Player may within 7 days after receipt of the Club's salary arbitration figure notify the Club that he does not wish to arbitrate and the matter shall be deemed withdrawn from arbitration. In such event, or in the event that neither the Club nor the Player submits to arbitration, the rights and obligations of the Club and Player shall be as they would have been had the salary arbitration procedure never been invoked. In the event the Club and Player reach agreement on salary before the arbitrator or arbitration panel reaches a decision, the matter shall be deemed withdrawn from arbitration.

(6) *Form of Submission.* The Player and the Club shall exchange with each other in advance of the hearing single salary figures for the coming season (which need not be figures offered during the prior negotiations) and then shall submit such figures to the arbitrator or arbitration panel. At the hearing, the Player and Club shall deliver to the arbitration panel a Uniform Player's Contract executed in duplicate, complete except for the salary figure to be inserted in paragraph 2. Upon submission of the salary issue to arbitration by either Player or Club, the

Player shall be regarded as a signed Player (unless the Player withdraws from arbitration as provided in paragraph (4) above).

(7) *Selection of Arbitrators.* The Association and the LRD shall annually select the arbitrators. In the event they are unable to agree by January 1 in any year, they jointly shall request that the American Arbitration Association furnish them lists of prominent, professional arbitrators. Upon receipt of such lists, the arbitrators shall be selected by alternately striking names from the lists. All cases shall be assigned to three-arbitrator panels. The Association and the LRD shall designate one arbitrator to serve as the panel chair.

(12) *Criteria*

(a) The criteria will be the quality of the Player's contribution to his Club during the past season (including but not limited to his overall performance, special qualities of leadership and public appeal), the length and consistency of his career contribution, the record of the Player's past compensation, comparative baseball salaries (see paragraph (13) below for confidential salary data), the existence of any physical or mental defects on the part of the Player, and the recent performance record of the Club including but not limited to its League standing and attendance as an indication of public acceptance (subject to the exclusion stated in subparagraph (b)(i) below). Any evidence may be submitted which is relevant to the above criteria, and the arbitration panel shall assign such weight to the evidence as shall appear appropriate under the circumstances. The arbitration panel shall, except for a Player with five or more years of Major League service, give particular attention, for comparative salary purposes, to the contracts of Players with Major League service not exceeding one annual service group above the Player's annual service group. This shall not limit the ability of a Player or his representative, because of special accomplishment, to argue the equal relevance of salaries of Players without regard to service, and the arbitration panel shall give whatever weight to such argument as is deemed appropriate.

(b) Evidence of the following shall not be admissible:

(i) The financial position of the Player and the Club;

(ii) Press comments, testimonials or similar material bearing on the performance of either the Player or the Club, except that recognized annual Player awards for playing excellence shall not be excluded;

(iii) Offers made by either Player or Club prior to arbitration;

(iv) The cost to the parties of their representatives, attorneys, etc.;

(v) Salaries in other sports or occupations.

(13) *Confidential Major League Salary Data.* For his or its confidential use, as background information, the arbitration panel will be given a tabulation showing the minimum salary in the Major Leagues and

salaries for the preceding season of all players on Major League rosters as of August 31, broken down by years of Major League service. The names and Clubs of the Players concerned will appear on the tabulation. In utilizing the salary tabulation, the arbitration panel shall consider the salaries of all comparable Players and not merely the salary of a single Player or group of Players.

(14) *Prohibition Regarding Competitive Balance Tax.* No participant in a salary arbitration shall refer in any fashion, either orally or in writing, to any of the provisions in Article XXIII (Competitive Balance Tax). No salary arbitrator or arbitration panel shall consider in any fashion any of the provisions in Article XXIII (Competitive Balance Tax).

ARTICLE XI—Grievance Procedure

For the purpose of providing an orderly and expeditious procedure for the handling and resolving of certain grievances and complaints, as hereinafter provided, the following shall apply as the exclusive remedy of the Parties.

A. Definitions

As used herein, the following terms shall have the meanings indicated:

(1) (a) "Grievance" shall mean a complaint which involves the existence or interpretation of, or compliance with, any agreement, or any provision of any agreement, between the Association and the Clubs or any of them, or between a Player and a Club, ...

(b) Notwithstanding the definitions of "Grievance" set forth in subparagraph (a) above, "Grievance" shall not mean a complaint which involves action taken with respect to a Player or Players by the Commissioner involving the preservation of the integrity of, or the maintenance of public confidence in, the game of baseball. Within 30 days of the date of the action taken, such complaint shall be presented to the Commissioner who promptly shall conduct a hearing in accordance with the Rules of Procedure attached hereto as Appendix A. The Commissioner shall render a written decision as soon as practicable following the conclusion of such hearing. The Commissioner's decision shall constitute full, final and complete disposition of such complaint, and shall have the same effect as a Grievance decision of the Arbitration Panel. In the event a matter filed as a Grievance in accordance with the procedure hereinafter provided in Section B gives rise to issues involving the integrity of, or public confidence in, the game of baseball, the Commissioner may, at any stage of its processing, order that the matter be withdrawn from such procedure and thereafter be processed in accordance with the procedure provided above in this subparagraph (b). The order of the Commissioner withdrawing such matter shall constitute a final determination of the procedure to be followed for the exclusive and complete disposition of such matter, and such order shall have the same effect as a Grievance decision of the Arbitration Panel. (See also Attachment 2.)

The Association may reopen this Agreement, with reference solely to Section A(1)(b) and Section C of this Article, upon the giving of 10 days' written notice at any time, based upon experience under the aforesaid Sections which, in its opinion, is unsatisfactory.

Any reopening notice served by the Association, in accordance with the foregoing, will be based only on actual experience with the operation of such Sections in the processing of grievances or complaints and such reopening cannot occur unless there is actual experience under such Sections.

(9) "Arbitration Panel" shall mean the impartial arbitrator or, where either Party so elects, a tripartite panel so empowered and composed of the impartial arbitrator and two party arbitrators, one appointed by the Association, the other appointed by the LRD. The impartial arbitrator, who shall in all instances be designated as the Panel Chairman, shall be appointed by agreement of the Association and the LRD. In the event the Association and the LRD are unable to agree upon the appointment of the impartial arbitrator, they jointly shall request that the American Arbitration Association furnish them a list of prominent, professional arbitrators. Upon receipt of said list, they shall alternate in striking names from the list until only one remains. The arbitrator whose name remains shall be deemed appointed as the impartial arbitrator.

At any time during the term of this Agreement either the Association or the LRD may terminate the appointment of the impartial arbitrator by serving written notice upon him and the other Party; provided that no such termination shall in any way impair the authority of the impartial arbitrator to render awards with respect to matters fully submitted to him. Within 30 days of any such termination, the Association and LRD shall either agree upon a successor impartial arbitrator or select a successor from an American Arbitration Association list, as set forth above. . . .

C. Special Procedure with Regard to Certain Disciplinary Action

Complaints involving a fine or suspension imposed upon a Player by the Vice President, On–Field Operations or the Commissioner for conduct on the playing field or in the ballpark shall be subject exclusively to this Section C, as follows:

(1) Any Player who believes that he has a justifiable complaint regarding such discipline may, within 7 days of his receipt of written notification of the discipline, appeal in writing to the President and Chief Operating Officer, if the discipline was imposed by the Vice President, On–Field Operations, or to the Commissioner, if the discipline was imposed by him, for a hearing. Upon receipt of the notice of appeal, the President and Chief Operating Officer or the Commissioner, as the case may be, shall designate a time and place for hearing the appeal, which hearing shall be commenced within 10 days from the date of receipt of

the appeal. . . . Such hearing shall be conducted in accordance with the Rules of Procedure attached hereto as Appendix A. The President and Chief Operating Officer or the Commissioner, as the case may be, shall render a written decision as soon as practicable following the conclusion of such hearing, and may affirm, modify, or revoke the disciplinary action originally imposed. The decision of the President and Chief Operating Officer or the Commissioner, as the case may be, shall constitute full, final and complete disposition of the complaint and shall have the same effect as a Grievance decision of the Arbitration Panel.

* * *

ARTICLE XII—Discipline

A. Just Cause

The Parties recognize that a Player may be subjected to disciplinary action for just cause by his Club, the Vice President, On–Field Operations or the Commissioner. Therefore, in Grievances regarding discipline, the issue to be resolved shall be whether there has been just cause for the penalty imposed.

If discipline imposed upon a Player is determined to be improper by reason of a final decision under this Grievance Procedure, the Player shall promptly be made whole.

* * *

ARTICLE XIX—Assignment of Player Contracts

A. Consent to Assignment

(1) The contract of a Player with ten or more years of Major League service, the last five of which have been with one Club, shall not be assignable to another Major League Club without the Player's written consent. No consent from a Player shall be considered effective until twenty-four hours from the Club's request to the Player for such consent. . . .

(2) (a) The contract of a Player with five or more years of Major League service . . . shall not be assigned otherwise than to another Major League Club, without the Player's written consent.

* * *

ARTICLE XX—Reserve System

B. Free Agency

(1) *Eligibility*

Following the completion of the term of his Uniform Player's Contract, any Player with 6 or more years of Major League service who has not executed a contract for the next succeeding season shall be eligible to become a free agent, subject to and in accordance with the provisions of this Section B.

(4) *Compensation*

(a) The former Club of a Player who: (i) became a free agent under this Section B; and (ii) ranks as a Type A, B or C Player as defined below [generally, star players], shall be entitled to receive compensation subject to the provisions of subparagraph (c) below. Such compensation shall consist solely of the amateur draft choices described in subparagraph (c) below and shall be awarded in the Major League Rule 4 Draft succeeding the Player's election of free agency.

* * *

ARTICLE XXIII—Competitive Balance Tax

B.   Determination of Competitive Balance Tax

(1) *Calculation of Tax.* Except as specifically provided in Section B(3) below, a Club with a final Actual Club Payroll that exceeds the Tax Threshold applicable in that Contract Year ("Tax Threshold") shall be assessed a Competitive Balance Tax on the difference between its final Actual Club Payroll and the Tax Threshold. A Club with a final Actual Club Payroll at or below the Tax Threshold shall incur no Competitive Balance Tax for that Contract Year.

(2) *Tax Thresholds.* The Tax Threshold shall be $117 Million in the 2003 Contract Year, $120.5 Million in the 2004 Contract Year, $128 Million in the 2005 Contract Year and $136.5 million in the 2006 Contract Year.

(3) *Tax Rates.* The Competitive Balance Tax rate applicable to a Club shall depend on the number of Contract Years during this Agreement in which the Club's Actual Club Payroll was above the Tax Threshold.

(a) The Competitive Balance Tax rate applicable in the 2003 Contract Year to a Club with an Actual Club Payroll above the Tax Threshold shall be 17.5%.

(b) The Competitive Balance Tax rate applicable in the 2004 or 2005 Contract Year to a Club with an Actual Club Payroll above the Tax Threshold for the first time during the Agreement shall be 22.5%. A Club with an Actual Club Payroll above the Tax Threshold in the 2006 Contact Year, and for the first time during the Agreement, shall be assessed no tax.

(c) The Competitive Balance Tax rate applicable to a Club with an Actual Club Payroll above the Tax Threshold for a second time during the Agreement shall be 30%. Notwithstanding the foregoing, a Club with an Actual Club Payroll above the Tax Threshold in the 2006 Contract Year for the second time but with an Actual Club Payroll in the 2005 Contract Year that was not above the Tax Threshold shall be assessed no tax.

(d) The Competitive Balance Tax rate applicable to a Club with an Actual Club Payroll above the Tax Threshold for a third or fourth consecutive time during the Agreement shall be 40%. The Competitive Balance Tax rate applicable in the 2006 Contract Year to a Club with an Actual Club Payroll that was above the Tax Threshold in the 2003 and 2005 Contract Years (but not in the 2004 Contract Year) shall be 30%. A Club with an Actual Club Payroll above the Tax Threshold in the 2006 Contract Year but with an Actual Club Payroll in the 2005 Contract Year that was not above the Tax Threshold shall be assessed no tax, even if the Club's Actual Club Payroll was above the Tax Threshold in the 2003 and 2004 Contract Years.

H. Uses Of Competitive Balance Tax Proceeds

Competitive Balance Tax proceeds collected pursuant to Section B(4) above shall be used as follows.

(1) The first $5 million of the proceeds (collected for any Contract Year) shall be held in reserve for the purposes described in paragraphs (5)(b)(ii), (5)(c)(ii)(C) and (5)(d)(iii) of Section E and, if the Parties agree based on experience under such Salary attribution rules, another $5 million, or such other figure to which the Parties agree, of proceeds (collected for any Contract Year) shall be held in reserve for such purposes. Any amount held in reserve pursuant to this paragraph (1), with accrued interest, shall be contributed to the Industry Growth Fund and used for the purposes set out in Article XXV if and when the Parties agree that there is no longer any need for such reserve.

(2) Fifty percent (50%) of the remaining proceeds collected for each Contract Year, with accrued interest, shall be used, as the Office of the Commissioner and the Association shall agree, to fund benefits to Players active during the term of this Agreement.

(3) Twenty-five percent (25%) of the remaining proceeds collected for each Contract Year, with accrued interest, shall be used, as the Office of the Commissioner and the Association shall agree, to fund projects and other efforts to develop baseball players in countries where organized high school baseball is not played.

(4) Twenty-five percent (25%) of the remaining proceeds collected for each Contract Year shall be contributed to the Industry Growth Fund and, with accrued interest, used for the purposes set out in Article XXV.

I. Sunset

There shall be no Competitive Balance Tax in place following the 2006 championship season, and the parties expressly acknowledge and agree that the provisions of this Article XXIII (except those concerning the collection and distribution of the Competitive Balance Tax proceeds for the 2006 Contract Year) shall not survive the expiration of this Agreement.

ARTICLE XXIV—The Revenue Sharing Plan

B. General Principles

(1) *Intent of the Plan.* The intent of the revenue sharing plan is to effect in each revenue sharing year the equivalent net transfer of revenue among the Clubs of $248.014 million at 100% implementation, based on 2001 "payment 5" local revenue data, plus such net transfer as may result from distributions of the Commissioner's Discretionary Fund.

[The lengthy and complex rules for calculating the transfers are omitted.]

NFL–NFLPA COLLECTIVE BARGAINING AGREEMENT

(1993–2007, as extended in 2002)

ARTICLE VI—NFLPA Agent Certification

***Section 1.* Exclusive Representation:** The NFLMC and the Clubs recognize that the NFLPA regulates the conduct of agents who represent players in individual contract negotiations with Clubs. The NFLMC and the Clubs agree that the Clubs are prohibited from engaging in individual contract negotiations with any agent who is not listed by the NFLPA as being duly certified by the NFLPA in accordance with its role as exclusive bargaining agent for NFL players.... The NFLPA agrees that it will not discipline, dismiss or decertify agents based upon the results they achieve or do not achieve in negotiating terms or conditions of employment with NFL Clubs.

ARTICLE IX—Non–Injury Grievance

***Section 1.* Definition:** Any dispute (hereinafter referred to as a "grievance") arising after the execution of this Agreement and involving the interpretation of, application of, or compliance with, any provision of this Agreement, the NFL Player Contract, or any applicable provision of the NFL Constitution and Bylaws pertaining to terms and conditions of employment of NFL players, will be resolved exclusively in accordance with the procedure set forth in this Article, except wherever another method of dispute resolution is set forth elsewhere in this Agreement, and except wherever the Settlement Agreement provides that the Special Master, Impartial Arbitrator, the Federal District Court or the Accountants shall resolve a dispute.

***Section 4.* Appeal:** If a grievance is not resolved after it has been filed and answered, either the player(s) or Club(s) involved, or the NFLPA, or the Management Council may appeal such grievance by filing a written notice of appeal with the Notice Arbitrator and mailing copies thereof to the party or parties against whom such appeal is taken, and either the NFLPA or the Management Council as may be appropriate....

Section 6. **Arbitration Panel:** There will be a panel of four (4) arbitrators, whose appointment must be accepted in writing by the NFLPA and the Management Council. The parties will designate the Notice Arbitrator within ten (10) days of the execution of this Agreement. In the event of a vacancy in the position of Notice Arbitrator, the senior arbitrator in terms of affiliation with this Agreement will succeed to the position of Notice Arbitrator, and the resultant vacancy on the panel will be filled according to the procedures of this Section. Either party to this Agreement may discharge a member of the arbitration panel by serving written notice upon the arbitrator and the other party to this Agreement between December 1 and 10 of each year, but at no time shall such discharges result in no arbitrators remaining on the panel. If either party discharges an arbitrator, the other party shall have two (2) business days to discharge any other arbitrator....

Section 7. **Hearing:** Each arbitrator will designate a minimum of twelve (12) hearing dates per year, exclusive of the period July 15 through September 10 for non-expedited cases, for use by the parties to this Agreement.... At the hearing, the parties to the grievance and the NFLPA and Management Council will have the right to present, by testimony or otherwise, and subject to Section 5, any evidence relevant to the grievance. All hearings will be transcribed....

Section 8. **Arbitrator's Decision and Award:** The arbitrator will issue a written decision within thirty (30) days of the submission of briefs, but in no event shall he consider briefs filed by either party more than sixty (60) days after receipt of the last transcript, unless the parties agree otherwise. The decision of the arbitrator will constitute full, final and complete disposition of the grievance, and will be binding upon the player(s) and Club(s) involved and the parties to this Agreement; provided, however, that the arbitrator will not have the jurisdiction or authority: (a) to add to, subtract from, or alter in any way the provisions of this Agreement or any other applicable document; or (b) to grant any remedy other than a money award, an order of reinstatement, suspension without pay, a stay of suspension pending decision, a cease and desist order, a credit or benefit award under the Bert Bell/Pete Rozelle NFL Player Retirement Plan, or an order of compliance, with a specific term of this Agreement or any other applicable document, or an advisory opinion pursuant to Article XIII (Committees), Section 1(c)....

Section 13. **Grievance Settlement Committee:** A grievance settlement committee consisting of the Executive Director of the NFLPA and the Executive Vice President for Labor Relations of the NFL shall have the authority to resolve any grievance filed under this Article. This committee shall meet periodically to discuss and consider pending grievances. No evidence will be taken at such meetings, except parties involved in the grievance may be contacted to obtain information about their dispute. If the committee resolves any grievance by mutual agreement of the two members, such resolution will be made in writing and will constitute full, final and complete disposition of the grievance and will be binding upon the player(s) and the Club(s) involved and the parties to this Agreement....

ARTICLE X—Injury Grievance

Section 1. **Definition:** An "injury grievance" is a claim or complaint that, at the time a player's NFL Player Contract was terminated by a Club, the player was physically unable to perform the services required of him by that contract because of an injury incurred in the performance of his services under that contract. All time limitations in this Article may be extended by mutual agreement of the parties.

Section 2. **Filing:** Any player and/or the NFLPA must present an injury grievance in writing to a Club, with a copy to the Management Council, within twenty-five (25) days from the date it became known or should have become known to the player that his contract had been terminated....

Section 3. **Answer:** The Club to which an injury grievance has been presented will answer in writing within seven (7) days. If the answer contains a denial of the claim, the general grounds for such denial will be set forth. The answer may raise any special defense, including but not limited to the following:

(a) That the player did not pass the physical examination administered by the Club physician at the beginning of the pre-season training camp for the year in question....; (b) That the player failed to make full and complete disclosure of his known physical or mental condition when questioned during the physical examination; (c) That the player's injury occurred prior to the physical examination and the player knowingly executed a waiver or release prior to the physical examination or his commencement of practice for the season in question which specifically pertained to such prior injury; (d) That the player's injury arose solely from a non-football-related cause subsequent to the physical examination; (e) That subsequent to the physical examination the player suffered no new football-related injury; (f) That subsequent to the physical examination the player suffered no football-related aggravation of a prior injury reducing his physical capacity below the level existing at the time of his physical examination as contemporaneously recorded by the Club physician.

Section 4. **Neutral Physician:** The player must present himself for examination by a neutral physician in the Club city or the Club city closest to the player's residence within twenty (20) days from the date of the grievance.... The neutral physician will not become the treating physician nor will the neutral physician examination involve more than one office visit without the prior approval of both the NFLPA and Management Council. The neutral physician may review any objective medical tests which all parties mutually agree to provide. The neutral physician is further authorized to perform any necessary diagnostic tests after consultation with the parties. The neutral physician is required to submit to the parties a detailed typewritten medical report of his examination. . . .

Section 5.   **Neutral Physician List:** The NFLPA and the Management Council will maintain a jointly approved list of neutral physicians, including at least two orthopedic physicians in each city in which a Club is located. . . .

Section 6.   **Appeal:** A grievance may be appealed to an arbitrator by filing of written notice of appeal with the chairman of the arbitration panel within thirty (30) days from the date of receipt of the neutral physician's written report.

Section 7.   **Arbitration Panel** There will be a panel of five (5) arbitrators, whose appointment must be accepted in writing by the NFLPA and the Management Council. The parties have designated Arthur Stark as the Chairman of the panel. In the event of a vacancy in the position of the Chairman of the panel, the senior arbitrator in terms of affiliation with this Agreement will succeed to the position of Chairman of the panel, and the resultant vacancy on the panel will be filled according to the procedures of this Section. Either party to this Agreement may discharge a member of the arbitration panel by serving written notice upon the arbitrator and the other party to this Agreement between December 1 and 10 of each year, but at no time shall such discharges result in no arbitrators remaining on the panel. . . .

Section 8.   **Hearing:** . . . . The arbitrator will issue a written decision within thirty (30) days of the submission of briefs but shall not consider briefs filed by either party more than sixty-five (65) days after receipt of the last transcript, unless the parties agree otherwise. The arbitrator's decision will be final and binding; provided, however, that no arbitrator will have the authority to add to, subtract from, or alter in any way any provision of this Agreement or any other applicable document. . . .

Section 9.   **Miscellaneous:** The arbitrator will consider the neutral physician's findings conclusive with regard to the physical condition of the player and the extent of an injury at the time of his examination by the neutral physician. The arbitrator will decide the dispute in light of this finding and such other issues or defenses which may have been properly submitted to him. . . .

ARTICLE XI—Commissioner Discipline

Section 1.   **League Discipline:** Notwithstanding anything stated in Article IX (Non–Injury Grievance):

(a) All disputes involving a fine or suspension imposed upon a player for conduct on the playing field other than as described in subsection (b) below, or involving action taken against a player by the Commissioner for conduct detrimental to the integrity of, or public confidence in, the game of professional football, will be processed exclusively as follows: The Commissioner will promptly send written notice of his action to the player, with a copy to the NFLPA. Within twenty (20) days following such written notification, the player affected thereby, or the NFLPA with the player's approval, may appeal in writing to the Commissioner.

(b) Fines or suspensions imposed upon players for unnecessary roughness or unsportsmanlike conduct on the playing field with respect to an opposing player or players shall be determined initially by a person being appointed by the Commissioner after consultation concerning the person being appointed with the Executive Director of the NFLPA, as promptly as possible after the event(s) in question. Such person will send written notice of his action to the player, with a copy to the NFLPA. Within ten (10) days following such notification, the player, or the NFLPA with his approval, may appeal in writing to the Commissioner.

(c) On receipt of a notice of appeal under subsection (a) or (b) above, the Commissioner will designate a time and place for a hearing to be commenced within ten (10) days thereafter, at which he or his designee (other than the person appointed in (b) above) will preside. . . . The hearing may be by telephone conference call, if the player so requests. As soon as practicable following the conclusion of such hearing, the Commissioner will render a written decision which will constitute full, final and complete disposition of the dispute and will be binding upon the player(s) and Club(s) involved in the parties to this Agreement with respect to that dispute. Any discipline imposed pursuant to subsection (b) above may only be affirmed, reduced, or vacated by the Commissioner in such decision, and may not be increased.

* * *

ARTICLE XV—Option Clause

Section 1. **Prohibition:** Commencing with the execution of this Agreement, the option clause contained in the NFL Player Contract shall be discontinued. Any option clause must be negotiated as a separate addendum to the revised NFL Player Contract form. Any negotiated option clause must state the dollar amount(s) to be paid to the player during the option year.

ARTICLE XVI—College Draft

Section 2. **Number of Choices:** . . . [T]he Draft shall consist of seven rounds, with each round consisting of the same number of selection choices as there will be Clubs in the NFL the following League Year, plus a maximum number of additional Compensatory Draft Selections equal to the number of Clubs then in the League, with such Compensatory Draft Selections reserved for Clubs losing certain Unrestricted Free Agents. . . .

Section 5. **Other Professional Teams:**

(a) . . . [I]f a player is drafted by a Club and, during the period between the Draft and the next annual Draft, signs a contract with, plays for or is employed by a professional football team not in the NFL during all or any part of the 12–month period following the initial Draft, then the drafting Club (or any assignee Club) shall retain the exclusive NFL rights to negotiate for and sign a contract with the player until the day of the Draft three League Years after the initial Draft, and shall thereafter have a Right of First Refusal as described herein, and the player may receive offers from any Club at any time thereafter....

Section 6. **Return to College:** If any college football player who becomes eligible for the Draft prior to exhausting his college football eligibility through participation is drafted by an NFL Club, and returns to college, the drafting Club's exclusive right to negotiate and sign a Player Contract with such player shall continue through the date of the Draft that follows the last season in which the player was eligible to participate in college football, and thereafter the player shall be treated and the Club shall have such exclusive rights as if he were drafted in such Draft by such Club (or assignee Club).

Section 9. **No Subsequent Draft:** If a player is drafted by a Club in an initial Draft and (a) does not sign a contract with a Club during the signing period set forth in Sections 4 through 6 above, and (b) is not drafted by any Club in the subsequent Draft, the player immediately becomes and Undrafted Rookie, with the right to negotiate and sign a Player Contract with any Club, and any Club is then free to negotiate for and sign a Player Contract with such player, without any Draft Choice Compensation between Clubs or First Refusal Rights of any kind, or any signing period.

ARTICLE XVII—Entering Player Pool

Section 1. **Definition:** For purposes of this Article XVII of this Agreement, the following terms shall have the meanings set forth below:

(a) "Entering Player Pool" means the League-wide limit on the total amount of Salary to which all of the NFL Clubs may contract for in singing Drafted Rookies (and certain amounts contracted to be paid to Undrafted Rookies as described below) during each League Year of this Agreement, as set forth below.

Section 3. **Calculation:**

(a) .... For the 2004–07 League Years, the Entering Player Pool shall consist on a League-wide basis of the amount of the Entering Player Pool for the immediately preceding League Year (excluding any formula allotments attributable to any Compensatory Draft Selections), increased by the same percentage as the increase in Projected DGR for that League Year over the prior year's DGR ..., up to a maximum of five percent (5%) per season, but shall not in any event decrease in actual amount from League Year to League Year....

(b) For each League Year of this Agreement, each Club shall have a Rookie Allocation, which shall be its proportional share of the Entering Player Pool, calculated based on the number, round, and position of the

Club's selection choices in the Draft. The Rookie Allocation formula shall be agreed upon by the NFL and the NFLPA and shall remain in effect for the duration of the Agreement, unless the NFL and the NFLPA otherwise agree.

(c) If, pursuant to Article XVI (College Draft), Section 2 and/or Article XX (Franchise and Transition Players), Section 13, a Club has one or more Compensatory Draft Selections, an amount shall be added to that Club's Rookie Allocation, and to the Entering Player Pool (notwithstanding subsection (b) above), based upon the amount allotted to selection choices of that round and position in calculating the Rookie Allocation (the "Formula Allotment").....

(d) Notwithstanding the above, nothing shall prevent the Club from signing a player for an amount in excess of the player's Formula Allotment, if the Club has Room available under its Rookie Allocation.

(e) In the event that the NFL holds a supplemental draft in addition to its annual Draft in advance of the next League Year's Draft, adjustments shall be made to the Entering Player Pool and Rookie Allocation in a manner to be agreed upon by the NFL and the NFLPA.

Section 4. **Operation:**

(a) No Club may enter into Player Contracts with Drafted Rookies that, standing alone or in the aggregate, provide for Salaries in the first League Year of such Player Contracts that would exceed the Club's Rookie Allocation for that year.

(e) No Player Contract signed by a Rookie may provide for an annual increase in Salary of more than 25% of the contract's first League Year Salary. For the purposes of the calculation in this section only, any amount of a signing bonus attributed to the player's Salary shall not be counted.

(f) The Player Contract of a Drafted Rookie or Undrafted Rookie may not be renegotiated for a one (1) year period following the date of the initial signing of such Player Contract, or until August 1 of the following League Year, whichever is later.

(g) Nothing in this Agreement is intended to or shall be construed to mean that any Rookie's Salary is predetermined by any Allocation or Formula Allotment.

ARTICLE XVIII—Veterans With Less Than Tree Accrued Seasons

Section 1. **Accrued Seasons Calculation:**

(a) For the purposes of calculating Accrued Seasons under this Agreement, a player shall receive one Accrued Season for each season during which he was on, or should have been on, full pay status for a total of six or more regular season games, but which, irrespective of the player's pay status, shall not include games for which the player was on: (i) the Exempt Commissioner Permission List, (ii) the Reserve PUP List as a result of a non-football injury, or (iii) a Club's Practice or Development Squad.

(b) For the purposes of calculating Accrued Seasons under this Agreement, ... a player shall not receive an Accrued Season for any League Year in which the player is under contract to a Club and in which he failed to report to such Club at least thirty days prior to the first regular season game of that season, or in which the player thereafter failed to perform his contract services for the Club for a material period of time, unless he demonstrates to the Impartial Arbitrator extreme personal hardship causing such failure to report or perform, such as severe illness or death in the family....

Section 2. **Negotiating Rights of Players With Less Than Three Accrued Seasons:** Any Veteran with less than three Accrued Seasons whose contract has expired may negotiate or sign a Player Contract only with his Prior Club, if on or before March 1 his Prior Club tenders the player a one year Player Contract with a Paragraph 5 Salary of at least the Minimum Active/Inactive List Salary applicable to that player. If the Prior Club has not by that date made the Required Tender or later withdraws such tender, the player shall be completely free to negotiate and sign a Player Contract with any Club, and any Club shall be completely free to negotiate and sign a Player Contract with such player, without any penalty or restriction, including, but not limited to, Draft Choice Compensation between Clubs or First Refusal Rights of any kind, or any signing period.

* * *

ARTICLE XIX—Veteran Free Agency

Section 1. **Unrestricted Free Agents:**

(a) Subject to the provisions of Article XX (Franchise and Transition Players), any player with five or more Accrued Seasons, or with four or more Accrued Seasons in any Capped Year, shall, at the expiration of his Player Contract, become an Unrestricted Free Agent. Such player shall be completely free to negotiate and sign a Player Contract with any Club, and any Club shall be completely free to negotiate and sign a Player Contract with such player, without penalty or restriction, ...

Section 2. **Restricted Free Agents:**

(a) Any Veteran player with three or more Accrued Seasons, but less than five Accrued Seasons (or less than four Accrued Seasons in any Capped Year), shall, at the expiration of his last Player Contract during such period, become a Restricted Free Agent. Any such player shall be completely free to negotiate and sign a Player Contract with any Club, and any Club shall be completely free to negotiate and sign a Player Contract with any such player, subject to the restrictions set forth in this Article.

(b) In order to receive the following specified Rights of First Refusal and/or Draft Choice Compensation with respect to a Restricted Free

Agent, the Prior Club of a Restricted Free Agent must tender the player a Qualifying Offer on or before the first date of the Restricted Free Agent Signing Period, as follows:

(i) For Restricted Free Agents with three Accrued Seasons:

(1) *Right of First Refusal*: one year Player Contract with Paragraph 5 Salary of at least $275,000;

(2) *Right of First Refusal and Draft Selection at Player's Original Draft Round*: one year Player Contract with a Paragraph 5 Salary of at least (a) $275,000, or (b) 110% of the player's prior year's Paragraph 5 Salary, whichever is greater; in addition, if option (b) applies, all other terms of the player's prior year contract are carried forward unchanged (this subsection is subject to the rules of subsection (c) below);

(3) *Right of First Refusal and One First Round Draft Selection*: one year Player Contract with a Paragraph 5 Salary of at least (a) $600,000, or (b) 110% of the player's prior year's Paragraph 5 Salary, whichever is greater; in addition, if option (b) applies, all other terms of the player's prior year contract are carried forward unchanged;

(4) *Right of First Refusal, One First Round Draft Selection, and One Third Round Draft Selection*: one year Player Contract with a Paragraph 5 Salary of at least (a) $800,000, or (b) 110% of the player's prior year's Paragraph 5 Salary, whichever is greater; in addition, if option (b) applies, all other terms of the player's prior year contract are carried forward unchanged.

(ii) For Restricted Free Agents with four Accrued Seasons (in Uncapped Years):

(1) *Right of First Refusal*: one year Player Contract with Paragraph 5 Salary of at least $325,000;

(2) *Right of First Refusal and Draft Selection at Player's Original Draft Round*: one year Player Contract with a Paragraph 5 Salary of at least (a) $325,000, or (b) 110% of the player's prior year's Paragraph 5 Salary, whichever is greater; in addition, if option (b) applies, all other terms of the player's prior year contract are carried forward unchanged (this subsection is subject to the rules of subsection (c) below);

(3) *Right of First Refusal and One First Round Draft Selection*: one year Player Contract with a Paragraph 5 Salary of at least (a) $700,000, or (b) 110% of the player's prior year's Paragraph 5 Salary, whichever is greater; in addition, if option (b) applies, all other terms of the player's prior year contract are carried forward unchanged; and

(4) *Right of First Refusal, One First Round Draft Selection, and One Third Round Draft Selection*: one year Player Contract with a Paragraph 5 Salary of at least (a) $900,000, or (b) 110%

of the player's prior year's Paragraph 5 Salary, whichever is greater; in addition, if option (b) applies, all other terms of the player's prior year contract are carried forward unchanged.

* * *

(e) The amounts of the Qualifying Offers specified in this section ($275,000, $325,000, $600,000, $700,000, $800,000 and $900,000) shall increase each League Year following the 1993 League Year by the same percentage as the increase in Projected DGR over the prior League Year's DGR (as defined in Article XXIV), up to a maximum of ten percent (10%) per League Year, but shall not in any event decrease in actual amount from League Year to League Year. Notwithstanding the foregoing, in no event shall Qualifying Offer amounts increase if the projected DGR for the League Year in question is not greater than the highest DGR of any previous League Year.

(f) A Restricted Free Agent shall have the option of accepting a one year NFL Player Contract for 110% of his Prior Year Paragraph 5 Salary (with all other terms of his prior year contract carried forward unchanged) in lieu of a Player Contract for the applicable alternative amount specified in this section, if he so wishes, regardless of which Player Contract is for a greater amount.

(g) In the event a Prior Club withdraws its Qualifying Offer, the Restricted Free Agent shall immediately become an Unrestricted Free Agent and shall be completely free to negotiate and sign a Player Contract with any Club, and any Club shall be completely free to negotiate and sign a Player Contract with any such player, without being subject to First Refusal, Draft Choice Compensation, Signing Period, or any other limitation of any kind.

ARTICLE XX—Franchise and Transition Players

Section 1. **Franchise Player Designations:** Except as set forth in Sections 3, 9, and 17 below, each Club shall be permitted to designate one of its players who would otherwise be an Unrestricted [or Restricted] Free Agent as a Franchise Player each season during the term of this Agreement. . . . Any Club that designates a Franchise Player shall be the only Club with which such Franchise Player may negotiate or sign a Player Contract, during the period the player is so designated, notwithstanding the number of his Accrued Seasons. . . .

Section 2. **Required Tender for Franchise Players:**

(a)-(b) [deleted]

(c) Any Club that designates a Franchise Player shall on the date the designation is made notify the player and the NFLPA which one of the following two potential required tenders the Club has selected:

(i) A one year NFL Player Contract for the average of the five largest Prior Year Salaries for players at the position at which the Franchise Player played most games during the prior League Year, or 120% of his Prior Year Salary, whichever is greater; if the Club extends the tender pursuant to this Subsection (c)(i), the player shall be permitted to negotiate a Player Contract with any Club as if he were a player subject to Section 5 below [where current Club holds a right of first refusal], except that Draft Choice Compensation of two first round draft selections shall be made with respect to such player in the event he signs with the New Club. . . . ; or

(ii) A one year NFL Player Contract of (1) the average of the five largest Salaries in Player Contracts for that League Year as of the end of the Restricted Free Agent Signing Period for that League Year . . ., for players at the position at which he played the most games during the prior League Year, or (2) the amount of the required tender under subsection (c)(i) above, whichever is greater.

* * *

Section 3. Transition Player Designations:

(a) Each Club shall be permitted to designate one Unrestricted Free Agent as a Transition Player between February 1 and February 15 in the Final League Year, . . . In addition, in each League Year during the term of this Agreement, each Club shall be permitted to designate one Unrestricted Free Agent as a Transition Player in lieu of designating a Franchise Player, if such Franchise Player designation is available to such Club, in addition to the Transition Player designations permitted by the immediately preceding sentence.

(b) Any Club that designates a Transition Player shall receive the Rights of First Refusal specified in this Article notwithstanding the number of his Accrued Seasons. Any Transition Player shall be completely free to negotiate and sign a Player Contract with any Club during the period from the first day of the League Year following the expiration of his last Player Contract to July 22, and any Club shall be completely free to negotiate and sign a Player Contract with such player, without penalty or restriction, including, but not limited to, Draft Choice Compensation between Clubs of any kind, subject only to the Prior Club's Right of First Refusal described in this Article.

Section 4. Required Tender for Transition Players:

(a) Any Club that designates a Transition Player shall be deemed on the first day of the League Year following the expiration of the player's last contract to have automatically tendered the player a one year NFL Player Contract for the average of the ten largest Prior Year Salaries for players at the position at which he played the most games during the prior League Year, or 120% of his Prior Year Salary, whichever is greater. . . .

ARTICLE XXIV—Guaranteed League–Wide Salary, Salary Cap & Minimum Team Salary

Section 1. Definitions: For purposes of this Article, and anywhere else specifically stated in this Agreement, the following terms shall have the meanings set forth below:

(a) **Defined Gross Revenues.**

(i) "Defined Gross Revenues" (also referred to as "DGR") means the aggregate revenues received or to be received on an accrual basis, for or with respect to a League Year during the term of this Agreement, by the NFL and all NFL Teams (and their designees), from all sources, whether known or unknown, derived from, relating to or arising out of the performance of players in NFL football games, with only the specific exceptions set forth below. The NFL and each NFL Team shall in good faith act and use their best efforts, consistent with sound business judgment, so as to maximize Defined Gross Revenues for each playing season during the term of this Agreement. Defined Gross Revenues shall include, without limitation:

(1) regular season, pre-season, and post-season gate receipts (net of admission taxes, and surcharges paid to stadium or municipal authorities which are deducted for purposes of calculating gate receipts subject to revenue sharing), including ticket revenue from "luxury boxes," suits and premium seating subject to gate receipt sharing among NFL Teams; and

(2) proceeds including Copyright Royalty Tribunal and extended market payments from the sale, license or other conveyance of the right to broadcast or exhibit NFL pre-season, regular season and play-off games on radio and television . . . ; and

(3) proceeds from the sale or conveyance of any right to receive any of the revenues described above.

(ii) The following is a nonexclusive list of examples of revenues received by the NFL and/or NFL Teams which are not derived from, and do not relate to or arise out of the performance of players in NFL football games (and are therefore not "DGR"): proceeds from the assignment, sale or trade of Player Contracts, proceeds from the sale of any existing NFL franchise (or any interest therein) or the grant of NFL expansion franchises, dues or capital contributions received by the NFL, fines, "revenue sharing" among NFL Teams, interest income, insurance recoveries, and sales of interests in real estate and other property.

* * *

Notwithstanding any other provision of this Agreement, the NFLPA and Class Counsel may agree, on a case-by-case basis, with no limitation on their exercise of discretion, not to include in DGR network television revenues to the extent that such revenue is used to fund the construction or renovation of a stadium that results in an increase of DGR and/or Excluded DGR.

(iii) Notwithstanding subsection 1(a)(i) above, the following shall be considered "Excluded DGR" and not included in Defined Gross Revenues: revenues derived from concessions, parking, local advertising and promotion, signage, magazine advertising, local sponsorship agreements, stadium clubs, luxury box income other than that included in subsection 1(a)(i)(1) above, sales of programs and novelties, and any categories of revenue (other than those listed in subsections 1(a)(i)(1)–(3) above) currently included under NFL Films and NFL Properties, Inc. and its subsidiaries....

(vii) The reasonableness and includability in DGR of [] allocations and transactions between Related Entities [3rd parties owned or controlled by a Club's owner(s)] shall be determined by the nationally recognized accounting firm jointly retained by the parties....

(x)(1) ... [E]xcept as specified in subsections (x)(2) through (x)(7) below, DGR shall include all revenues from Personal Seat Licenses ("PSLs") received by, or received by a third party and used, directly or indirectly, for the benefit of, the NFL or any Team or Team Affiliate, without any deduction for taxes or other expenses. Such revenues shall be allocated in equal portions, commencing in the League Year in which they are received, over the remaining life of the PSL, subject to a maximum allocation period of fifteen years; ....

(x)(2) To the extent that PSL revenues are used to pay for the construction of a new stadium or stadium renovation(s) that increase DGR (regardless of whether the stadium is owned by a public authority or a private entity ...), *and* if such PSL revenues have received a waiver of any League requirement of sharing of "gross receipts," then such PSL revenues will not be included in a Particular League Year in DGR or in Excluded DGR [up to a maximum of the amount that DGR is increased by such expenditures].

* * *

Section 2. **Trigger For Guaranteed League-wide Salary, Salary Cap, and Minimum Team Salary:** ... If in any League Year the total Player Costs for all NFL Teams equals or exceeds 67% of actual Defined Gross Revenues, there shall be a Guaranteed League-wide Salary, Salary Cap, and Minimum Team Salary in the amounts set forth below for the next League Year and all subsequent League Years, unless the Salary Cap is removed pursuant to Section 4(b)(ii)(4) below. Notwithstanding the immediately preceding sentence, there will be no Guaranteed League-wide Salary, Salary Cap or Minimum Team Salary in the Final League Year.

Section 3. **Guaranteed League-wide Salary:** In any League Year in which a Salary Cap is in effect there shall be a Guaranteed League-wide Salary of 58% of actual Defined Gross Revenues. In the event that the Player Costs for all NFL Teams during any League Year in which a Salary Cap is in effect are less than 58% of actual Defined Gross Revenues for such season, then, on or before April 15 of the next League Year, the NFL shall pay an amount equal to such deficiency directly to players who played on NFL Teams during such season pursuant to the reasonable allocation instructions of the NFLPA.

Section 4. **Salary Cap Amounts:**

(a) Subject to the adjustments set forth below, the amount of the Salary Cap for each NFL Team in years that it is in effect shall be (1) in the 2002 League Year, 64% of the Projected Defined Gross Revenues, less League-wide Projected Benefits, divided by the number of Teams playing in the NFL during such year; (2) in the 2003 League Year, 64.25% of the Projected Defined Gross Revenues, less League-wide Projected Benefits, divided by the number of Teams playing in the NFL during such year; and (3) in the 2004 League Year, 64.75% of the Projected Defined Gross revenues, less League-wide Projected benefits, divided by the number of Teams playing in the NFL during such year; (4) in the 2005 League Year, 65.5% of the Projected Defined Gross revenues, less League-wide Projected benefits, divided by the number of Teams playing in the NFL during such year; and (5) in the 2006 League Year, 64.5% of the Projected Defined Gross revenues, less League-wide Projected benefits, divided by the number of Teams playing in the NFL during such year . . . .

(b) The foregoing Salary Cap amounts shall be adjusted as follows:

(i) The actual dollar amount of the Salary Cap shall not be less than the actual dollar amount of any Salary Cap in effect during the preceding League Year; provided, however, that at no time shall the Projected Benefits, plus the amount of the Salary Cap multiplied by the number of Teams in the NFL, exceed 70% of the Projected Defined Gross Revenues.

(ii) If the total Player Costs of the NFL Teams during any League Year in which the Salary Cap is in effect falls below:

(1) 59% of actual Defined Gross Revenues, then the Salary Cap percentage for the next League Year shall be increased by 1% of Projected Defined Gross Revenues;

(2) 58% of actual Defined Gross Revenues, then the Salary Cap percentage for the next League Year shall be increased by 2% of Projected Defined Gross Revenues;

(3) 57% of actual Defined Gross Revenues, then the Salary Cap percentage for the next League Year shall be increased by 3% of Projected Defined Gross Revenues;

(4) 56% of actual Defined Gross Revenues, then there shall be no Salary Cap for the next League Year or any succeeding League Year unless and until the Salary Cap again becomes effective in accordance with Section 2 of this Article.

Section 5. **Minimum Team Salary:**

(a) With respect to each League Year for which a Salary Cap is in effect, there shall be a guaranteed Minimum Team Salary of 56% of Projected Defined Gross Revenues, less League-wide Projected Benefits, divided by the then current number of teams in the NFL. Each Team shall be required to have a Team Salary of at least the Minimum Team Salary at the end of each League Year.

(b) Nothing contained herein shall preclude a Team from having a Team Salary in excess of the Minimum Team Salary, provided it does not exceed the Salary Cap.

(c) Any shortfall in the Minimum Team Salary at the end of a League Year shall be paid, on or before April 15 of the next League Year, by the Teams having such shortfall, directly to the players who were on such Teams' roster at any time during the season, pursuant to reasonable allocation instructions of the NFLPA.

***Section 7.* Valuation of Player Contracts:** Notwithstanding any provision in a Player Contract to the contrary or when such payments are actually made, the following rules shall apply in determining the amount of a player's Salary that is to be included in Team Salary in a particular League Year for purposes of the Salary Cap:

(a) **Paragraph 5.**

(i) The highest applicable Salary set forth in Paragraph 5 of the NFL Player Contract shall be included in Team Salary in the year earned, ...

(ii) **Deferred Salary.** Any Paragraph 5 Salary to be earned in a particular year but not to be paid until after the next League Year shall be considered "Deferred Salary" and will be included in Team Salary during the League Year earned at its present value based on the Treasury Note rate published in The Wall Street Journal on March 1 in the year earned. . . .

(b) **Signing Bonuses.**

(i) **Proration.** The total amount of any signing bonus shall be prorated over the term of the Player Contract in determining Team and Player Salary, except that:

(1) Signing bonuses agreed to in a Capped Year may not be prorated more than three years beyond the Final Capped Year. . . .

(2) Any contract year in which the player has the right to terminate based upon events within his sole control shall not be counted as a contract year for purposes of proration. . . .

[*Side Letter 11/1/95: Sec. 1*

[This agreement applies to] any multiyear Player Contract not unconditionally approved by the Commissioner as of the date hereof, other than any multiyear Player Contract executed in the last Capped Year of this Agreement, that extends from a Capped Year into any Uncapped Year. For purposes of determining Team Salary, if (i) the sum of the player's Paragraph 5 Salary, roster bonuses that are based upon the player making any of the Club's roster categories without limitation, and reporting bonuses during all Capped Years of the Subject Contract (but, if there are fewer than three remaining Capped Years, during the first three years of the Subject Contract) is in the aggregate less than (ii) the portion of the Subject Contract's signing bonus that would be allocated to those League Years if the signing bonus were prorated equally over the term of the Subject Contract, then: the difference of the amounts calculated pursuant to (ii) and (i) of this sentence, up to 50% of the portion of the signing bonus that would otherwise be allocated to the Uncapped Years (the "Difference"), shall be deducted in equal portions from those Uncapped Years and reallocated in equal portions over the Capped Years of the Subject Contract (or, if there are fewer than three Capped Years within the term of the Subject Contract, over the first three years of the Subject Contract). For purposes of this Paragraph, a renegotiation shall be treated as if it is an entirely new Player Contract.]

(3) If a Player Contract provides for an increase in Salary upon the assignment of such contract to another NFL Team, such increase shall be included in the player's Salary upon such assignment and be attributable to the Team paying the bonus.

(ii) **Acceleration.**

(1) For any player removed from the Team's roster on or before June 1, any unamortized signing bonus amounts will be included in Team Salary for such League Year. If such acceleration puts a Team over the Salary Cap, the Team will have seven days to conform with the Salary Cap, but may not sign any players until there is Room to do so under the Salary Cap.

(2) For any player removed from the Team's roster after June 1, any unamortized signing bonus amounts for future years will be included fully in Team Salary at the start of the next League Year.

(3) In the event that a player who has had a signing bonus allocated over the years of his Player Contract is traded, or whose Contract is assigned to another team pursuant to the NFL's waiver procedure, then such signing bonus shall be accelerated as in subsection (ii)(1) above and the assignee Team's Team Salary will not include any portion of the signing bonus.

(4) Any contract year that the player has the right to terminate based upon a contingency shall count as a contract year for purposes of proration until the contingency is fulfilled, at which time any amounts attributed to such year shall be accelerated and included immediately in Team Salary. To the extent that such acceleration puts the Team over its Salary Cap, the difference shall be deducted from its Salary Cap for the following year.

* * *

(c) **Incentives.**

(i) Any and all incentive amounts, including but not limited to performance bonuses, shall be included in Team Salary if they are "likely to be earned" during such League Year based upon the player's and/or Team's performance during the prior year. In the case of a Rookie, or a Veteran who did not play during the prior season, in the event that the NFL and the NFLPA cannot agree as to whether such performance bonus is "likely to be earned," such disputes shall be referred to the Impartial Arbitrator. Any incentive within the sole control of the player (e.g., non-guaranteed reporting bonuses, off-season workout and weight bonuses) shall be deemed "likely to be earned."

(ii) At the end of a season, if performance bonuses actually earned resulted in a Team's paying Salary in excess of the Salary Cap, then the amount by which the Team exceeded the Salary Cap as a result of such actually paid performance bonuses shall be subtracted from the Team's Salary Cap for the next League Year.

(iii) At the end of a season, if performance bonuses previously included in a Team's Team Salary but not actually earned exceed performance bonuses actually earned but not previously included in Team Salary, an amount shall be added to the Team's Salary Cap for the next League Year equaling the amount, if any, by which such overage exceeds the Team's Room under the Salary Cap at the end of a season.

(e) **Other Amounts.**

(i) **Loans.** The principal amount of any loan made, guaranteed, or collateralized by a Team or its Team Affiliate to a player shall be included in Team Salary. However, when a player pays back any portion of the principal amount of any such loan, such amount will be added to the Team's Salary Cap to the extent previously included in Team Salary.

(ii) **Salary Advances.** The full amount of any Salary advance paid to a player will be included immediately in Salary and Team Salary.

(iii) **Non-Cash Provisions.** The fair market value of all non-cash provisions (e.g., automobiles, houses, insurance policies) shall be included in Team Salary during the year in which such provision is made. If the parties cannot agree on the fair market value of such provisions, such dispute will be submitted to the Impartial Arbitrator.

ARTICLE XXV—Enforcement of the Salary Cap and Entering Player Pool

Section 3. **Special Master Action:** Any individual player or the NFLPA acting on that player's or any number of players' behalf, the NFL and any Club may bring an action before the Special Master alleging a violation of Article XVII (Entering Player Pool) and/or Article XXIV (Guaranteed League-wide Salary, Salary Cap & Minimum Team Salary) of this Agreement. Issues of relief and liability shall be determined in the same proceeding. The complaining party shall bear the burden of demonstrating by a clear preponderance of the evidence that the challenged conduct was in violation of Article XVII (Engineering Player Pool) and/or Article XXIV (Guaranteed League-wide Salary, Salary Cap & Minimum Team Salary).

Section 4. **Commissioner Disapproval:** In the event the Commissioner disapproves any Player Contract as being in violation of Article XVII (Entering Player Pool) and/or Article XXIV (Guaranteed League-wide Salary, Salary Cap & Minimum Team Salary), he shall at the time of such disapproval notify the NFLPA, all affected Clubs, and all affected players of such disapproval in writing and the reasons therefor. Except as required by the terms of this Agreement, nothing in this Agreement is intended to affect (i) any authority of the Commissioner to approve or disapprove Player Contracts and (ii) the effect of the Commissioner's approval or disapproval on the validity of such Player Contracts.

Section 5. **Special Master Review:** In the event that the Commissioner disapproves a Player Contract pursuant to Section 4 above, the NFLPA, any affected Club, and any affected player shall have the right within thirty (30) days of such person's notice of such disapproval to initiate a proceeding before the Special Master to determine whether such contract is in violation of Articles XVII (Entering Player Pool) and/or Article XXIV (Guaranteed League-wide Salary, Salary Cap & Minimum Team Salary). The Special Master shall review the dispute *de novo*, and shall have the authority to approve such Player Contracts in lieu of the Commissioner's approval, or confirm the Commissioner's disapproval. In the event the Commissioner's disapproval is upheld, the player and the Club shall have ten (10) days to attempt to renegotiate such Player Contract notwithstanding any other time period set forth in this Agreement. The Special Master does not have the authority to impose any revisions to such Player Contract on the player or the Club.

Section 6. **Sanctions:** (a) *Players and Agents.* In the event that the Special Master finds a violation of subsection 1(a) or 1(b) of this Article [dealing with Undisclosed Terms of Circumvention of the Salary Cap], for each such violation: (i) (1) the Special Master may impose a fine of up to $250,000 on any player or player agent found to have committed such violation, and (2) shall, unless the parties to this Agreement otherwise agree, order the player to disgorge any undisclosed compensation found to have been paid in violation of Section1 of this Article unless the player establishes by a preponderance of the evidence that he was unaware of the violation; and (ii) the Commissioner shall be authorized to void any Player Contract(s) that was (or were) the direct cause of such violation.

(b) *Clubs.* In the event that the Special Master finds a violation of Section 1(a) of this Article ["Undisclosed Terms"], for each such violation, the Commissioner shall be authorized to: (i) impose a fine of up to $3,500,000, payable to the NFL, upon any Club found to have committed such violation; (ii) order the forfeiture of up to a maximum of two draft choices (without limitation as to round) by the Club found to have committed such violation; (iii) impose a fine of up to $250,000 on any Club executive or other Club personnel found to have committed such violation; and/or (iv) suspend for up to one year any Club executive or other Club personnel found to have committed such violation. In the event that the Special Master finds a violation of subsection 1(b) of this Article ["Circumvention"], for each such violation, the Special Master may: (i) impose a fine of up to $3,500,000, payable to the NFL, upon any Club found to have committed such violation; and (ii) impose a fine of up to $250,000 on any Club executive or other Club personnel found to have committed such violation. In addition, in the event that the Special

Master finds a violation of subsection 1(b) of this Article ["Circumvention"], for each such violation, the Commissioner (i) shall be authorized to order the forfeiture of up to a maximum of two draft choices (without limitation as to round) by the Club found to have committed such violation; and (ii) shall, unless the parties agree otherwise, suspend for up to one year any Club executive or other Club personnel found to have committed such violation. . . .

(c) . . . . For each League Year after the 2000 League Year, each of the maximum fines set forth in Paragraph 6 shall increase by the same percentage as the increase in Projected DGR for that League Year over the Prior Year's DGR (up to a maximum of ten percent (10%) per League Year). . . .

ARTICLE XXVI—Special Master

Section 1. **Appointment:** The parties agree that the Special Master appointed by the Court pursuant to the Final Consent Judgment in *White v. NFL* shall have exclusive jurisdiction to enforce the terms of Articles I, XIV, XVI–XXI, XXIV–XXX, and LVI–LVIII of this Agreement that specifically provide for resolution by the Special Master (except as provided in those Articles with respect to disputes determined by the Impartial Arbitrator) and shall hold hearings on alleged violations thereof, subject to review by the Court in the manner set forth below.

Section 2. **Scope of Authority:** The powers of the Court and the Special Master and the rights of the parties in any enforcement proceeding shall be as set forth in Rules 53(a), (c), (d) and (e) of the Federal Rules of Civil Procedure; provided, however, that:

(a) The Special Master shall make findings of fact and recommendation of relief including, without limitation, damages (including damages referred to in Articles XXVIII (Anti–Collusion), Section 9), contempt and specific performance;

(b) The Court shall accept the Special Master's findings of fact unless clearly erroneous and the Special Master's recommendations of relief unless based upon clearly erroneous findings of fact, incorrect application of the law, or abuse of discretion; except that, as to any finding concerning Article XXVIII (Anti–Collusion), any imposition of a fine of $1 million or more, or any finding that would permit termination of this Agreement, review shall be *de novo*; . . . .

ARTICLE XXVII—Impartial Arbitrator

Section 1. **Selection:** The parties shall agree upon an Impartial Arbitrator who shall have exclusive jurisdiction to determine disputes that are specifically referred to the Impartial Arbitrator pursuant to the express terms of this Agreement.

Section 2. **Scope of Authority:** The powers of the Impartial Arbitrator and the rights of the parties in any proceeding before him or her shall be solely to determine disputes that are specifically referred to the Impartial Arbitrator pursuant to the express terms of this Agreement. In no event shall the Impartial Arbitrator have any authority to add to, subtract from, or alter in any way the provisions of this Agreement.

ARTICLE LVII—Mutual Reservation
Of Rights: Labor Exemption

Section 1. **Rights Under Law:** ... Subject to the provisions of this Article, upon the expiration or termination of this Agreement or the Settlement Agreement, the Parties shall be free to make any available argument that any provision or practice authorized by this Agreement or the Settlement Agreement is or is not then a violation of the antitrust laws, or is or is not then entitled to any labor exemption.

Section 2. **Labor Exemption:** In effectuation of this Agreement, the Parties agree that the labor exemption from the antitrust laws applies during the express term of this Agreement and to any conduct of the NFL and the NFLPA taken in accordance with the terms of this Agreement during its express term.

Section 3. **CBA Expiration:**

(a) Following the expiration of the express term of this Agreement, then, if the NFLPA is in existence as a union, the Parties agree that none of the Class Members (as defined in the Settlement Agreement) nor any player represented by the NFLPA shall be able to commence an action, or assert a claim, under the antitrust laws for conduct occurring, until either: (i) the Management Council and NFLPA have bargained to impasse; or (ii) six months after such expiration, whichever is later; at that time, the Parties reserve any arguments they may make regarding the application of the labor exemption.

(b) The Parties agree that, after the expiration of the express term of this Agreement, in the event that at that time or any time thereafter a majority of players indicate that they wish to end the collective bargaining status of the NFLPA on or after expiration of this Agreement, the NFL and its Clubs and their respective heirs, executors, administrators, representatives, agents, successors and assigns waive any rights they may have to assert any antitrust labor exemption defense based upon any claim that the termination by the NFLPA of its status as a collective bargaining representative is or would be a sham, pretext, ineffective, requires additional steps, or has not in fact occurred.

————

COLLECTIVE BARGAINING AGREEMENT BETWEEN
THE NATIONAL BASKETBALL ASSOCIATION
AND THE NATIONAL BASKETBALL
PLAYERS ASSOCIATION

(1998–2005)

[Note: This agreement expires in 2005 and will be replaced by a new one that may have substantially different terms than those

set forth herein. **The excerpts below from the old agreement, however, may be illustrative of the general framework for the NBA's salary cap system, grievance arbitration, and drug testing and controls that likely will emerge.]**

ARTICLE II—Uniform Player Contract

Section 1. **Required Form.** The Player Contract to be entered into by each player and the Team by which he is employed shall be a Uniform Player Contract in the form annexed hereto as Exhibit A.

Section 2. **Limitation on Amendments.**

(a) Except as provided in Sections 3, 8, and 9 of this Article, no amendments to the form of Uniform Player Contract provided for by Section 1 of this Article shall be permitted.

* * *

Section 3. **Allowable Amendments.** In their individual contract negotiations, a player and a Team may amend the provisions of a Uniform Player Contract, but only in the following respects:

(a) By agreeing upon provisions (to be set forth in Exhibit 1 to a Uniform Player Contract) with respect to the Cash Compensation to be paid or amounts to be loaned to the player for rendering the services described in such Contract.

(b) By agreeing upon provisions with respect to any form of Non–Cash Compensation to be paid or provided to the player for rendering the services described in such Contract.

(c) By agreeing upon provisions with respect to bonuses, or increases or reductions in Cash Compensation, for (i) the player's execution of a Uniform Player Contract (a "signing bonus"), (ii) the exercise or non-exercise of an option pursuant to Articles VII and XII, (iii) the player's achievement of agreed-upon benchmarks relating to his performance as a player, (iv) the player's achievement or non-achievement of agreed-upon benchmarks relating to his physical condition or academic achievement, or (v) the Team's performance during a particular NBA Season, subject to the limitations imposed by paragraph 3(c) of the Uniform Player Contract. Any amendment agreed upon pursuant to subsections (c)(iii), (iv), or (v) above must be structured so as to provide an incentive for positive achievement by the player (under (c)(iii) and (iv)) and the Team (under (c)(v)).

[*9 permissible deviations from specific terms in the Uniform Player Contract are omitted.*]

ARTICLE VII—Team Salary, Salary Cap, and Minimum Team Salary

* * *

Section 2. **Calculation of Salary Cap and Minimum Team Salary.**

(a) **Salary Cap.**

(1) For each Season during the term of this Agreement, there shall be a Salary Cap. The Salary Cap for each Season will equal the greater of:

    (i)   1996–97: $24.3 million

          1997–98: $25.0 million

          1998–99: $26.0 million

          1999–00: $27.0 million

          2000–01: $28.0 million

(the "Guaranteed Minimum Salary Caps"); or

(ii) 48.04% of Projected [Basketball Related Income or "BRI"], less Projected Benefits (as defined in Article IV, Section 2(a)), plus or minus any Salary Cap adjustments (pursuant to subsection (d) below), divided by (A) 27 with respect to the 1996–1997 Season, and (B) 29 with respect to each remaining Season of the Agreement (the "Calculated Salary Cap").

* * *

(b) **Minimum Team Salary.**

(1) For each Season during the term of this Agreement, there shall be a Minimum Team Salary equal to 75% of the Salary Cap for such Season.

(2) In the event that, by the conclusion of the Salary Cap Year for a Season, a Team has failed to make aggregate Salary payments and/or incur aggregate Salary obligations equal to or greater than the applicable Minimum Team Salary for that Season, the NBA shall cause such Team to make such payments (to be disbursed to the players on such Team pro rata for in accordance with such other formula as may be reasonably determined by the Players Association).

(3) Nothing contained herein shall preclude a Team from having a Team Salary in excess of the Minimum Team Salary, provided that the Team's Team Salary does not exceed the Salary Cap plus any additional amounts authorized pursuant to the Exceptions set forth in this Article VII.

* * *

Section 5. Operation of Salary Cap.

(a) **Basic Rule.** A Team's Team Salary may not exceed the Salary Cap at any time unless the Team is using one of the Exceptions set forth in Section 6 below.

(b) **Room.** Subject to the provisions of this Section 5, any Team with Room may enter into a Player Contract that calls for a Salary in the first Season of such Contract that would not exceed the Team's then-current Room.

(c) **20% Rule.**

(1) Except as provided in Sections 5(d) (Banked Room), 6(b)(1) (Qualifying Veteran Free Agent), and 7(b) (First Round Pick Extensions) below, for each Season of a Player Contract after the first Season, and for each Season of an Extension after the first Season of the extended term (including, in either case, any Season following the Effective Date of an Option or an Early Termination Option), the player's Salary, excluding performance bonuses, may increase over the previous Season's Salary, excluding performance bonuses, by no more than (i) 20% of the Regular Salary for the first Season of the Contract, or (ii) in the case of an Extension, 20% of the Regular Salary for the last Season of the original term of the Contract.

(2) In the event that the first Season of a Contract provides for performance bonuses, the total amount of Likely Bonuses in each subsequent Season of the Contract may increase by up to 20% of the amount of Likely Bonuses in the first Season, and the total amount of Unlikely Bonuses in each subsequent Season may increase by up to 20% of the amount of Unlikely Bonuses in the first Season. With respect to an Extension, in the event that the last Season of the original term of the Contract provides for performance bonuses, the amount of Likely Bonuses and Unlikely Bonuses in each Season of the Extension after the first Season of the extended term may increase by up to 20% of the amount of Likely Bonuses and Unlikely Bonuses, respectively, in the last Season of the original term.

(d) **Banked Room.** In the event the first Season of a Player Contract results in Banked Room, the unused portion of such Banked Room may be used in any subsequent Season to provide for an increase in Salary and Unlikely Bonuses over the previous Season's Salary in excess of that permitted by the 20% Rule.

* * *

(f) **Performance Bonuses.**

(1) No Team may enter into a Player Contract containing a performance bonus for the first Season of the Contract that, if earned or paid during the first Season covered by such Contract, would result in the Team's Team Salary exceeding the Room under which it is signing the Contract. For the sole purpose of determining whether a Team has Room for a new Unlikely Bonus, the Team's Room shall be deemed reduced by all Unlikely Bonuses in Contracts approved by the Commissioner that may be paid to all of the Team's players that entered into Player Contracts (including Renegotiations) during that Salary Cap Year.

* * *

Section 6. **Exceptions to the Salary Cap.**

There shall be the following exceptions to the rule that a Team's Team Salary may not exceed the Salary Cap:

(a) **Existing Contracts.** A Team may exceed the Salary Cap to the extent of its current contractual commitments, provided that such contracts satisfied the provisions of this Article VII when entered into or were entered into prior to the execution date of this Agreement in accordance with the rules then in effect.

(b) **Veteran Free Agent Exception.** Beginning on the July 1 following the last Season covered by a Veteran Free Agent's Player Contract, such player may enter into a new Player Contract with his Prior Team (or, in the case of a player selected in an Expansion Draft that year, with the Team that selected such player in an Expansion Draft) as follows:

(1) If the player is a Qualifying Veteran Free Agent, the new Player Contract may provide for Salary of any amount for any Season of the Contract.

(2) If the player is a Non–Qualifying Veteran Free Agent, the new Player Contract may provide for a Salary for the first Season of up to the greater of (i) 120% of the Regular Salary for the final Season of the player's prior Contract, plus 120% of any Likely Bonuses and Unlikely Bonuses, respectively, called for in the final Season covered by the player's prior Contract, or (ii) 120% of the Minimum Annual Salary for the then-current Season. Salary increases and increases in Unlikely Bonuses in subsequent Seasons shall be governed by the 20% Rule.

(3) If the player is an Early Qualifying Veteran Free Agent, the new Player Contract must cover at least two Seasons and may provide for a Salary for the first Season of up to the greater of (i) 175% of the Regular Salary for the final Season covered by his prior Contract, plus 175% of any Likely Bonuses and Unlikely Bonuses, respectively, called for in the final Season covered by the player's prior Contract, or (ii) 108% of the Average Player Salary for the prior Season (or if the prior Season's Average Player Salary has not been determined, 108% of the Estimated Average Player Salary for the prior Season). Salary increases and increases in Unlikely Bonuses in subsequent Seasons shall be governed by the 20% Rule.

(c) **Disabled Player Exceptions.**

(1) Subject to the rules set forth in subsection (i) below, a Team may, in accordance with the rules set forth in this subsection (c), sign or acquire one Replacement Player to replace a player who, as a result of a Disabling Injury or Illness (as defined below) is unable to render playing services (the "Disabled Player"). Such Replacement Player's Contract may provide a Salary for the first Season of up to the lessor of (i) 50% of the Disabled Player's Salary at the time the Disabling Injury or Illness occurred, or (ii) 108% of the Average

Player Salary for the prior Season (or, if the prior Season's Average Player Salary has not been determined, 108% of the Estimated Average Player Salary for the prior Season). Salary increases and increases in Unlikely Bonuses for subsequent Seasons shall be governed by the 20% Rule.

* * *

(e) **Rookie Exception.** A Team may enter into a Rookie Scale Contract in accordance with Article VIII.

(f) **Minimum Annual Salary Exception.** A Team may sign a player to a one-year Player Contract at the Minimum Annual Salary applicable to that player (or, if the Contract is signed during the Regular Season, a prorated portion of such Minimum Annual Salary based on the number of remaining Regular Season days covered by the Contract).

(g) **Assigned Player Exception.**

(1) Subject to the rules set forth in subsection (j) below, a Team may, for a period of one year following the date of the assignment of a Player Contract to another Team, replace the Traded Player with one or more players acquired by assignment as follows:

(i) a Team may replace a Traded Player with one or more Replacement Players whose Player Contracts are acquired simultaneously and whose post-assignment Salaries for the then-current Season, in the aggregate, are no more than an amount equal to 115% of the pre-assignment Salary (or Base Year Compensation, if applicable) of the Traded Player, plus $100,000.

* * *

(2) Except as provided in subsection (g)(3) below, and notwithstanding subsection (j) below, a Team with a Team Salary below the Salary Cap may acquire one or more players by assignment whose post-assignment Salaries, in the aggregate, are no more than an amount equal to the Team's Room plus $100,000.

* * *

ARTICLE VIII—Rookie Scale

Section 1. **Rookie Scale Contracts.**

Except as provided in Sections 2 and 3 below, beginning with the 1995 NBA Draft, the following rules shall apply to every Rookie Scale Contract:

(a) Each Rookie Scale Contract shall cover a period of three Seasons.

(b) A Rookie Scale Contract shall provide in each of the three Seasons covered by the Contract at least 80% of the applicable Rookie Scale Amount in Current Cash Compensation. Components of Salary in excess of 80%, if any, are subject to individual negotiation, except that (i) in no event may Salary plus Unlikely Bonuses in any Season exceed

120% of the applicable Rookie Scale Amount, and (ii) a Rookie Scale Contract may not provide for a signing bonus (except for "foreign player payments" in excess of $250,000 made in accordance with Article VII, Section 3(f)) or a loan. A Rookie Scale Contract may provide for a payment schedule in any Season that is more favorable to the player than that called for under paragraph 2 of the Contract, provided that no payments for any Season are made prior to the July 1 preceding such Season.

* * *

ARTICLE XII—Option Clauses

Section 1. **Team Options.**

A Player Contract shall not contain any option in favor of the Team, except an Option (as defined in Article I, Section 1 (ae)) that: (i) is specifically negotiated between a Veteran or a Rookie (other than a First Round Pick) and a Team; (ii) authorizes the extension of such Contract for no more than one year beyond the stated term; (iii) is exercisable only once; and (iv) provides that the Salary payable with respect to the option year is no less than 100% of the Salary payable with respect to the last year of the stated term of such Contract and that all other non-monetary terms applicable in the last year of the stated term of such Contract shall be applicable in the option year.

Section 2. **Player Options.**

A Player Contract shall not contain any option in favor of the player, except:

(a) an Option that: (i) is specifically negotiated between a Veteran or a Rookie (other than a First Round Pick) and a Team; (ii) authorizes the extension of such Contract for no more than one year beyond the stated term; (iii) is exercisable only once; and (iv) provides that the Salary payable with respect to the option year is no less than 100% of the Salary payable with respect to the last year of the stated term of such Contract and that all other non-monetary terms applicable in the last year of the stated term of such Contract shall be applicable in the option year; and/or

(b) an Early Termination Option (or "ETO") (as defined in Article I, Section 1(p)), provided that such ETO is exercisable only once and takes effect no earlier than the end of the third year of the Contract.
* * *

ARTICLE XXXI—Grievance and Arbitration Procedure

Section 1. **Scope.**

(a) Any dispute (such dispute hereinafter being referred to as a "Grievance") involving the interpretation or application of, or compliance with, the provisions of this Agreement or the provisions of a Player Contract (except as provided in paragraph 9 of a Uniform Player Contract), including a dispute concerning the validity of a Player Contract, shall be resolved exclusively by the Grievance Arbitrator in accordance with the procedures set forth in this Article; provided, however, that disputes arising under Articles VII, VIII, X, XI, XII, XIII, XIV, XV, XVI, XXXVI, XXXVIII, and XXXIX shall be determined by the System Arbitrator provided for in Article XXXII.

(b) The Grievance Arbitrator shall also have jurisdiction over disputes involving player discipline, to the extent set forth in Section 8 below.

* * *

Section 5.   Arbitrator's Decision and Award.

(a) Except as set forth in Section 10 below, the Grievance Arbitrator shall render an Award as soon as practicable, but in no event more than thirty (30) days following the conclusion of a Grievance hearing or the submission of post-hearing briefs where applicable. That Award may be accompanied by a written opinion, or the written opinion may follow within a reasonable time thereafter. The Award shall constitute full, final and complete disposition of the Grievance, and shall be binding upon the player(s) and Team(s) involved and the parties to this Agreement.

* * *

(c) In any Grievance that involves an action taken by the Commissioner (or his designee) concerning (i) the preservation of the integrity of, or the maintenance of public confidence in, the game of basketball, and (ii) a fine and/or suspension that results in a financial impact to the player of more than $25,000, the Grievance Arbitrator shall apply an ''arbitrary and capricious'' standard of review.

* * *

Section 7.   Injury Grievances. (a) Disputes arising under paragraphs 7, 16(b), or 16(c) of a Uniform Player Contract as to (i) whether a player was in sufficiently good condition to play skilled basketball, (ii) whether the player was injured as a direct result of participating in any basketball practice or game played for the Club, and/or (iii) whether such injury disabled the player and/or rendered him unfit to play skilled basketball, shall be processed and determined in the same manner as a Grievance under Sections 2–6 of this Article XXXI, except that if a party to such Grievance so elects, a physician designated by the President of the American College of Orthopedic Surgeons (or such other similar organization as the parties agree may be most appropriate to the issues in dispute) and who has no relationship with any party covered by this Agreement shall conduct a physical examination of the player and shall perform the functions of the Grievance Arbitrator. The physician so designated shall render a written decision which shall constitute full, final and complete disposition of the dispute, and shall be binding upon the player(s) and Team(s) involved and the parties to this Agreement.

Any fees or costs associated with the physician's determination will be borne equally by both sides. * * *

Section 8.   **Special Procedures with Respect to Player Discipline.**

(a) Any dispute involving (i) a fine or suspension imposed upon a player by the Commissioner (or his designee) for conduct on the playing court, or (ii) action taken by the Commissioner (or his designee) concerning the preservation of the integrity of, or the maintenance of public confidence in, the game of basketball resulting in a financial impact to the player of $25,000 or less, shall be processed exclusively as follows:

(i) Within 20 days following written notification of the action taken by the Commissioner (or his designee), a player affected thereby or the Players Association may appeal in writing to the Commissioner.

(ii) The Commissioner shall designate a time and place for hearing, which shall be commenced within 10 days following his receipt of the notice of appeal.

(iii) As soon as practicable following the conclusion of such hearing, the Commissioner shall render a written decision, which decision shall constitute full, final and complete disposition of the dispute, and shall be binding upon the Player(s) and Club(s) involved and the parties to this Agreement.

(iv) In the event such appeal involves a fine or suspension imposed by the Commissioner's designee, the Commissioner, as a consequence of such appeal and hearing, shall have authority only to affirm or reduce such fine or suspension, and shall not have authority to increase such fine or suspension.

(b) In the event a matter filed as a Grievance in accordance with the provisions of Section 2(d) gives rise to issues involving the integrity of, or public confidence in, the game of basketball, and the financial impact to the player of the action being grieved is $25,000 or less, the Commissioner may, at any stage of its processing, order that the matter be withdrawn from such processing and thereafter be processed in accordance with the procedure provided in Section 8(a).

* * *

ARTICLE XXXII—System Arbitrator

Section 1.   **Jurisdiction and Authority.** The NBA and the Players Association shall agree upon a System Arbitrator, who shall have exclusive jurisdiction to determine any and all disputes arising under Articles VII, VIII, X, XI, XII, XIII, XIV, XV, XVI, XXXVI, XXXVIII, and XXXIX of this Agreement; provided, however, that any claim or dispute arising under such Articles involving the NBA, any Team, the Players Association or any player, which is specifically under the terms of this Agreement to be determined in accordance with the Expedited Procedures described in Article XXXI, Section 12 above, shall be determined by the Grievance Arbitrator provided for in Article XXXI. The System Arbitrator shall hold hearings on alleged violations of the foregoing articles, subject to review by the Appeals Panel, in the manner set forth below.

* * *

(c) Rulings of the System Arbitrator shall upon their issuance constitute full, final and complete disposition of the dispute, shall be binding upon the parties to this Agreement and upon any player(s) or Team(s) involved, and shall be followed by them unless a notice of appeal is served by the appealing party upon the responding party an filed with the System Arbitrator within 10 days of the date of the decision of the System Arbitrator appealed from. If and when a decision of the System Arbitrator is reversed or modified by the Appeals Panel, the effect of such reversals or modification shall be deemed by the parties to be retroactive to the time of issuance of the ruling of the System Arbitrator. The parties may seek appropriate relief to effectuate and enforce this provision.

* * *

[Although no language was included in the 1996 NBA–NBPA Collective Bargaining Agreement relating to drug testing and penalties for drug use, in a side letter attached to the CBA the NBPA Executive Director, Simon Gourdine, and the NBA Commissioner, David Stern, agreed to continue during the term of the agreement the same provisions that were contained in Article XXXIII of the 1988 Collective Bargaining Agreement, reproduced below.]

ARTICLE XXXIII—NBA Anti–Drug Program
(1988 NBA–NBPA Collective Bargaining Agreement)

Section 1. Any player who has been convicted of or has pled guilty to a crime involving the use, possession, or distribution of any of the substances set forth in Exhibit J annexed hereto (the "prohibited substances") or has been found through the procedures set forth in Sections 6 or 7 below to have used, possessed, or distributed any of the prohibited substances, shall, without exception, immediately be dismissed and permanently disqualified from any further association with the NBA or any of its Teams, and such player's Player Contract shall be rendered null and void and of no further force or effect, subject to the provisions of paragraph 6(d) of the Uniform Player Contract. Such dismissal and permanent disqualification shall be mandatory and may not be rescinded or reduced by the player's Club or the NBA.

Section 2. (a) During the term of this Agreement, any player, except a player referred to in Section 9 below, who comes forward voluntarily to seek treatment of a problem involving the use of drugs, will be provided with appropriate counseling and medical assistance, at the expense of his Club. The term "comes forward voluntarily," * * *

shall be deemed to mean that the player has directly communicated his desire to come forward voluntarily to either the office of the Players Association or the NBA League Office. * * *

(b) Any player who comes forward voluntarily shall be required to report to and commence the treatment prescribed by the ASAP Program at Van Nuys Hospital under the supervision of Dr. Dave Lewis (or such other organization as may be designated by the NBA and the Players Association) (hereinafter "drug program's counselors") within ten (10) days of the time he comes forward voluntarily. * * *

(c) Any player who completes the treatment prescribed by the drug program's counselors shall be required to comply with such "after-care" program as may be prescribed by the drug program's counselors, * * *.

(d) Any player who, after "coming forward voluntarily," fails to comply with his in-patient treatment or with his aftercare (as set forth above and as may be supplemented from time to time), as prescribed and determined by the drug program's counselors, shall be suspended, without pay. Such suspension shall continue until the player has, in the opinion of the drug program's counselors, resumed full compliance with his in-patient treatment or after-care.

(e) Except as provided in Section 2(b) and 2(d) above, no penalty of any kind will be imposed on such player and, provided he complies with the terms of his prescribed treatment, he will continue to receive his salary during the term of his treatment, for a period of up to three months of in-patient care in a facility approved by the drug program's counselors * * * and such outpatient care as may be required by that facility.

Section 3. The NBA and the Players Association shall jointly appoint an independent expert (the "Expert") who shall be a person experienced in the field of drug abuse detection and enforcement. The Expert shall serve for the duration of this Agreement; provided, however, that as of each September 1, either the NBA or the Players Association may discharge the Expert by serving 30 days' prior written notice upon him and upon the other party. * * *

Section 4. (a) In the event that either the NBA or the Players Association has information that gives it reasonable cause to believe that a player may have been engaged in the use, possession, or distribution of a prohibited substance, including information that a player may have been engaged in such conduct during the period beginning three months prior to his entry into the NBA, such party shall request a conference with the other party and the expert * * *. [T]he Expert shall immediately decide whether there is reasonable cause to believe that the player in question may have been engaged in the use, possession, or distribution of a prohibited substance. If the Expert decides that such reasonable cause to believe exists, the Expert shall thereupon issue an Authorization for Testing with respect to such player in the form annexed hereto as Exhibit K.

(b) If any player publicly acknowledges the use, possession or distribution of a prohibited substance, but does not "come forward voluntarily" in accordance with Section 2 above, either the NBA or the Players Association may request a conference with the other party and the Expert, in accordance with subsection (a) above, and the Expert, at such conference, shall deem such public acknowledgement to be reasonable cause to believe that the player in question may have been engaged in the use, possession or distribution of a prohibited substance and shall issue an Authorization for Testing with respect to such player.

Section 6. (a) Immediately upon the Expert's issuance of an Authorization for Testing with respect to a particular player, the NBA shall arrange for such player to undergo the testing procedures, as set forth in Exhibit L annexed hereto, no more than four times during the six-week period commencing with the issuance of the Authorization for Testing. Such testing procedures may be administered at any time, in the discretion of the NBA, without prior notice to the player. In the event that any of the testing procedures produces a positive result, the player shall be deemed to have used a prohibited substance and shall suffer the penalty set forth in Section 1 above, and shall be so notified by the Commissioner. Any player refusing to submit to a testing procedure, pursuant to an Authorization for Testing at the time set by the NBA, shall be deemed to have produced a positive result for such testing procedure and shall suffer the penalty set forth in Section 1 above.

(b) Any player, after "coming forward voluntarily" who [without a documented explanation, satisfactory to the NBA and the Players Association]: (i) fails to appear for any of his Team's scheduled games; or (ii) misses, during any consecutive seven-day period, any two airplane flights on which his team is scheduled to travel, any two Team practices, or a combination of any one practice and any one Team flight, must appear at his Team's office and submit to a urine test, to be conducted by the NBA, within 24 hours of the game for which the player failed to appear or within 24 hours of the second missed flight or practice or combination of one missed flight and one missed practice, as the case may be. If any such test is "positive" for a "prohibited substance," the player will be deemed to have "come forward voluntarily" again or be subject to the penalty set forth in Section 1 above, as the case may be. For purposes of this paragraph, a player who fails to appear within the required 24–hour period and submit himself for any such test (absent a documented explanation, satisfactory to the NBA and the Players Association) shall be deemed to have tested "positive" for a "prohibited substance." * * *

(c) No Uniform Player Contract entered into after the date hereof shall include any term or provision which modifies, contradicts, changes or is inconsistent with paragraph 6(d) to the Uniform Player Contract or provides for the testing of a player for illegal substances. Any term or provision of a currently effective Uniform Player Contract which is inconsistent with paragraph 6(d) to the Uniform Player Contract shall be deemed null and void only to the extent of the inconsistency.

Section 7. In the event that either the NBA or the Players Association determines that there is sufficient evidence to demonstrate that a player has engaged in the use, possession, or distribution of a prohibited substance, or has received treatment for use of a prohibited substance other than in accordance with the terms of this agreement, it may, in lieu of requesting the testing procedure set forth in Section 4 through 6, request a hearing on the matter before the Impartial Arbitrator. If the Impartial Arbitrator concludes that the player has used, possessed, or distributed a prohibited substance, or has received treatment other than in accordance with the terms of this agreement, the player shall suffer the penalty set forth in Section 1 above, notwithstanding the fact that the player has not undergone the testing procedure set forth in Section 6.

Section 8. The NBA and the Players Association agree that neither of them will divulge to any other party, including their respective members and the player and Team involved (other than as required by the Testing Procedure set forth in Section 6 above) (i) that it has received information regarding the use, possession, or distribution of a prohibited substance by a player; (ii) that it is considering requesting, has requested, or has had a conference with the Expert; (iii) any information disclosed to the Expert; and (iv) the results of any conference with the Expert.

Section 9. Any player who, after previously requesting and receiving treatment for a drug problem, again comes forward voluntarily to seek such treatment, or any player who the drug program'' counselors have determined has suffered a relapse and requires further treatment, or any player who has tested positive or has been deemed to have tested ''positive'' under Section 6(b) above, shall be suspended, without pay, during any period in which such subsequent treatment prevents his rendering of the playing services called for by his Uniform Player Contract, but shall not suffer the penalty set forth in Section 1 above. Any subsequent use, possession or distribution of a prohibited substance, even if voluntarily disclosed, shall result in the imposition of the penalty set forth in Section 1 above.

Section 10. Notwithstanding the provisions of Section 1 above, after a period of at least two years from the time of a player's dismissal and permanent disqualification, such player may apply for reinstatement as a player in the NBA. However, such player shall have no right to reinstatement under any circumstance and the reinstatement shall be granted only with the prior approval of both the Commissioner and Player Association. The approval of the Commissioner and the Players Association shall rest in their absolute and sole discretion, and their decision shall be final, binding and unappealable. * * * The granting of an application for reinstatement may be conditioned upon periodic testing of the player or such other terms as may be agreed upon by the NBA and the Players Association. [The Club for which the player previously played] shall have 30 days in which to tender the player a contract with a stated term of at least one year and calling for a Salary at least equal to the Salary last paid to the player. If within 30 days of his receipt of such tender, the player does not accept it, he shall thereupon be deemed a Restricted Free Agent, subject to a Right of First Refusal. If the Club fails to make such tender within 30 days of notification by the player of his reinstatement, the player shall thereupon be deemed an Unrestricted Free Agent.

Section 11. (a) In addition to the testing procedures set forth in Section 6, * * * all players who have not previously played in a NBA regular season game may be required to undergo the testing procedures set forth in Exhibit L annexed hereto, no more than one time during regular training camp * * *. Such testing procedures may be administered * * * without prior notice to the player. * * *

(b) (1) Any player who has produced a positive result or has been deemed to have produced a positive result pursuant to Section 11(a) above, shall immediately be suspended, without pay, and such player's Player Contract shall be rendered null and void and of no further force or effect.

(2) After a period of at least one year from the time of a player's suspension pursuant to subsection (1) above, such player may apply for reinstatement as a player in the NBA. However, such player shall have no right to reinstatement shall be granted only with the prior approval of both the Commissioner and the Players Association. The Commissioner and Players Association will consider applications for reinstatement only if the player has, in the opinion of the drug program's counselors, successfully completed any in-patient treatment and after-care prescribed by the drug program's counselors. The approval of the Commissioner and the Players Association shall rest in their absolute and sole discretion, and their decision shall be final, binding, and unappealable.

* * *

Section 12. (a) Except as expressly provided in Section 6 and 11 above, there shall be no other screening or testing for the prohibited substances conducted by the NBA or NBA clubs, and no player shall be required to undergo such screening or testing. * * * Notwithstanding the foregoing, any player who has acknowledged the use of a prohibited substance by entering a treatment program, shall be subject to such screening or testing as may be determined by the drug program" counselors, in addition to the testing provided for in Section 6(b) above. The frequency and duration of any screening or testing, as determined by the drug program's counselors, shall not exceed three times a week for a period of more than one year following in-patient treatment.

(b) The penalties set forth in this Article XXXIII shall be the exclusive penalties to be imposed upon a player for the use, possession or distribution of a "prohibited substance."

NHL–NHLPA COLLECTIVE BARGAINING AGREEMENT

(1998–2004)

[Note: The NHL–NHLPA agreement expires in 2004, just after this book goes to print. Predictions at that time were for a lengthy lockout and for substantial revisions to the old agreement. Thus, the only terms in the old agreement set forth here relate to the unique salary arbitration system utilized in the NHL, which may well survive in large part in the next agreement.]

Article 12—Salary Arbitration

12.1 Eligibility.

(a) A player is eligible to elect salary arbitration if the player meets the qualifications set forth in the following chart and in Section 12.1(b) below:

First Contract Signing Age	Minimum Level of Professional Experience Required to be Eligible for Salary Arbitration
18–20	5 years professional experience
21	4 years professional experience
22–23	3 years professional experience
24	2 years professional experience
25 and older	1 year professional experience

A player aged 18 or 19 earns a year of "professional experience" by playing ten or more NHL games (regular season and/or playoffs) in a given season. A player aged 20 or above (or who turns 20 between September 16 and December 31 of the year in which he signs his first Player Contract) earns a year of professional experience by playing ten or more professional games under NHL contract in a given season.

(b) Only players who qualify as Restricted Free Agents as described in Section 10.2 and who have not signed an Offer Sheet may elect salary arbitration.

(c) As used in this Article, "age," including "First Contract Signing Age," means a player's age on September 15 of the calendar year in which he first signs a Player Contract regardless of his actual age on the date he signs such contract.

12.5. *Rules of Procedure*

* * *

(f) Evidence.

(i) Subject to the limitations set forth in subsection (iii) below, the parties may present whatever witnesses, affidavits, documents and other relevant evidence they choose to present at the hearing. The Arbitrator, on behalf of any party, or on his own behalf, may call witnesses or request documents or other evidence as he deems necessary to resolve the dispute. The Arbitrator in his discretion shall be the judge of the relevancy and materiality of the evidence offered and/or the weight, if any, to attach to any evidence and shall not be bound by any formal legal rules of evidence. . . .

(ii) The parties may offer evidence of the following:

(A) the overall performance, including official statistics prepared by the League (both offensive and defensive) of the Player in the previous season or seasons;

(B) the number of games played by the Player, his injuries or illnesses during the preceding seasons;

(C) the length of service of the Player in the League and/or with the Club;

(D) the overall contribution of the Player to the competitive success or failure of his Club in the preceding season;

(E) any special qualities of leadership or public appeal not inconsistent with the fulfillment of his responsibilities as a playing member of his team;

(F) the overall performance in the previous season or seasons of any player(s) who is alleged to be comparable to the party Player whose salary is in dispute; and

(G) (1) The compensation of any player(s) who is alleged to be comparable to the party Player, provided, however, that in applying this or any of the above subparagraphs, the Arbitrator shall not consider a player(s) to be comparable to the party Player unless a party to the arbitration has contended that the player(s) is comparable; nor shall the Arbitrator consider the Compensation or performance of a player(s) unless a party to the arbitration has contended that the player(s) is comparable.

(2) To the extent a non-cash economic item does not have an attributed value set forth in the player's contract or any addenda thereto, the parties shall attribute a value thereto by mutual agreement or, failing to reach such agreement, then such value shall be determined by the Impartial Arbitrator.

(iii) The following categories of evidence are inadmissible and shall not be considered by the Arbitrator:

(1) Any contract the terms of which began when the player party to such contract was not a Group II Player;

(2) Any contract entered into by an Unrestricted Free Agent, including contracts signed by players after the player's Club has exercised a walk-away right pursuant to Section 12.6;

(3) Qualifying Offers made by the Club pursuant to Section 10.2;

(4) Any prior offers or history or negotiations between the Player and the Club;

(5) Testimonials, videotapes, newspaper columns, press game reports or similar materials;

(6) Any reference to actual or potential walk-away rights;

(7) Any award issued by an arbitrator as to which a Club exercises its walk-away pursuant to Section 12.6;

(8) The financial condition of the Club or the League.

(iv) In each League Year, the League and the NHLPA shall agree on a Joint Exhibit setting forth the Compensation terms contained in all then current contracts of League players. . . .

* * *

(m) Salary Arbitration Decision.

(i) Each salary arbitration decision must be issued by fax to each of the parties within 48 hours of the close of the hearing, provided that for arbitrations held on Friday, within 72 hours of the close of the hearing.

(ii) The decision of the Arbitrator shall establish:

(A) the term of the contract, based upon the Club's election of a one or two year contract, as set forth in its brief and as consistent with this Article;

(B) the base salary to be paid to the Player by the Club for the season(s) in respect to which the arbitration is conducted;

(C) the bonuses, if any, which are appropriate in the circumstances;

(D) the inclusion or otherwise of a "minor league clause" (or clauses) and the amount of base salary to be paid under each of the season(s) in respect to which the arbitration is requested;

(E) a brief statement of the reasons for the decision, including identification of any comparable(s) relied on.

* * *

12.6. Walk–Away Rights.

(a) If a Club has elected to arbitrate a one year contract, and the award issued is for $550,000 or more per annum, then the Club may, within 72 hours after the award of the Arbitrator is issued (or if a Club has any other player still eligible for salary arbitration at that time and for whom a decision has not been rendered by an Arbitrator at that time, and the Club still has a walk-away right available to it in such League Year pursuant to paragraph (d) below, 72 hours after the award of the Arbitrator for such other player is issued), notify the player, the NHLPA and the NHL in writing that it does not intend to tender to the player a Player Contract based on the award as determined by the Arbitrator. Upon receipt of that notice, the player shall automatically be deemed to be an Unrestricted Free Agent, subject to the provisions of paragraphs (c) and (d) below.

(b) If a Club has elected to arbitrate a two year contract and the award issued is for $550,000 or more per annum, then the Club may, within 72 hours after the award of the Arbitrator is issued (or, if a Club has any other player still eligible for salary arbitration at that time and for whom a decision has not been rendered by an Arbitrator at that time, and the Club still has a walk-away right available to it in such League Year pursuant to paragraph (d) below, 72 hours after the award of the Arbitrator for such other player is issued), notify the player, the NHLPA and the NHL in writing that it does not intend to tender to the player a two year Player Contract based on the award as determined by the Arbitrator. Upon receipt of that notice by either the player or the NHL, the player and the Club shall enter into a one year Player Contract providing for the Compensation set forth in the award and the player will automatically be deemed to be an Unrestricted Free Agent at the conclusion of that one year Player Contract subject to the provisions of paragraphs (c) and (d) below.

(c) If a Club exercises its walk-away right, the following applies:

(i) If the player accepts an offer from a New Club in respect of that year of the contract which the Prior Club has walked-away from that is less than 80% of the award for such year, the Prior Club may, within seven (7) days after the date it receives the applicable Offer Sheet, elect to match the offer of the New Club and the Player and the Prior Club shall enter into a Player Contract on those terms and conditions; or

(ii) The player may (A) within seven (7) days after receipt of notice from the player's Prior Club that the Prior Club elects to walk-away from the arbitration award, in respect of the Prior Club's request for a one year contract, or (B) by July 15 of the League Year following the expiry of the first year of the award issued by the Arbitrator where the Club had requested a two-year contract, in either case by written notice to the Club, elect to enter into a Player Contract with the Club on the terms and conditions set forth in the Prior Club's Qualifying Offer. If such election is timely exercises, the Club must enter into such contract and, at the end of the term thereof, the Player shall be a free agent subject to the provisions of Article 10.

(d) Notwithstanding the provisions of paragraphs (a) and (b) above, a Club may exercise the walk-away rights referred to therein not more than 3 times in any contiguous two League Years and in any event not more than twice in any League Year. If a Club exercises its walk-away right with respect to a two year award, the walk-away right shall be deemed to be exercised in the first year of the two-year contract.

(d) The dollar amount of $550,000 set forth in each paragraphs (a) and (b) above, shall be increased on an annual basis at the same percentage rate of increase as the Average League Salary, with the commencement of the 1996/97 League Year being the first year such increase shall take effect. . . .

D. STANDARD PLAYER CONTRACTS

MAJOR LEAGUE (BASEBALL) UNIFORM PLAYER'S CONTRACT

Parties

Between _____, herein called the Club, and _____, herein called the Player.

Employment

1. The Club hereby employs the Player to render, and the Player agrees to render, skilled services as a baseball player during the year(s) _____ including the Club's training season, the Club's exhibition games, the Club's playing season, the Division Series, the League Championship Series and the World Series (or any other official series in which the Club may participate and in any receipts of which the Player may be entitled to share).

Payment

2. For performance of the Player's services and promises hereunder the Club will pay the Player the sum of $ _____ in semi-monthly installments after the commencement of the championship season(s) covered by this contract except as the schedule of payments may be modified by a special covenant. Payment shall be made on the day the amount becomes due, regardless of whether the Club is "home" or "abroad." If a monthly rate of payment is stipulated above, it shall begin with the commencement of the championship season (or such subsequent date as the Players s services may commence) and end with the termination of the championship season and shall be payable in semi-monthly installments as above provided.

Nothing herein shall interfere with the right of the Club and the Player by special covenant herein to mutually agree upon a method of payment whereby part of the Player's salary for the above year can be deferred to subsequent years.

If the Player is in the service of the Club for part of the championship season only, he shall receive such proportion of the sum above mentioned, as the number of days of his actual employment in the championship season bears to the number of days in the championship season. Notwithstanding the rate of payment stipulated above, the minimum rate of payment to the Player for each day of service on a Major League Club shall be at the applicable rate set forth in Article VI(B)(1) of the Basic Agreement between the Thirty Major League Clubs

130

and the Major League Baseball Players Association, effective September 30, 2002 ("Basic Agreement"). The minimum rate of payment for Minor League service for all Players (a) signing a second Major League contract (not covering the same season as any such Player's initial Major League contract) or a subsequent Major League contract, or (b) having at least one day of Major League service, shall be at the applicable rate set forth in Article VI(B)(2) of the Basic Agreement.

Payment to the Player at the rate stipulated above shall be continued throughout any period in which a Player is required to attend a regularly scheduled military encampment of the Reserve of the Armed Forces or of the National Guard during the championship season.

Loyalty

3.(a) The Player agrees to perform his services hereunder diligently and faithfully, to keep himself in first-class physical condition and to obey the Club's training rules, and pledges himself to the American public and to the Club to conform to high standards of personal conduct, fair play and good sportsmanship.

Baseball Promotion

3.(b) In addition to his services in connection with the actual playing of baseball, the Player agrees to cooperate with the Club and participate in any and all reasonable promotional activities of the Club and Major League Baseball, which, in the opinion of the Club, will promote the welfare of the Club or professional baseball, and to observe and comply with all reasonable requirements of the Club respecting conduct and service of its team and its players, at all times whether on or off the field.

Pictures and Public Appearances

3.(c) The Player agrees that his picture may be taken for still photographs, motion pictures or television at such times as the Club may designate and agrees that all rights in such pictures shall belong to the Club and may be used by the Club for publicity purposes in any manner it desires. The Player further agrees that during the playing season he will not make public appearances, participate in radio or television programs or permit his picture to be taken or write or sponsor newspaper or magazine articles or sponsor commercial products without the written consent of the Club, which shall not be withheld except in the reasonable interests of the Club or professional baseball.

PLAYER REPRESENTATIONS

Ability

4.(a) The Player represents and agrees that he has exceptional and unique skill and ability as a baseball player; that his services to be rendered hereunder are of a special, unusual and extraordinary character which gives them peculiar value which cannot be reasonably or adequately compensated for in damages at law, and that the Player's breach of this contract will cause the Club great and irreparable injury and damage. The Player agrees that, in addition to other remedies, the Club shall be entitled to injunctive and other equitable relief to prevent a breach of this contract by the Player, including, among others, the right to enjoin the Player from playing baseball for any other person or organization during the term of his contract.

Condition

4.(b) The Player represents that he has no physical or mental defects known to him and unknown to the appropriate representative of the Club which would prevent or impair performance of his services.

Interest in Club

4.(c) The Player represents that he does not, directly or indirectly, own stock or have any financial interest in the ownership or earnings of any Major League Club, except as hereinafter expressly set forth, and covenants that he will not hereafter, while connected with any Major League Club, acquire or hold any such stock or interest except in accordance with Major League Rule 20(e).

Service

5(a) The Player agrees that, while under contract, and prior to expiration of the Club's right to renew this contract, he will not play baseball otherwise than for the Club, except that the Player may participate in post-season games under the conditions prescribed in the Major League Rules. Major League Rule 18(b) is set forth herein.

Other Sports

5.(b) The Player and the Club recognize and agree that the Player's participation in certain other sports may impair or destroy his ability and skill as a baseball player. Accordingly, the Player agrees that he will not engage in professional boxing or wrestling; and that, except with the written consent of the Club, he will not engage in skiing, auto racing, motorcycle racing, sky diving, or in any game or exhibition of football, soccer, professional league basketball, ice hockey or other sport involving a substantial risk of personal injury.

Assignment

6.(a) The Player agrees that his contract may be assigned by the Club (and reassigned by any assignee Club) to any other Club in accordance with the Major League Rules. The Club and the Player may, without obtaining special approval, agree by special covenant to limit or eliminate the right of the Club to assign this contract.

Medical Information

6.(b) The Player agrees:

(1) that the Club's physician and any other physician consulted by the Player pursuant to Regulation 2 of this contract or Article XIII(D) of the Basic Agreement may furnish to the Club all relevant medical information relating to the Player; and

(2) that, should the Club contemplate an assignment of this contract to another Club or Clubs, the Club's physician may furnish to the physicians and officials of such other Club or Clubs all relevant medical information relating to the Player.

No Salary Reduction

6.(c) The amount stated in paragraph 2 and in special covenants hereof which is payable to the Player for the period stated in paragraph 1 hereof shall not be diminished by any such assignment, except for failure to report as provided in the next subparagraph (d).

Reporting

6.(d) The Player shall report to the assignee Club promptly (as provided in the Regulations) upon receipt of written notice from the Club of the assignment of this contract. If the Player fails to so report, he shall not be entitled to any payment for the period from the date he receives written notice of assignment until he reports to the assignee Club.

Obligations of Assignor and Assignee Clubs

6.(e) Upon and after such assignment, all rights and obligations of the assignor Club hereunder shall become the rights and obligations of the assignee Club; provided, however, that

(1) The assignee Club shall be liable to the Player for payments accruing only from the date of assignment and shall not be liable (but the assignor Club shall remain liable) for payments accrued prior to that date.

(2) If at any time the assignee is a Major League Club, it shall be liable to pay the Player at the full rate stipulated in paragraph 2 hereof for the remainder of the period stated in paragraph 1 hereof and all prior assignors and assignees shall be relieved of liability for any payment for such period.

(3) Unless the assignor and assignee Clubs agree otherwise, if the assignee Club is a Minor League Baseball Club, the assignee Club shall be liable only to pay the Player at the rate usually paid by said assignee Club to other Players of similar skill and ability in its classification and the assignor Club shall be liable to pay the difference for the remainder of the period stated in paragraph I hereof between an amount computed at the rate stipulated in paragraph 2 hereof and the amount so payable by the assignee Club.

Moving Allowances

6.(f) The Player shall be entitled to moving allowances under the circumstances and in the amounts set forth in Articles VII(F) and VIII of the Basic Agreement.

TERMINATION

By Player

7.(a) The Player may terminate this contract, upon written notice to the Club, if the Club shall default in the payments to the Player provided for in paragraph 2 hereof or shall fail to perform any other obligation agreed to be performed by the Club hereunder and if the Club shall fail to remedy such default within ten (10) days after the receipt by the Club of written notice of such default. The Player may also terminate this contract as provided in subparagraph (d)(4) of this paragraph 7. (See Article XV(I) of the Basic Agreement.)

By Club

7.(b) The Club may terminate this contract upon written notice to the Player (but only after requesting and obtaining waivers of this contract from all other Major League Clubs) if the Player shall at any time:

> (1) fail, refuse or neglect to conform his personal conduct to the standards of good citizenship and good sportsmanship or to keep himself in first-class physical condition or to obey the Club's training rules; or

> (2) fail, in the opinion of the Club's management, to exhibit sufficient skill or competitive ability to qualify or continue as a member of the Club's team; or

> (3) fail, refuse or neglect to render his services hereunder or in any other manner materially breach this contract.

7.(c) If this contract is terminated by the Club, the Player shall be entitled to termination pay under the circumstances and in the amounts set forth in Article IX of the Basic Agreement. In addition, the Player shall be entitled to receive an amount equal to the reasonable traveling expenses of the Player, including first-class jet air fare and meals en route, to his home city.

Procedure

7.(d) If the Club proposes to terminate this contract in accordance with subparagraph (b) of this paragraph 7, the procedure shall be as follows:

> (1) The Club shall request waivers from all other Major League Clubs. Such waivers shall be good for two (2) business days only. Such waiver request must state that it is for the purpose of terminating this contract and it may not be withdrawn.

(2) Upon receipt of waiver request, any other Major League Club may claim assignment of this contract at a waiver price of $1.00, the priority of claims to be determined in accordance with the Major League Rules.

(3) If this contract is so claimed, the Club shall, promptly and before any assignment, notify the Player that it had requested waivers for the purpose of terminating this contract and that the contract had been claimed.

(4) Within five (5) days after receipt of notice of such claim, the Player shall be entitled, by written notice to the Club, to terminate this contract on the date of his notice of termination. If the Player fails to so notify the Club, this contract shall be assigned to the claiming Club.

(5) If the contract is not claimed, the Club shall promptly deliver written notice of termination to the Player at the expiration of the waiver period.

7.(e) Upon any termination of this contract by the Player, all obligations of both Parties hereunder shall cease on the date of termination, except the obligation of the Club to pay the Player's compensation to said date.

Rules

9.(a) The Club and the Player agree to accept, abide by and comply with all provisions of the Major League Constitution, and the Major League Rules, or other rules or regulations in effect on the date of this Uniform Player's Contract, which are not inconsistent with the provisions of this contract or the provisions of any agreement between the Major League Clubs and the Major League Baseball Players Association, provided that the Club, together with the other Major League Clubs and Minor League Baseball, reserves the right to modify, supplement or repeal any provision of said Constitution, Major League Rules or other rules and regulations in a manner not inconsistent with this contract or the provisions of any then existing agreement between the Major League Clubs and the Major League Baseball Players Association.

Disputes

9.(b) All disputes between the Player and the Club which are covered by the Grievance Procedure as set forth in the Basic Agreement shall be resolved in accordance with such Grievance Procedure.

Publication

9.(c) The Club, the Vice President, On–Field Operations and the Commissioner, or any of them, may make public the findings, decision and record of any inquiry, investigation or hearing held or conducted, including in such record all evidence or information given, received, or obtained in connection therewith.

Renewal

10.(a) Unless the Player has exercised his right to become a free agent as set forth in the Basic Agreement, the Club may retain reservation rights over the Player by instructing the Office of the Commissioner to tender to the Player a contract for the term of the next year by including the Player on the Central Tender Letter that the Office of the Commissioner submits to the Players Association on or before December 20 (or if a Sunday, then on or before December 18) in the year of the last playing season covered by this contract. (See Article XX(A) of and Attachment 12 to the Basic Agreement.) If prior to the March 1 next succeeding said December 20, the Player and the Club have not agreed upon the terms of such contract, then on or before ten (10) days after said March 1, the Club shall have the right by written notice to the Player at his address following his signature hereto, or if none be given, then at his last address of record with the Club, to renew this contract for the period of one year on the same terms, except that the amount payable to the Player shall be such as the Club shall fix in said notice; provided, however, that said amount, if fixed by a Major League Club, shall be in an amount payable at a rate not less than as specified in Article VI, Section D, of the Basic Agreement. Subject to the Player's rights as set forth in the Basic Agreement, the Club may renew this contract from year to year.

10.(b) The Club's right to renew this contract, as provided in subparagraph (a) of this paragraph 10, and the promise of the Player not to play otherwise than with the Club have been taken into consideration in determining the amount payable under paragraph 2 hereof.

Governmental Regulation—National Emergency

11. This contract is subject to federal or state legislation, regulations, executive or other official orders or other governmental action, now or hereafter in effect respecting military, naval, air or other governmental service, which may directly or indirectly affect the Player, Club or the League and subject also to the right of the Commissioner to suspend the operation of this contract during any national emergency during which Major League Baseball is not played.

Supplemental Agreements

The Club and the Player covenant that this contract, the Basic Agreement and the Agreement Re Major League Baseball Players Benefit Plan effective April 1, 2003 and applicable supplements thereto fully set forth all understandings and agreements between them, and agree that no other understandings or agreements, whether heretofore or hereafter made, shall be valid, recognizable, or of any effect whatsoever, unless expressly set forth in a new or supplemental contract executed by the Player and the Club (acting by its President or such other officer as shall have been thereunto duly authorized by the President or Board of Directors as evidenced by a certificate filed of record with the Commissioner) and complying with the Major League Rules.

Special Covenants: [Signing or performance bonuses, no-trade clauses, salary guarantees, or other special benefits for the player not inconsistent with the collective bargaining agreement may be added onto the contract here.]

[SIGNED by the player, a representative of the club, and the commissioner]

REGULATIONS

1.   The Club's playing season for each year covered by this contract and all renewals hereof shall be as fixed by Major League Baseball.

2.   The Player, when requested by the Club, must submit to a complete physical examination at the expense of the Club, and if necessary to treatment by a regular physician or dentist in good standing. Upon refusal of the Player to submit to a complete medical or dental examination, the Club may consider such refusal a violation of this regulation and may take such action as it deems advisable under Regulation 5 of this contract. Disability directly resulting from injury sustained in the course and within the scope of his employment under this contract shall not impair the right of the Player to receive his full salary for the period of such disability or for the season in which the injury was sustained (whichever period is shorter), together with the reasonable medical and hospital expenses incurred by reason of the injury and during the term of this contract or for a period of up to two years from the date of initial treatment for such injury, whichever period is longer, but only upon the express prerequisite conditions that (a) written notice of such injury, including the time, place, cause and nature of the injury, is served upon and received by the Club within twenty days of the sustaining of said injury and (b) the Club shall have the right to designate the doctors and hospitals furnishing such medical and hospital services. Failure to give such notice shall not impair the rights of the Player, as herein set forth, if the Club has actual knowledge of such injury. All workmen's compensation payments received by the Player as compensation for loss of income for a specific period during which the Club is paying him in full, shall be paid over by the Player to the Club. Any other disability may be grounds for suspending or terminating this contract.

3.   The Club will furnish the Player with two complete uniforms, exclusive of shoes, unless the Club requires the Player to wear non-standard shoes in which case the Club will furnish the shoes. The uniforms will be surrendered by the Player to the Club at the end of the season or upon termination of this contract.

4.   The Player shall be entitled to expense allowances under the circumstances and in the amounts set forth in Article VII of the Basic Agreement.

5.   For violation by the Player of any regulation or other provision of this contract, the Club may impose a reasonable fine and deduct the amount thereof from the Player's salary or may suspend the Player

without salary for a period not exceeding thirty days or both. Written notice of the fine or suspension or both and the reason therefor shall in every case be given to the Player and the Players Association. (See Article XII of the Basic Agreement.)

6.   In order to enable the Player to fit himself for his duties under this contract, the Club may require the Player to report for practice at such places as the Club may designate and to participate in such exhibition contests as may be arranged by the Club, without any other compensation than that herein elsewhere provided, for a period beginning not earlier than thirty-three (33) days prior to the start of the championship season, provided, however, that the Club may invite players to report at an earlier date on a voluntary basis in accordance with Article XIV of the Basic Agreement. The Club will pay the necessary traveling expenses, including the first class jet air fare and meals en route of the Player from his home city to the training place of the Club, whether he be ordered to go there directly or by way of the home city of the Club. In the event of the failure of the Player to report for practice or to participate in the exhibition games, as required and provided for, he shall be required to get into playing condition to the satisfaction of the Club's team manager, and at the Player's own expense, before his salary shall commence.

7.   In case of assignment of this contract, the Player shall report promptly to the assignee Club within 72 hours from the date he receives written notice from the Club of such assignment, if the Player is then not more than 1,600 miles by most direct available railroad route from the assignee Club, plus an additional 24 hours for each additional 800 miles.

Post–Season Exhibition Games. Major League Rule 18(b) provides:

(b) EXHIBITION GAMES. No player shall participate in any exhibition game during the period between the close of the Major League championship season and the following training season, except that, with the consent of the player's Club and permission of the Commissioner, a player may participate in exhibition games for a period of not less than 30 days, such period to be designated annually by the Commissioner. Players who participate in barnstorming during this period cannot engage in any Winter League activities.

Player conduct, on and off the field, in connection with such post-season exhibition games shall be subject to the discipline of the Commissioner. The Commissioner shall not approve of more than three players of any one Club on the same team. The Commissioner shall not approve of more than three players from the joint membership of the World Series participants playing in the same game.

No player shall participate in any exhibition game with or against any team which, during the current season or within one year, has had any ineligible player or which is or has been during the current season or within one year, managed and controlled by an ineligible player or by any person who has listed an ineligible player under an assumed name or who otherwise has violated, or attempted to violate, any exhibition game contract; or with or against any team which, during said season or within one year, has played against teams containing such ineligible players, or so managed or controlled. Any player who participates in such a game in violation of this Rule 18 shall be fined not less than $50 nor more than $500, except that in no event shall such fine be less than the consideration received by such player for participating in such game.

SAMPLE A—BASEBALL SALARY GUARANTEE ADDENDUM TO UNIFORM PLAYER'S CONTRACT

A. AGREEMENT TO PAY IF THE CONTRACT IS NOT TERMINATED

So long as this contract is not terminated, the Club agrees to pay the Player in full the salary stipulated in Paragraph 2 of the contract; provided, however, that the Club shall be relieved of its obligation to pay salary during any period that the Player fails to render his services under the contract due to:

(1) Voluntary retirement as an active Player;

(2) Strike by the Major League Baseball Players' Association;

(3) Placement on any of the lists set out in Major League Rule 15;

(4) Suspension by the Club or by action of the League President or the Commissioner of Baseball;

(5) Physical or mental incapacity or death due to or attributable to: (a) Self-injury, suicide or attempted suicide; (b) Drug or alcohol abuse; (c) The acts, activities or sports prohibited by the contract; (d) His own criminal or felonious act (including civil or criminal incarceration as a form of incapacity); (e) Participation in the following activities or sports

B. AGREEMENT TO PAY SALARY IN THE EVENT OF TERMINATION OF THE CONTRACT

(1) The Club agrees that if the contract is terminated because the Player fails, in the opinion of the Club's management, to exhibit sufficient skill or competitive ability to qualify to continue as a member of the Club's team (Paragraph 7(b)(2) of the contract), the Player shall continue to receive the unpaid balance of the salary stipulated in Paragraph 2 of the contract for the term of the contract; provided, however, that the foregoing agreement to continue the Player's salary applies only in those situations where insufficient skill or competitive ability does not result from the Player's misconduct or the Player's unlawful or contractually prohibited acts, which include the following acts:

(a) The Player's failure, refusal or neglect to conform his personal conduct to the standards of good citizenship and good sportsmanship or to keep himself in first-class condition or to obey the Club's training rules (Paragraph 7(b)(1) of the contract); or

(b) The Player's failure, refusal or neglect or render services under the contract or in any other manner materially breach the contract (Paragraph 7(b)(3) of the contract); or

(c) The Player's failure to render his services due to physical or mental incapacity or death directly or indirectly due to or attributable to: (1) participation in the following activities or sports _____; (2) self-injury, suicide or attempted suicide; (3) drug or alcohol abuse; (4) acts, activities or sports prohibited by the contract; (5) his own criminal or felonious act (including civil or criminal incarceration as a form of incapacity).

In the event the contract is terminated and during its term the Player signs a player contract with another Club or Clubs, notwithstanding anything to the contrary in this Paragraph B the Club's total obligations to the Player (including amounts deferred to later years, if any) in any year shall be reduced by the amounts which the Player earns during that year from any Club or Clubs, including amounts deferred to later years, if any, and bonuses.

In the event the Player refuses to accept a reasonable Major League contract offered by a Club other than the Club which released him, the Player shall forfeit that portion of salary which would not have been payable had he accepted such other contract.

(2) If the Club terminates the contract pursuant to Paragraph 7(b)(1) or 7(b)(3) of the contract, all obligations of both parties hereunder, including the obligation to pay the player in full the salary stipulated in Paragraph 2 of the contract, shall cease on the date of termination, except the obligation to pay the player compensation earned to said date.

[alternatively]

SAMPLE B—BASEBALL SALARY GUARANTEE

ADDENDUM TO UNIFORM PLAYER'S CONTRACT

A.1.   In addition to the payments set forth in paragraph 2 of the Contract the Club shall make the following payments (subject to applicable withholding) to Player.

(i) For the signing of the Contract, _____ on or before _____; and

(ii) For personal services to be rendered by Player during the term of this Contract, _____ per year for each commencing

_____ and continuing to and including _____, payable during each such year in equal monthly installments.

A.2. The Club agrees that the payments due to the Player as compensation (pursuant to paragraph 2 of this Contract and paragraph A.1. of this Addendum) shall be payable by the Club to Player and shall remain the obligation of the Club, despite the inability of the Player to perform the services as a baseball player as provided for under the Contract, except as hereinafter provided in this Addendum. Accordingly, all such compensation shall be payable by the Club to the Player (except as hereinafter provided in its Addendum) despite the fact that Player's inability to so perform said services is due to a failure of Player to display sufficient professional skills, or to the death of the Player, or to a physical handicap or disability (whether incurred on or off the baseball field or during the championship season or the off-season). In the event of the death of the Player, all such compensation due thereafter shall be payable by Club to Player's estate or the designee named in a written instrument filed by the Player with the Club. If the Club shall be obligated to pay Player (or his estate) compensation despite the inability of Player to perform services as a baseball player as provided for under the Contract, such payments shall be made at the same time and in the same installments as provided in paragraph 2 of the Contract or paragraph A.1. of this Addendum.

A.3. If the Club shall be obligated to pay Player compensation under paragraph 2 of this Contract despite the inability of Player to perform services as a baseball player, Player shall, nevertheless, on a full time basis for the remaining years through _____ (but only during the championship season), perform such services for the Club as management shall from time to time determine. Such services may include services in public relations, management, coaching or similar capacities, but the type of such services shall take into account the nature of the disability.

A.4. The obligations of the Club under paragraph A.2. of this Contract to pay compensation to Player, or, in the even of death, to his estate, despite his inability to perform services, is subject only to the following conditions:

(a) The Club shall have the option of terminating this Contract upon written notice to the Player, which termination shall release the Club from all of its obligations, liabilities, and responsibilities hereunder accruing from and after the occurrence of an injury which impairs the Player's ability to play baseball, or death of the Player, if said injury or death:

(i) results from the Player participating or engaging in, from and after the date of execution of this Contract up to and including the last day of the _____ Championship season, the following: (A) auto or motorcycle racing, piloting of aircraft, fencing, parachuting, skydiving, gliding, hang gliding, karate, judo, football, snow or water skiing, soccer, ice hockey, or (B) any other sport or pastime involving a substantial risk of personal injury, or (C) without the prior written consent of the Club, in organized or in professional athletics except in his employment by the Club.

(ii) is proximately caused by: (A) suicide, attempted suicide, or intentionally self-inflicted injury, (B) a felonious act by Player, or occurs in the commission thereof, (C) illegal drug use, drug abuse or use of alcoholic beverages by the Player.

(b) The Club shall also have the option of terminating the Contract upon written notice to the Player, which termination shall release the Club from all of its obligations, liabilities, and responsibilities hereunder accruing from and after the following events: (i) a final conviction of a felony; (ii) an unjustifiable refusal to render his professional service; (iii) voluntary retirement by the Player; (iv) a material breach of this Contract.

(c) Should the Club not exercise its option to terminate the Contract pursuant to this paragraph A.4. it shall be released of its obligations, liabilities, and responsibilities hereunder only during the period the Player is unable to or does not render his professional services.

For the purposes of paragraph 4(b) of the Contract, Player confirms that he knows of no mental or physical defects which he has and accordingly, has not advised the Club of any such defects.

———

NFL PLAYER CONTRACT

THIS CONTRACT is between _____, hereinafter "Player," and _____, a _____ (corporation) (limited partnership) (partnership), hereinafter "Club," operating under the name of the _____ as a member of the National Football League, hereinafter "League." In consideration of the promises made by each to the other, Player and Club agree as follows:

1.   TERM. This contract covers _____ football season(s), and will begin on the date of execution or March 1, _____, whichever is later, and end on February 28 or 29, _____, unless extended, terminated, or renewed as specified elsewhere in this contract.

2.   EMPLOYMENT AND SERVICES. Club employs Player as a skilled football player. Player accepts such employment. He agrees to give his best efforts and loyalty to the Club, and to conduct himself on and off the field with appropriate recognition of the fact that the success of professional football depends largely on public respect for and approval of those associated with the game. Player will report promptly for and participate fully in Club's official mandatory mini-camp(s), official pre-season training camp, all Club meetings and practice sessions, and all pre-season, regular season and post-season football games scheduled for or by Club. If invited, Player will practice for and play in any all-star football game sponsored by the League. Player will not participate in any

football game not sponsored by the League unless the game is first approved by the League.

3. OTHER ACTIVITIES. Without prior written consent of the Club, Player will not play football or engage in activities related to football otherwise than for Club or engage in any activity other than football which may involve a significant risk of personal injury. Player represents that he has special, exceptional and unique knowledge, skill, ability, and experience as a football player, the loss of which cannot be estimated with any certainty and cannot be fairly or adequately compensated by damages. Player therefore agrees that Club will have the right, in addition to any other right which Club may possess, to enjoin Player by appropriate proceedings from playing football or engaging in football-related activities other than for Club or from engaging in any activity other than football which may involve a significant risk of personal injury.

4. PUBLICITY AND NFLPA GROUP LICENSING PROGRAM.

(a) Player grants to Club and the League, separately and together, the authority to use his name and picture for publicity and the promotion of NFL Football, the League or any of its member clubs in newspapers, magazines, motion pictures, game programs and roster manuals, broadcasts and telecasts, and all other publicity and advertising media, provided such publicity and promotion does not constitute an endorsement by Player of a commercial product. Player will cooperate with the news media, and will participate upon request in reasonable activities to promote the Club and the League. Player and National Football League Players Association, hereinafter "NFLPA," will not contest the rights of the League and its member clubs to telecast, broadcast, or otherwise transmit NFL Football or the right of NFL Films to produce, sell, market, or distribute football game film footage, except insofar as such broadcast, telecast, or transmission of footage is used in any commercially marketable game or interactive use. The League and its member clubs, and Player and the NFLPA, reserve their respective rights as to the use of such broadcasts, telecasts or transmissions of footage in such games or interactive uses, which shall be unaffected by this subparagraph.

(b) Player hereby assigns to the NFLPA and its licensing affiliates, if any, the exclusive right to use and to grant to persons, firms, or corporations (collectively "licensees") the right to use his name, signature facsimile, voice, picture, photograph, likeness, and/or biographical information (collectively "image") in group licensing programs. Group licensing programs are defined as those licensing programs in which a licensee utilizes a total of six (6) or more NFL player images on products that are sold at retail or used as promotional or premium items. Player retains the right to grant permission to a licensee to utilize his image if that licensee is not concurrently utilizing the images of five (5) or more other NFL players on products that are sold at retail or are used as promotional or premium items. If Player's inclusion in a particular

NFLPA program is precluded by an individual exclusive endorsement agreement, and Player provides the NFLPA with timely written notice of that preclusion, the NFLPA will exclude Player from that particular program. In consideration for this assignment of rights, the NFLPA will use the revenues it receives from group licensing programs to support the objectives as set forth in the By-laws of the NFLPA. The NFLPA will use its best efforts to promote the use of NFL player images in group licensing programs, to provide group licensing opportunities to all NFL players, and to ensure that no entity utilizes the group licensing rights granted to the NFLPA without first obtaining a license from the NFLPA. This paragraph shall be construed under New York law without reference to conflicts of law principles. The assignment in this paragraph shall expire on December 31 of the later of (a) the third year following the execution of this contract, or (b) the year in which this contract expires. Neither Club nor the League is a party to the terms of this paragraph, which is included herein solely for the administrative convenience and benefit of Player and the NFLPA. The terms of this subparagraph apply unless, at the time of execution of this contract, Player indicates by striking out this subparagraph (b) and marking his initials adjacent to the stricken language his intention to not participate in the NFLPA Group Licensing Program. Nothing in this subparagraph shall be construed to supersede or any way broaden, expand, detract from, or otherwise alter in any way whatsoever, the rights of NFL Properties, Inc. as permitted under Article V (Union Security), Section 4 of the 1993 Collective Bargaining Agreement ("CBA").

5. COMPENSATION. For performance of Player's services and all other promises of Player, Club will pay Player a yearly salary as follows:

$_____ for the _____ season; [additional lines if necessary]

In addition, Club will pay Player such earned performance bonuses as may be called for in this contract; Player's necessary traveling expenses from his residence to training camp; Player's reasonable board and lodging expenses during pre-season training and in connection with playing pre-season, regular season, and post-season football games outside Club's home city; Player's necessary traveling expenses to and from pre-season, regular season, and post-season football games outside Club's home city; Player's necessary traveling expenses to his residence if this contract is terminated by Club; and such additional compensation, benefits and reimbursement of expenses as may be called for in any collective bargaining agreement in existence during the term of this contract. (For purposes of this contract, a collective bargaining agreement will be deemed to be "in existence" during its stated term or during any period for which the parties to that agreement agree to extend it.)

6. PAYMENT. Unless this contract or any collective bargaining agreement in existence during the term of this contract specifically provides otherwise, Player will be paid 100% of his yearly salary under this contract in equal weekly or bi-weekly installments over the course of

the applicable regular season period, commencing with the first regular season game played by Club in each season. Unless this contract specifically provides otherwise, if this contract is executed or Player is activated after the beginning of the regular season, the yearly salary payable to Player will be reduced proportionately and Player will be paid the weekly or bi-weekly portions of his yearly salary becoming due and payable after he is activated. Unless this contract specifically provides otherwise, if this contract is terminated after the beginning of the regular season, the yearly salary payable to Player will be reduced proportionately and Player will be paid the weekly or bi-weekly portions of his yearly salary having become due and payable up to the time of termination.

7. DEDUCTIONS. Any advance made to Player will be repaid to Club, and any properly levied Club fine or Commissioner fine against Player will be paid, in cash on demand or by means of deductions from payments coming due to the Player under this contract, the amount of such deductions to be determined by Club unless this contract or any collective bargaining agreement in existence during the term of this contract specifically provides otherwise.

8. PHYSICAL CONDITION. Player represents to Club that he is and will maintain himself in excellent physical condition. Player will undergo a complete physical examination by the Club physician upon Club request, during which physical examination Player agrees to make full and complete disclosure of any physical or mental condition known to him which might impair his performance under this contract and to respond fully and in good faith when questioned by the Club physician about such condition. If Player fails to establish or maintain his excellent physical condition to the satisfaction of the Club physician, or make the required full and complete disclosure and good faith responses to the Club physician, then Club may terminate this contract.

9. INJURY. Unless this contract specifically provides otherwise, if Player is injured in the performance of his services under this contract and promptly reports such injury to the Club physician or trainer, then Player will receive such medical and hospital care during the term of this contract as the Club physician may deem necessary, and will continue to receive his yearly salary for so long, during the season of injury only and for no subsequent period covered by this contract, as Player is physically unable to perform the services required of him by this contract because of such injury. If Player's injury in the performance of his services under this contract results in his death, the unpaid balance of his yearly salary for the season of injury will be paid to his stated beneficiary, or in the absence of a stated beneficiary, to his estate.

10. WORKERS' COMPENSATION. Any compensation paid to Player under this contract or under any collective bargaining agreement in existence during the term of this contract for a period during which he is entitled to workers' compensation benefits by reason of temporary total, permanent total, temporary partial, or permanent partial disability will be deemed an advance payment of workers' compensation benefits

due Player, and Club will be entitled to be reimbursed the amount of such payment out of any award of workers' compensation.

11. SKILL, PERFORMANCE AND CONDUCT. Player understands that he is competing with other players for a position on Club's roster within the applicable player limits. If at any time, in the sole judgment of Club, Player's skill or performance has been unsatisfactory as compared with that of other players competing for positions on Club's roster, or if Player has engaged in personal conduct reasonably judged by Club to adversely affect or reflect on Club, then Club may terminate this contract. In addition, during the period any salary cap is legally in effect, this contract may be terminated if, in Club's opinion, Player is anticipated to make less of a contribution to Club's ability to compete on the playing field than another player or players whom Club intends to sign or attempts to sign, or another player or players who is or are already on Club's roster, and for whom Club needs room.

12. TERMINATION. The rights of termination set forth in this contract will be in addition to any other rights of termination allowed either party by law. Termination will be effective upon the giving of written notice, except that Player's death, other than as a result of injury incurred in the performance of his services under this contract, will automatically terminate this contract. If this contract is terminated by Club and either Player or Club so requests, Player will promptly undergo a complete physical examination by the Club physician.

13. INJURY GRIEVANCE. Unless a collective bargaining agreement in existence at the time of termination of this contract by Club provides otherwise, the following injury grievance procedure will apply: If Player believes that at the time of termination of this contract by Club he was physically unable to perform the services required of him by this contract because of an injury incurred in the performance of his services under this contract, Player may, within 60 days after examination by the Club physician, submit at his own expense to examination by a physician of his choice. If the opinion of Player's physician with respect to his physical ability to perform the services required of him by this contract is contrary to that of the Club's physician, the dispute will be submitted within a reasonable time to final and binding arbitration by an arbitrator selected by Club and Player or, if they are unable to agree, one selected in accordance with the procedures of the American Arbitration Association on application by either party.

14. RULES. Player will comply with and be bound by all reasonable Club rules and regulations in effect during the term of this contract which are not inconsistent with the provisions of this contract or of any collective bargaining agreement in existence during the term of this contract. Player's attention is also called to the fact that the League functions with certain rules and procedures expressive of its operation as a joint venture among its member clubs and that these rules and practices may affect Player's relationship to the League and its member clubs independently of the provisions of this contract.

15. INTEGRITY OF GAME. Player recognizes the detriment to the League and professional football that would result from impairment of public confidence in the honest and orderly conduct of NFL games or the integrity and good character of NFL players. Player therefore acknowledges his awareness that if he accepts a bribe or agrees to throw or fix an NFL game; fails to promptly report a bribe offer or an attempt to throw or fix an NFL game; bets on an NFL game; knowingly associates with gamblers or gambling activity; uses or provides other players with stimulants or other drugs for the purpose of attempting to enhance on-field performance; or is guilty of any other form of conduct reasonably judged by the League Commissioner to be detrimental to the League or professional football, the Commissioner will have the right, but only after giving Player the opportunity for a hearing at which he may be represented by counsel of his choice, to fine Player in a reasonable amount; to suspend Player for a period certain or indefinitely; and/or to terminate this contract.

16. EXTENSION. Unless this contract specifically provides otherwise, if Player becomes a member of the Armed Forces of the United States or any other country, or retires from professional football as an active player, or otherwise fails or refuses to perform his services under this contract, then this contract will be tolled between the date of Player's induction into the Armed Forces, or his retirement, or his failure or refusal to perform, and the later date of his return to professional football. During the period this contract is tolled, Player will not be entitled to any compensation or benefits. On Player's return to professional football, the term of this contract will be extended for a period of time equal to the number of seasons (to the nearest multiple of one) remaining at the time the contract was tolled. The right of renewal, if any, contained in this contract will remain in effect until the end of any such extended term.

17. ASSIGNMENT. Unless this contract specifically provides otherwise, Club may assign this contract and Player's services under this contract to any successor to Club's franchise or to any other Club in the League. Player will report to the assignee Club promptly upon being informed of the assignment of his contract and will faithfully perform his services under this contract. The assignee club will pay Player's necessary traveling expenses in reporting to it and will faithfully perform this contract with Player.

18. FILING. This contract will be valid and binding upon Player and Club immediately upon execution. A copy of this contract, including any attachment to it, will be filed by Club with the League Commissioner within 10 days after execution. The Commissioner will have the right to disapprove this contract on reasonable grounds, including but not limited to an attempt by the parties to abridge or impair the rights of any other club, uncertainty or incompleteness in expression of the parties' respective rights and obligations, or conflict between the terms of this contract and any collective bargaining agreement then in existence. Approval will be automatic unless, within 10 days after receipt of

this contract in his office, the Commissioner notifies the parties either of disapproval or of extension of this 10–day period for purposes of investigation or clarification pending his decision. On the receipt of notice of disapproval and termination, both parties will be relieved of their respective rights and obligations under this contract.

19. DISPUTES. During the term of any collective bargaining agreement, any dispute between Player and Club involving the interpretation or application of any provision of this contract will be submitted to final and binding arbitration in accordance with the procedure called for in any collective bargaining agreement in existence at the time the event giving rise to any such dispute occurs.

20. NOTICE. Any notice, request, approval or consent under this contract will be sufficiently given if in writing and delivered in person or mailed (certified or first class) by one party to the other at the address set forth in this contract or to such other address as the recipient may subsequently have furnished in writing to the sender.

21. OTHER AGREEMENTS. This contract, including any attachment to it, sets forth the entire agreement between Player and Club and cannot be modified or supplemented orally. Player and Club represent that no other agreement, oral or written, except as attached to or specifically incorporated in this contract, exists between them. The provisions of this contract will govern the relationship between Player and Club unless there are conflicting provisions in any collective bargaining agreement in existence during the term of this contract, in which case the provisions of the collective bargaining agreement will take precedence over conflicting provisions of this contract relating to the rights or obligations of either party.

22. LAW. This contract is made under and shall be governed by the laws of the State of _____.

23. WAIVER AND RELEASE. Player waives and releases any claims that he may have arising out of, related to, or asserted in the lawsuit entitled White v. National Football League, including, but not limited to, any such claim regarding past NFL Rules, the College Draft, Plan B, the first refusal/compensation system, the NFL Player Contract, pre-season compensation, or any other term or condition of employment, except any claims asserted in Brown v. Pro Football, Inc. This waiver and release also extends to any conduct engaged in pursuant to the Stipulation and Settlement Agreement in White ("Settlement Agreement") during the express term of that Settlement Agreement or any portion thereof. This waiver and release shall not limit any rights Player may have to performance by the Club under this Contract or Player's rights as a member of the White class to object to the Settlement Agreement during its review by the court in Minnesota. This waiver and release is subject to Article XIV (NFL Player Contract), Section 3(c) of the CBA.

24. OTHER PROVISIONS.

(a) Each of the undersigned hereby confirms that (i) this contract, renegotiation, extension or amendment sets forth all components of the player's remuneration for playing professional football (whether such compensation is being furnished directly by the Club or by a related or affiliated entity); and (ii) there are not undisclosed agreements of any kind, whether express or implied, oral or written, and there are no promises, undertakings, representations, commitments, inducements, assurances of intent, or understandings of any kind that have not been disclosed to the NFL involving consideration of any kind to be paid, furnished or made available to Player or any entity or person owned or controlled by, affiliated with, or related to Player, either during the term of this contract or thereafter.

(b) Each of the undersigned further confirms that, except insofar as any of the undersigned may describe in an addendum to this contract, to the best of their knowledge, no conduct in violation of the Anti–Collusion rules of the Settlement Agreement took place with respect to this contract. Each of the undersigned further confirms that nothing in this contract is designed or intended to defeat or circumvent any provisions of the Settlement Agreement, including but not limited to the Rookie Pool and Salary Cap provisions; however, any conduct permitted by the CBA and/or the Settlement Agreement shall not be considered a violation of this confirmation.

(c) The Club further confirms that any information regarding the negotiation of this contract that it provided to the Neutral Verifier was, at the time the information was provided, true and correct in all material respects.

25. SPECIAL PROVISIONS. [Signing or performance bonuses, no-trade clauses, salary guarantees, or other special benefits for the player not inconsistent with the collective bargaining agreement may be added onto the contract here.]

[SIGNED by the player, a representative of the club, and the player's agent]

E. AGENT RELATED REGULATIONS AND STATUTES

UNIFORM ATHLETE AGENTS ACT (2000)

(Adopted in 28 States as of April 2004)

SECTION 2. DEFINITIONS. In this [Act]:

(1) "Agency contract" means an agreement in which a student-athlete authorizes a person to negotiate or solicit on behalf of the student-athlete a professional-sports-services contract or an endorsement contract.

(2) "Athlete agent" means an individual who enters into an agency contract with a student-athlete or, directly or indirectly, recruits or solicits a student-athlete to enter into an agency contract. The term includes an individual who represents to the public that the individual is an athlete agent....

(8) "Professional-sports-services contract" means an agreement under which an individual is employed, or agrees to render services, as a player on a professional sports team, with a professional sports organization, or as a professional athlete.

(12) "Student-athlete" means an individual who engages in, is eligible to engage in, or may be eligible in the future to engage in, any intercollegiate sport. If an individual is permanently ineligible to participate in a particular intercollegiate sport, the individual is not a student-athlete for purposes of that sport.

SECTION 4. ATHLETE AGENTS: REGISTRATION REQUIRED; VOID CONTRACTS

(a) Except as otherwise provided in subsection (b), an individual may not act as an athlete agent in this State without holding a certificate of registration under Section 6 or 8.

(b) Before being issued a certificate of registration, an individual may act as an athlete agent in this State for all purposes except signing an agency contract, if: (1) a student-athlete or another person acting on behalf of the student-athlete initiates communication with the individual; and (2) within seven days after an initial act as an athlete agent, the individual submits an application for registration as an athlete agent in this State.

(c) An agency contract resulting from conduct in violation of this section is void and the athlete agent shall return any consideration received under the contract.

Comment

The intent of this section is to make the registration requirement as broad as constitutionally permissible consistent with the minimum contacts theory of *International Shoe Company v. Washington*, 326 U.S. 310 (1945). Agents must register in each State in which they have established minimum contacts. For example, an individual in State A contacting a student-athlete in State B is acting as an athlete agent in both States and is therefore required to register in both States.

SECTION 5. REGISTRATION AS ATHLETE AGENT; FORM; REQUIREMENTS

(a) An applicant for registration shall submit an application for registration to the [Secretary of State] in a form prescribed by the [Secretary of State]. [An application filed under this section is a public record.] The application must be in the name of an individual and, except as otherwise provided in subsection (b), signed or otherwise authenticated by the applicant under penalty of perjury and state or contain: [lengthy list of detailed categories of information relating to the applicant's personal, professional, and disciplinary/criminal history, clients, partners and associates, education, and references].

(b) An individual who has submitted an application for, and holds a certificate of, registration or licensure as an athlete agent in another State, may submit a copy of the application and certificate in lieu of submitting an application in the form prescribed pursuant to subsection (a). The [Secretary of State] shall accept the application and the certificate from the other State as an application for registration in this State. . . .

Comment

. . . .Subsection (b) provides for reciprocal use of applications in States which have adopted the Uniform Act. The need for an agent to comply with substantially different application procedures in multiple jurisdictions is eliminated. It is the first of a number of reciprocity provisions found in the act which are intended to ease the burden placed on agents by substantially different registration requirements and to simplify enforcement of the act. Absence of reciprocity provisions in existing acts is a primary reason why the Uniform Act is needed.

SECTION 6. CERTIFICATE OF REGISTRATION; ISSUANCE OR DENIAL; RENEWAL

(b) The [Secretary of State] may refuse to issue a certificate of registration if the [Secretary of State] determines that the applicant has engaged in conduct that has a significant adverse effect on the applicant's fitness to act as an athlete agent. . . .

(f) A certificate of registration or a renewal of a registration is valid for [two] years.

SECTION 7.   SUSPENSION, REVOCATION, OR REFUSAL TO RENEW REGISTRATION

[(a)] The [Secretary of State] may suspend, revoke, or refuse to renew a registration for conduct that would have justified denial of registration under Section 6(b).

[(b) The [Secretary of State] may deny, suspend, revoke, or refuse to renew a certificate of registration or licensure only after proper notice and an opportunity for a hearing. The [Administrative Procedures Act] applies to this [Act].]

SECTION 9.   REGISTRATION AND RENEWAL FEES.   An application for registration or renewal of registration must be accompanied by a fee in the following amount: [amount(s) open for determination by each state].

SECTION 10.   REQUIRED FORM OF CONTRACT.

(a) An agency contract must be in a record, signed or otherwise authenticated by the parties.

(b) An agency contract must state or contain:

(1) the amount and method of calculating the consideration to be paid by the student-athlete for services to be provided by the athlete agent under the contract and any other consideration the athlete agent has received or will receive from any other source for entering into the contract or for providing the services;

(2) the name of any person not listed in the application for registration or renewal of registration who will be compensated because the student-athlete signed the agency contract;

(3) a description of any expenses that the student-athlete agrees to reimburse;

(4) a description of the services to be provided to the student-athlete;

(5) the duration of the contract; and

(6) the date of execution.

(c) An agency contract must contain, in close proximity to the signature of the student-athlete, a conspicuous notice in boldface type in capital letters stating:

WARNING TO STUDENT–ATHLETE

IF YOU SIGN THIS CONTRACT:

(1) YOU MAY LOSE YOUR ELIGIBILITY TO COMPETE AS A STUDENT–ATHLETE IN YOUR SPORT;

(2) IF YOU HAVE AN ATHLETIC DIRECTOR, WITHIN 72 HOURS AFTER ENTERING INTO THIS CONTRACT, BOTH YOU AND YOUR ATHLETE AGENT MUST NOTIFY YOUR ATHLETIC DIRECTOR; AND

(3) YOU MAY CANCEL THIS CONTRACT WITHIN 14 DAYS AFTER SIGNING IT. CANCELLATION OF THIS CONTRACT MAY NOT REINSTATE YOUR ELIGIBILITY.

(d) An agency contract that does not conform to this section is voidable by the student-athlete. If a student-athlete voids an agency contract, the student-athlete is not required to pay any consideration under the contract or to return any consideration received from the athlete agent to induce the student-athlete to enter into the contract.

(e) The athlete agent shall give a record of the signed or otherwise authenticated agency contract to the student-athlete at the time of execution.

SECTION 11. NOTICE TO EDUCATIONAL INSTITUTION

(a) Within 72 hours after entering into an agency contract or before the next scheduled athletic event in which the student-athlete may participate, whichever occurs first, the athlete agent shall give notice in a record of the existence of the contract to the athletic director of the educational institution at which the student-athlete is enrolled or the athlete agent has reasonable grounds to believe the student-athlete intends to enroll.

(b) Within 72 hours after entering into an agency contract or before the next athletic event in which the student-athlete may participate, whichever occurs first, the student-athlete shall inform the athletic director of the educational institution at which the student-athlete is enrolled that he or she has entered into an agency contract.

SECTION 12. STUDENT–ATHLETE'S RIGHT TO CANCEL

(a) A student-athlete may cancel an agency contract by giving notice of the cancellation to the athlete agent in a record within 14 days after the contract is signed.

(b) A student-athlete may not waive the right to cancel an agency contract.

(c) If a student-athlete cancels an agency contract, the student-athlete is not required to pay any consideration under the contract or to return any consideration received from the athlete agent to induce the student-athlete to enter into the contract.

SECTION 14. PROHIBITED CONDUCT

(a) An athlete agent, with the intent to induce a student-athlete to enter into an agency contract, may not: (1) give any materially false or misleading information or make a materially false promise or representation; (2) furnish anything of value to a student-athlete before the student-athlete enters into the agency contract; or (3) furnish anything of value to any individual other than the student-athlete or another registered athlete agent.

(b) An athlete agent may not intentionally: (1) initiate contact with a student-athlete unless registered under this [Act]; (2) refuse or fail to retain or permit inspection of the records required to be retained by Section 13; (3) fail to register when required by Section 4; (4) provide materially false or misleading information in an application for registration or renewal of registration; (5) predate or postdate an agency contract; or (6) fail to notify a student-athlete before the student-athlete signs or otherwise authenticates an agency contract for a particular sport that the signing or authentication may make the student-athlete ineligible to participate as a student-athlete in that sport.

SECTION 15.   CRIMINAL PENALTIES. An athlete agent who violates Section 14 is guilty of a [misdemeanor] [felony] and, upon conviction, is punishable by [_____].

SECTION 16.   CIVIL REMEDIES

(a) An educational institution has a right of action against an athlete agent or a former student-athlete for damages caused by a violation of this [Act]. In an action under this section, the court may award to the prevailing party costs and reasonable attorney's fees.

(b) Damages of an educational institution under subsection (a) include losses and expenses incurred because, as a result of the conduct of an athlete agent or former student-athlete, the educational institution was injured by a violation of this [Act] or was penalized, disqualified, or suspended from participation in athletics by a national association for the promotion and regulation of athletics, by an athletic conference, or by reasonable self-imposed disciplinary action taken to mitigate sanctions likely to be imposed by such an organization. . . .

SECTION 17.   ADMINISTRATIVE PENALTY. The [Secretary of State] may assess a civil penalty against an athlete agent not to exceed [$25,000] for a violation of this [Act].

NFLPA REGULATIONS GOVERNING CONTRACT ADVISORS

Introduction

In 1994, the Officers and Player Representatives of the National Football League Players Association ("NFLPA") adopted the NFLPA Regulations Governing Contract Advisors ("Regulations") for persons who desired to provide representation services to players (including rookies) by conducting individual contract negotiations and/or assisting in or advising with respect to such negotiations with the member Clubs of the National Football League ("NFL"). . . .

Persons serving or wishing to serve as the NFLPA's "agent" pursuant to these provisions of the CBA, which persons are herein referred to as "Contract Advisors," shall be governed by these Regulations.

SECTION 1—SCOPE OF REGULATIONS

A.   Persons Subject to Regulations—No person (other than a player representing himself) shall be permitted to conduct individual contract negotiations on behalf of a player and/or assist in or advise with respect to such negotiations with NFL Clubs after the effective date of these Regulations unless he/she is (1) currently certified as a Contract Advisor pursuant to these Regulations; (2) signs a Standard Representation Agreement with the player (See Section 4; Appendix D); and (3) files a fully executed copy of the Standard Representation Agreement with the NFLPA, along with any contract(s) between the player and the Contract Advisor for other services to be provided.

B.   Activities Covered—The activities of Contract Advisors which are governed by these Regulations include: the providing of advice, counsel, information or assistance to players with respect to negotiating their individual contracts with Clubs and/or thereafter in enforcing those contracts; the conduct of individual compensation negotiations with the Clubs on behalf of players; and any other activity or conduct which directly bears upon the Contract Advisor's integrity, competence or ability to properly represent individual NFL players and the NFLPA in individual contract negotiations, including the handling of player funds, providing tax counseling and preparation services, and providing financial advice and investment services to individual players.

SECTION 2—CERTIFICATION

After the effective date of these Regulations, any person who wishes to perform the functions of a Contract Advisor as described in Section 1 above must be certified by the NFLPA. . . .

C.   Grounds for Denial for Certification—Grounds for denial of Certification shall include, but not be limited to, the following:

- The applicant has made false or misleading statements of a material nature in his/her application;

- The applicant has misappropriated funds, or engaged in other specific acts such as embezzlement, theft or fraud, which would render him/her unfit to serve in a fiduciary capacity on behalf of players;

- The applicant has engaged in any other conduct that significantly impacts adversely on his/her credibility, integrity or competence to serve in a fiduciary capacity on behalf of players;

- The applicant is unwilling to swear or affirm that he/she will comply with these Regulations and any amendments hereto and/or that he/she will abide by the fee structure contained in the Standard Representation Agreement incorporated into these Regulations;

• The applicant has been denied certification by another professional sports players association;

• The applicant directly or indirectly solicited a player for representation as a Contract Advisor during the period of time between the filing of his/her Application for Certification and Certification by the NFLPA;

• The applicant has not received a degree from an accredited four year college/university, unless excepted from this requirement. . . .

D. Appeal from Denial of Certification—In the event an Application for Certification is denied pursuant to this Section, the applicant shall be notified in writing (by confirmed facsimile or overnight delivery) of the reasons for the denial. The applicant may appeal such action to the Arbitrator appointed pursuant to Section 5 of these Regulations. . . .

E. Suspension or Revocation of Certification—At any time subsequent to granting Certification to a Contract Advisor, the NFLPA may, based upon information brought to its attention or acting on its own initiative, immediately revoke such Certification pursuant to Section 6(B) hereof, or propose the suspension or revocation of such Certification on any ground that would have provided a basis for denying Certification in the first place (see Section 2(C)) and/or for conduct prohibited in Section 3(B)(1) through 3(B)(27) of these Regulations and/or for failing to engage in the conduct required in Section 3(A)(1) through 3(A)(17) of these Regulations. . . . The Contract Advisor may challenge any such proposed suspension or revocation by appealing such action pursuant to Section 6(B) through 6(H). The appeal to arbitration shall constitute the exclusive method of challenging any proposed suspension or revocation of Certification.

G. Expiration of Certification—The Certification of any Contract Advisor who has failed to negotiate and sign a player to an NFL Player Contract (excluding Practice Squad Contracts) for at least one NFL player during any three-year period shall automatically expire at the end of such three-year period.

SECTION 3—STANDARD CODE OF CONDUCT FOR CONTRACT ADVISORS

The objective of the NFLPA in implementing these Regulations is to enable players to make an informed selection of a Contract Advisor and to help assure that the Contract Advisor will provide effective representation at fair, reasonable, and uniformly applicable rates to those individual players he/she represents, and to avoid any conflict of interest which could potentially compromise the best interests of NFL players.

A. General Requirements—Consistent with this objective, a Contract Advisor shall be required to:

(1) Disclose on his/her Application and thereafter upon request of the NFLPA all information relevant to his/her qualifications to serve as a Contract Advisor, including, but not limited to, background, special training, experience in negotiations, past representation of professional athletes, and relevant business associations or memberships in professional organizations;

(2) Pay an application fee pursuant to Section 2 above unless waived;

(3) Pay the annual fee in a timely manner . . . ;

(4) Attend an NFLPA seminar on individual contract negotiations each year;

(5) Comply with the maximum fee schedule and all other provisions of these Regulations and any amendments thereto;

(6) Execute and abide by the printed Standard Representation Agreement with all players represented and file with the NFLPA a copy of that fully executed Agreement along with any other contract(s) for additional services that the Contract Advisor has executed with the player . . . . ;

(7) Advise the affected player and report to the NFLPA any known violations by an NFL Club of a player's individual contract or of his rights under any applicable Collective Bargaining Agreement;

(8) Sign and provide the NFLPA and the club with a copy of any player contract negotiated with that club within 48 hours after the contract is executed . . . . ;

(9) Provide on or before May 1 each year, to every player who he/she represents, with a copy to the NFLPA, an itemized statement covering the period beginning March 1 of the prior year through February 28 or 29 of that year, which separately sets forth both the fee charged to the player for, and any expenses incurred in connection with, the performance of the following services: (a) individual player salary negotiations, (b) management of the player's assets, (c) financial, investment, legal, tax and/or other advice to the player, and (d) any other miscellaneous services;

(10) Permit a person or firm authorized by a former or current player-client to conduct an audit of all relevant books and records pertaining to any services provided to that player;

(11) Complete a notarized updated Application for Certification on or before an annual date to be determined by the NFLPA . . . . ;

(13) Provide the NFLPA with all materials that the NFLPA deems relevant with respect to any investigation conducted pursuant to these Regulations and in all other respects cooperate fully with the NFLPA;

(14) Fully comply with applicable state and federal laws;

(15) Become and remain sufficiently educated with regard to NFL structure and economics, applicable Collective Bargaining Agreements and other governing documents, basic negotiating techniques, and developments in sports law and related subjects. To ascertain whether the Contract Advisor is sufficiently educated with regard to the above-related subjects, the NFLPA may require a Contract Advisor to pass a Contract Advisor examination....;

(16) Disclose in an addendum attached to the Standard Representation Agreement between the Contract Advisor and player, the names and current positions of any NFL management personnel or coaches whom Contract Advisor represents or has represented in matters pertaining to their employment by or association with any NFL club;

(17) Act at all times in a fiduciary capacity on behalf of players.

B. Prohibited Conduct— Contract Advisors are prohibited from:

(1) Representing any player in individual contract negotiations with any Club unless he/she (i) is an NFLPA Certified Contract Advisor; (ii) has signed the Standard Representation Agreement with such player; and (iii) has filed a copy of the Standard Representation Agreement with the NFLPA along with any other contract(s) or agreement(s) between the player and the Contract Advisor;

(2) Providing or offering money or any other thing of value to any player or prospective player to induce or encourage that player to utilize his/her services;

(3) Providing or offering money or any other thing of value to a member of the player's or prospective player's family or any other person for the purpose of inducing or encouraging that person to recommend the services of the Contract Advisor;

(4) Providing materially false or misleading information to any player or prospective player in the context of recruiting the player as a client or in the course of representing that player as his Contract Advisor;

(5) Representing or suggesting to any player or prospective player that his/her NFLPA Certification is an endorsement or recommendation by the NFLPA of the Contract Advisor or the Contract Advisor's qualifications or services;

(6) Directly or indirectly borrowing money from any player (whether or not the player is a client), either by receiving the funds directly from the player or by the player providing collateral for or agreeing to guarantee a loan to the Contract Advisor by another party;

(7) Holding or seeking to hold, either directly or indirectly, a financial interest in any professional football club or in any other business entity when such investment could create an actual conflict

of interest or the appearance of a conflict of interest in the representation of NFL players;

(8) Engaging in any other activity which creates an actual or potential conflict of interest with the effective representation of NFL players;

(9) Soliciting or accepting money or anything of value from any NFL Club in a way that would create an actual or apparent conflict with the interests of any player that the Contract Advisor represents;

(10) Negotiating and/or agreeing to any provision in a player contract which deprives or purports to deprive that player of any benefit contained in any collectively bargained agreement between the NFL and the NFLPA or any other provision of any applicable documents which protect the working conditions of NFL players;

(11) Negotiating and/or agreeing to any provision in any agreement involving a player which directly or indirectly violates any stated policies or rules established by the NFLPA;

(12) Concealing material facts from any player whom the Contract Advisor is representing which relate to the subject of the player's individual contract negotiation;

(13) Failing to advise the player and to report to the NFLPA any known violations by an NFL Club of a player's individual contract;

(14) Engaging in unlawful conduct and/or conduct involving dishonesty, fraud, deceit, misrepresentation, or other activity which reflects adversely on his/her fitness as a Contract Advisor or jeopardizes his/her effective representation of NFL players;

(15) Failure to comply with the maximum fee provisions contained in Section 4 of these Regulations;

(16) Circumventing the maximum fee provisions contained in Section 4 of these Regulations by knowingly and intentionally increasing the fees that Contract Advisor charges or otherwise would have charged the player for other services including, but not limited to, financial consultation, money management, and/or negotiating player endorsement agreements;

(17) Failing to provide to each player represented and the NFLPA the annual statements required by Section 3(A)(9) of these Regulations and/or failing to provide the NFLPA copies of all agreements between the Contract Advisor and each player as required by Section 3(A)(6) of these Regulations;

(18) Filing any lawsuit or other proceeding against a player for any matter which is subject to the exclusive arbitration provisions contained in Section 5 of these regulations;

(19) Violating the confidentiality provisions of the National Football League Policy and Program for Substances of Abuse. The

NFLPA Executive Director in consultation with the Disciplinary Committee may fine a Contract Advisor in accordance with the terms of the National Football League Policy and Program for Substances of Abuse. Such fine, if imposed, shall be in addition to, and not a substitute for, discipline which may be imposed pursuant to Section 6 of these Regulations;

(20) Failing to disclose in writing to any player represented by Contract Advisor any fee paid or received by Contract Advisor to or from a third party in return for providing services to that player;

(21)(a) Initiating any communication, directly or indirectly, with a player who has entered into a Standard Representation Agreement with another Contract Advisor and such Standard Representation Agreement is on file with the NFLPA if the communication concerns a matter relating to the: (i) Player's current Contract Advisor; (ii) Player's current Standard Representation Agreement; (iii) Player's contract status with any NFL Club(s); or (iv) Services to be provided by prospective Contract Advisor either through a Standard Representation Agreement or otherwise.

(b) If a player, already a party to a Standard Representation Agreement, initiates communication with a Contract Advisor relating to any of the subject matters listed in Section 3(B)(21)(a) the Contract Advisor may continue communications with the Player regarding any of those matters.

(c) Section 3(B)(21) shall not apply to any player who has less than sixty (60) days remaining before his NFL Player Contract expires, and he has not yet signed a new Standard Representation Agreement.

(d) Section 3(B)(21) shall not prohibit a Contract Advisor from sending a player written materials which may be reasonably interpreted as advertising directed at players in general and not targeted at a specific player;

(22) Conditioning the signing of a Standard Representation Agreement upon the signing of a contract for other services or the performance of other services by the Contract Advisor or any affiliated entity; or [vice versa];

(23) Attempting to circumvent or circumventing relevant portions of Section 4(B)(5);

(24) Affiliating with or advising players to use the services of a person who is not an NFLPA Registered Player Financial Advisor for purposes of providing financial advice to the player; or acting as a "Financial Advisor" and/or providing "Financial Advice" to an NFL player as those terms are defined in the NFLPA Regulations and Code of Conduct Governing Registered Player Financial Advisors, without first becoming a Registered Player Financial Advisor pursuant to the NFLPA Regulations and Code of Conduct Governing Registered Player Financial Advisors;

(25) Entering into any business relationship with another Contract Advisor to share fees and/or provide negotiation services for players during a time period commencing when a Disciplinary Complaint has been filed against such Contract Advisor pursuant to Section 6 of these Regulations and ending when disciplinary sanctions become final or, if the sanctions include a suspension or revocation of Certification, at the end of the period of the suspension or revocation of Certification, whichever is later;

(26) Directly or indirectly soliciting a prospective rookie player for representation as a Contract Advisor ... if that player has signed a Standard Representation Agreement prior to a date which is thirty (30) days before the NFL Draft and if thirty (30) days have not elapsed since the Agreement was signed and filed with the NFLPA;

(27) Violating any other provision of these Regulations.

A Contract Advisor who engages in any prohibited conduct as defined above shall be subject to discipline in accordance with the procedures of Section 6 of these Regulations.

SECTION 4—AGREEMENTS BETWEEN CONTRACT ADVISORS AND PLAYERS; MAXIMUM FEE

A. Standard Form—Any agreement between a Contract Advisor and a player ..., which is not in writing in the pre-printed form attached hereto as Appendix D or which does not meet the requirements of these Regulations, shall not be enforceable against any player and no Contract Advisor shall have the right to assert any claim against the player for compensation on the basis of such a purported contract.

B. Contract Advisor's Compensation

1. The maximum fee which may be charged or collected by a Contract Advisor shall be three percent (3%) of the "compensation" (as defined within this Section) received by the player in each playing season covered by the contract negotiated by the Contract Advisor.

2. The Contract Advisor and player may agree to any fee which is less than the maximum fee set forth in (1) above.

3. As used in this Section 4(B), the term "compensation" shall be deemed to include only salaries, signing bonuses, reporting bonuses, roster bonuses, and any performance incentives earned by the player during the term of the contract (including any option year) negotiated by the Contract Advisor....

4. A Contract Advisor is prohibited from receiving any fee for his/her services until and unless the player receives the compensation upon which the fee is based. [There is a lengthy and complex exception if a player earns deferred compensation.]

5. A Contract Advisor who is found to have violated Section 3(B)(2) or (3) of these Regulations shall not be entitled to a fee for services

provided to a player who was the subject of an improper inducement under Section 3(B)(2) or (3). In the event that the Contract Advisor collects any fees from the player before a finding of such violation, he/she shall be required to reimburse the player for such fees. If the improper inducement was a loan of money or property which was to be repaid or returned to the Contract Advisor, the money or property need not be repaid or returned by the player who was the subject of the improper inducement under Section 3(B)(2) or (3). This Section 4(B)(5) shall not be subject to any waiver by player....

SECTION 5—ARBITRATION PROCEDURES

A. Disputes—This arbitration procedure shall be the exclusive method for resolving any and all disputes that may arise from the following: (1) Denial by the NFLPA of an Applicant's Application for Certification; (2) Any dispute between an NFL player and a Contract Advisor with respect to the conduct of individual negotiations by a Contract Advisor; (3) The meaning, interpretation or enforcement of a fee agreement; (4) Any other activities of a Contract Advisor within the scope of these Regulations; and/or (5) A dispute between two or more Contract Advisors with respect to whether or not a Contract Advisor interfered with the contractual relationship of a Contract Advisor and player....

D. Arbitrator—The NFLPA shall select a skilled and experienced person to serve as the outside impartial Arbitrator for all cases arising hereunder.

E. Hearing—After receipt of the grievance documents ..., the Arbitrator shall select a time and place for a hearing on the dispute, giving due consideration to the convenience of the parties involved and the degree of urgency for resolution of the dispute.... The Arbitrator may, at his/her discretion, order discovery in disputes between Contract Advisors filed pursuant to Section 5(A)(5).... [T]he Arbitrator shall issue a written decision. At the hearing, the grievant shall have the burden of proving, by a preponderance of the evidence, the allegations of the grievance. Such decision shall constitute full, final and complete disposition of the grievance, and will be binding upon the player and Contract Advisor involved; provided, however, that the Arbitrator will not have the jurisdiction or authority to add to, subtract from, or alter in any way the provisions of these Regulations or any other applicable document....

SECTION 6—OVERSIGHT AND COMPLIANCE PROCEDURE

A. Disciplinary Committee—The President of the NFLPA shall appoint a three to five person Disciplinary Committee which may prosecute disciplinary procedures against Contract Advisors who violate these Regulations. Any action taken shall be by a majority vote of the Disciplinary Committee members....

E.   Appeal—The Contract Advisor against whom a Complaint has been filed under this Section may appeal the Disciplinary Committee's proposed disciplinary action to the outside Arbitrator by filing a written Notice of Appeal with the Arbitrator within twenty (20) days following Contract Advisor's receipt of notification of the proposed disciplinary action. . . . The failure of Contract Advisor to file a timely appeal shall be deemed to constitute an acceptance of the discipline which shall then be promptly imposed.

G.   Conduct of Hearing—At the hearing of any Appeal pursuant to this Section 6, the Disciplinary Committee shall have the burden of proving, by a preponderance of the evidence, the allegations of its Complaint. The Committee and the Contract Advisor shall be afforded a full opportunity to present, through testimony or otherwise, their evidence pertaining to the action or conduct of the Contract Advisor alleged to be in violation of the Regulations. . . . The Arbitrator shall decide two issues: (1) whether the Contract Advisor has engaged in or is engaging in prohibited conduct as alleged by the Committee; and (2) if so, whether the discipline proposed by the Committee should be affirmed or modified. Such decision shall be made in the form of an appropriate written order reflecting the Arbitrator's opinion and shall be final and binding upon all parties.

NFLPA PLAYER–AGENT STANDARD REPRESENTATION AGREEMENT

This AGREEMENT made this _____ day of _____, 20___, by and between _____ (hereinafter "Player") and _____ (hereinafter "Contract Advisor")

WITNESSETH:

In consideration of the mutual promises made by each to the other, Player and Contract Advisor agree as follows:

1.   General Principles

This Agreement is entered into pursuant to and in accordance with the National Football League Players Association (hereinafter "NFLPA") Regulations Governing Contract Advisors (hereinafter "the Regulations") effective December 1, 1994, and as amended thereafter from time to time.

2.   Representatives

Contract Advisor represents that in advance of executing this Agreement, he/she has been duly certified as a Contract Advisor by the NFLPA. Player acknowledges that the NFLPA certification of the Contract Advisor is neither a recommendation of the Contract Advisor, nor a warranty by NFLPA of the Contract Advisor's competence, honesty, skills, or qualifications.

Contract Advisor hereby discloses that he/she (check one): [ ] represents or has represented; [ ] does not represent and has not represented NFL management personnel in matters pertaining to their employment by or association with any NFL club. (If Contract Advisor responds in the affirmative, Contract Advisor must attach a written addendum to this Agreement listing names and positions of those NFL Personnel represented).

3. Contract Services

Player hereby retains Contract Advisor to represent, advise, counsel, and assist Player in the negotiation, execution, and enforcement of this playing contract(s) in the National Football League.

In performing these services, Contract Advisor acknowledges that he/she is acting in a fiduciary capacity on behalf of Player and agrees to act in such manner as to protect the best interests of Player and assure effective representation of Player in individual contract negotiations with NFL Clubs. Contract Advisor shall be the exclusive representative for the purpose of negotiating player contracts for Player. However, Contract Advisor shall not have the authority to bind or commit Player to enter into any contract without actual execution thereof by Player. Once Player agrees to and executes his player contract, Contract Advisor agrees to also sign the player contract and send a copy (by facsimile or overnight mail) to the NFLPA and the NFL Club within 48 hours of execution by Player.

If Player and Contract Advisor have entered into any other agreements or contracts relating to services other than the individual negotiating services described in this Section (e.g. financial advice, tax preparation):

A.   Describe the nature of the other services covered by the separate agreements:

_____

_____

_____

B.   Contract Advisor and Player hereby acknowledge that Player was given the opportunity to enter into any of the agreements described in Paragraph 3A above and this Standard Representation Agreement, without the signing of one agreement being conditioned upon the signing of any of the other agreements in violation of Section 3(B)(21) of the NFLPA Regulations Governing Contract Advisors.

_____   _____
Contract Advisor   Player

4. Compensation for Services

If Contract Advisor succeeds in negotiating an NFL Player Contract acceptable to Player and signed by Player during the term hereof, Contract Advisor shall receive a fee of three percent (3%) of the compensation received by Player for each such playing season, unless a lesser percent (%) or amount has been agreed to by the parties and is noted in the space below.

The parties hereto have agreed to the following lesser fee.

_____

_____

_____

In computing the allowable fee pursuant to this Section 4 the term "compensation" shall include only base salaries, signing bonuses, reporting bonuses, roster bonuses and any performance incentives actually received by Player. The term "compensation" shall not include any "honor" incentive bonuses (i.e. ALL PRO, PRO BOWL, Rookie of the Year), or any collectively bargained benefits.

5. Payment of Contract Advisor's Fee

Contract Advisor shall not be entitled to receive any fee for the performance of his/her services pursuant to this Agreement until Player receives the compensation upon which the fee is based.

However, Player may enter into an agreement with Contract Advisor to pay any fee attributable to deferred compensation due and payable to Player in advance of when the deferred compensation is paid to Player, provided that Player has performed the services necessary under his contract to entitle him to the deferred compensation. Such fee shall be reduced to its present value as specified in the NFLPA Regulations (see Section 4(b)). Such an agreement must also be in writing, with a copy sent to the NFLPA.

In no case shall Contract Advisor accept, directly or indirectly, payment of any fees hereunder from Player's club. Further, Contract Advisor is prohibited from discussing any aspect of his/her fee arrangement hereunder with any club.

6. Expenses

Play shall reimburse Contract Advisor for all reasonable and necessary communication expenses (i.e. telephone and postage) actually incurred by Contract Advisor in connection with the negotiation of Player's NFL contract. Player also shall reimburse Contract Advisor for all reasonable and necessary travel expenses actually incurred by Contract Advisor during the term hereof in the negotiation of Player's NFL contract, but only if such expenses and approximate amounts thereof are approved in advance by Player. Player shall promptly pay all such expenses upon receipt of an itemized, written statement from Contract Advisor.

After each NFL season and prior to the first day of May following each season for which Contract Advisor has received fees and expenses, Contract Advisor must send to Player (with a copy of the NFLPA) an itemized statement covering the period March 1 through February 28th or 29th of that year. Such statement shall set forth both the fees charged to Player for, and any expenses incurred in connection with, the performance of the following services: (a) individual player salary negotiations, (b) management of player's assets, (c) financial, investment, legal, tax and/or other advice, and (d) any other miscellaneous services.

7. Disclaimer of Liability

Player and Contract Advisor agree that they are not subject to the control or direction of any other person with respect to the timing, place, manner or fashion in which individual negotiations are to be conducted pursuant to this Agreement (except to the extent that Contract Advisor shall comply with NFLPA Regulations) and that they will save and hold harmless the NFLPA, its officers, employees and representatives from any liability whatsoever with respect to their conduct or activities relating to or in connection with this Agreement or such individual negotiations.

8. Disputes

Any and all disputes between Player and Contract Advisor involving the meaning, interpretation, application, or enforcement of this Agreement or the obligations of the parties under this Agreement shall be resolved exclusively through the arbitration procedures set forth in Section 5 of the NFLPA Regulations Governing Contract Advisors.

9. Notices

All notices hereunder shall be effective if sent by certified mail, postage prepaid to the following addresses.

If to the Contract Advisor: _____

_____

If to the Player: _____

_____

10. Entire Agreement

This Agreement, along with the NFLPA Regulations, set forth the entire agreement between the parties hereto and cannot be amended, modified or changed orally. Any written amendments or changes shall be effective only to the extent that they are consistent with the Standard Representation Agreement as approved by the NFLPA.

11. Filing

This contract is signed in quadruplicate. Contract Advisor agrees to deliver two (2) copies to the NFLPA within five (5) days of its execution;

one (1) copy to the Player; and retain one (1) copy for his/her files. Contract Advisor further agrees to submit any other executed agreements between Player and Contract Advisor to NFLPA.

12. Term

The term of this Agreement shall begin on the date hereof and shall remain in effect until such time that it is terminated by either party in which case termination of this Agreement shall be effective five (5) days after written notice of termination is given to the other party. Notice shall be effective for purposes of this paragraph if sent by certified mail, postage prepaid, return receipt request to the appropriate address contained in this Agreement. Notwithstanding the above, if this Standard Representation Agreement is being signed by a prospective rookie player (a "Rookie" shall be defined as a person who has never signed an NFL Player Contract) prior to the date which is thirty (30) days before the NFL Draft, then this Agreement shall not be terminable by player until at least 30 days after it has been signed by player.

If termination pursuant to the above provision occurs prior to the completion of negotiations for an NFL player contract(s) acceptable to Player and signed by Player, Contract Advisor shall be entitled to compensation for the reasonable value of the services performed in the attempted negotiation of such contract(s) provided such services and time spent thereon are adequately documented by Contract Advisor. If termination pursuant to the above provision occurs after Player has signed an NFL player contract negotiated by Contract Advisor, Contract Advisor shall be entitled to the fee prescribed in Section 4 above for negotiation of such contract(s).

In the event that Player is able to renegotiate any contract(s) previously negotiated by Contract Advisor prior to expiration thereof, Contract Advisor shall still be entitled to the fee he/she would have been paid pursuant to Section 4 above as if such original contract(s) had not been renegotiated. If Contract Advisor represents Player in renegotiation of the original contract(s), the fee for such renegotiation shall be based solely upon the amount by which the compensation in the renegotiated contract(s) exceeds the compensation in the original contract(s), whether or not Contract Advisor negotiated the original contract(s).

If the Contract Advisor's certification is suspended or revoked by the NFLPA or the Contract Advisor is otherwise prohibited by the NFLPA from performing the services he/she has agreed to perform herein, this Agreement shall automatically terminate, effective as of the date of such suspension or termination.

13. Governing Law

This Agreement shall be construed, interpreted and enforced according to the laws of the State of _____.

Contract Advisor and Player recognize that certain state statutes regulating sports agents require specified language in the player/agent contract. The parties therefore agree to the following additional language as required by state statute.

EXAMINE THIS CONTRACT CAREFULLY BEFORE SIGNING IT

IN WITNESS WHEREOF, the parties hereto have hereunder signed their names as hereinafter set forth.

_____

(CONTRACT ADVISOR)
_____

(Street Address or P.O. Box)   (City, State, Zip Code)
_____

(Telephone)   (Fax Number)
_____

(PLAYER)
_____

(Street Address or P.O. Box)   (City, State, Zip Code)
_____

(In-Season Telephone)   (Off-Season Telephone)
_____

(Player's Birthdate)   **(College/University)**
_____

Print Name and Signature of PARENT or GUARDIAN (if Player is under 21 Years of Age)
_____

(Street Address)
_____

(City, State, Zip Code)
_____

(Telephone)
_____

F. MISCELLANEOUS DOCUMENTS

NCAA CONSTITUTION (2004)

Art. 1. Name, Purposes and Fundamental Policy

1.3.1 Basic Purpose. The competitive athletics programs of member institutions are designed to be a vital part of the educational system. A basic purpose of this Association is to maintain intercollegiate athletics as an integral part of the educational program and the athlete as an integral part of the student body and, by so doing, retain a clear line of demarcation between intercollegiate athletics and professional sports.

Art. 2. Principles for Conduct of Intercollegiate Athletics

2.1 THE PRINCIPLE OF INSTITUTIONAL CONTROL AND RESPONSIBILITY

2.1.1 Responsibility for Control. It is the responsibility of each member institution to control its intercollegiate athletics program in compliance with the rules and regulations of the Association. The institution's chief executive officer is responsible for the administration of all aspects of the athletics program, including approval of the budget and audit of all expenditures.

2.1.2 Scope of Responsibility. The institution's responsibility for the conduct of its intercollegiate athletics program includes responsibility for the actions of its staff members and for the actions of any other individual or organization engaged in activities promoting the athletics interests of the institution.

2.9 THE PRINCIPLE OF AMATEURISM. Student-athletes shall be amateurs in an intercollegiate sport, and their participation should be motivated primarily by education and by the physical, mental and social benefits to be derived. Student participation in intercollegiate athletics is an avocation, and student-athletes should be protected from exploitation by professional and commercial enterprises.

Art. 6. Institutional Control

6.4 RESPONSIBILITY FOR ACTIONS OF OUTSIDE ENTITIES

6.4.1 Independent Agencies or Organizations. An institution's "responsibility" for the conduct of its intercollegiate athletics program shall include responsibility for the acts of an independent agency, corporate entity (e.g., apparel or equipment manufacturer) or other organization when a member of the institution's executive or athletics administration, or an athletics department staff member, has knowledge that such agency, corporate entity or other organization is promoting the institution's intercollegiate athletics program.

6.4.2 Representatives of Athletics Interests. An institution's "responsibility" for the conduct of its intercollegiate athletics program shall include responsibility for the acts of individuals, a corporate entity (e.g., apparel or equipment manufacturer) or other organization when a member of the institution's executive or athletics administration or an athletics department staff member has knowledge or should have knowledge that such an individual, corporate entity or other organization:

(a) Has participated in or is a member of an agency or organization as described in Constitution 6.4.1;

(b) Has made financial contributions to the athletics department or to an athletics booster organization of that institution;

(c) Has been requested by the athletics department staff to assist in the recruitment of prospective student-athletes or is assisting in the recruitment of prospective student-athletes;

(d) Has assisted or is assisting in providing benefits to enrolled student-athletes; or

(e) Is otherwise involved in promoting the institution's athletics program.

NCAA OPERATING BY–LAWS (2004)

Art. 12. Amateurism

12.02.3 Professional Athlete. A professional athlete is one who receives any kind of payment, directly or indirectly, for athletics participation except as permitted by the governing legislation of the Association.

12.1 GENERAL REGULATIONS. An individual must comply with the following to retain amateur status. (See Bylaw 14 regarding the eligibility restoration process.)

12.1.1 Amateur Status. An individual loses amateur status and thus shall not be eligible for intercollegiate competition in a particular sport if the individual:

(a) Uses his or her athletics skill (directly or indirectly) for pay in any form in that sport;

(b) Accepts a promise of pay even if such pay is to be received following completion of intercollegiate athletics participation;

(c) Signs a contract or commitment of any kind to play professional athletics, regardless of its legal enforceability or any consideration received;

(d) Receives, directly or indirectly, a salary, reimbursement of expenses or any other form of financial assistance from a professional sports organization based upon athletics skill or participation, except as permitted by NCAA rules and regulations;

(e) Competes on any professional athletics team (per Bylaw 12.02.4), even if no pay or remuneration for expenses was received;

(f) Subsequent to initial full-time collegiate enrollment, enters into a professional draft (see also Bylaws 12.2.4.2.1 and 12.2.4.2.3); or

(g) Enters into an agreement with an agent.

12.1.1.1 Prohibited Forms of Pay. "Pay" as used in Bylaw 12.1.1 above includes, but is not limited to, the following:

12.1.1.1.1 *Salary, Gratuity or Compensation.* Any direct or indirect salary, gratuity or comparable compensation.

12.1.1.1.2 *Division or Split of Surplus.* Any division or split of surplus (bonuses, game receipts, etc.) .

12.1.1.1.3 *Educational Expenses.* Educational expenses not permitted by the governing legislation of this Association (see Bylaw 15 regarding permissible financial aid to enrolled student-athletes).

12.1.1.1.3.1 *Educational Expenses—Prior to Collegiate Enrollment.* A prospective student athlete may receive educational expenses (i.e., tuition, fees, room and board, and books) prior to collegiate enrollment from any individual or entity other than an agent, professional sports team/organization or a representative of an institution's athletics interests, provided such expenses are disbursed directly through the recipient's educational institution (e.g., high school, preparatory school).

12.1.1.1.3.2 *Educational Expenses from Outside Sports Team or Organization—Subsequent to Collegiate Enrollment.* Educational expenses provided to an individual subsequent to collegiate enrollment by an outside sports team or organization that are based in any degree upon the recipient's athletics ability [except as specified in Bylaw 15.2.5.4–(h)], ...

12.1.1.1.3.2.1 *Educational Expenses—U.S. Olympic Committee.* A student-athlete may receive educational expenses awarded by the U.S. Olympic Committee (or, for international student-athletes, expenses awarded by the equivalent organization of a foreign country) pursuant to the applicable conditions set forth in Bylaw 15.2.5.5.

12.1.1.1.3.2.2 *Educational Expenses—U.S. National Governing Body.* A student-athlete may receive educational expenses awarded by a U.S. national governing body (or, for international student-athletes, expenses awarded by the equivalent organization of a foreign country) pursuant to the applicable conditions set forth in Bylaw 15.2.5.5.

12.1.1.1.4 *Expenses, Awards and Benefits.* Excessive or improper expenses, awards and benefits (see Bylaw 16 regarding permissible awards, benefits and expenses to enrolled student-athletes).

12.1.1.1.4.1 *Cash or Equivalent Award.* Cash, or the equivalent thereof (e.g., trust fund), as an award for participation in competition at any time, even if such an award is permitted under the rules governing an amateur, noncollegiate event in which the individual is participating. An award or a cash prize that an individual could not receive under NCAA legislation may not be forwarded in the individual's name to a different individual or agency.

12.1.1.1.4.3 *Expenses from Outside Team or Organization.* Expenses received from an outside amateur sports team or organization in excess of actual and necessary travel, room and board expenses, and apparel and equipment . . . for competition and practice held in preparation for such competition. Practice must be conducted in a continuous time period preceding the competition except for practice sessions conducted by a national team. . . .

12.1.1.1.4.3.1 *Expenses/Benefits Related to Olympic Games.* It is permissible for members of an Olympic team to receive all nonmonetary benefits and awards provided to members of an Olympic team beyond actual and necessary expenses, including entertainment, equipment, clothing, long distance telephone service, Internet access, and any other item or service for which it can be demonstrated that the same benefit is available to all members of that nation's Olympic team or the specific sport Olympic team in question.

12.1.1.1.4.3.2 *Operation Gold Grant.* An individual may accept funds that are administered by the United States Olympic Committee pursuant to its Operation Gold program.

12.1.1.1.4.5 *Expenses from Sponsor Other Than Parents/Legal Guardians or Nonprofessional Sponsor of Event.* Actual and necessary expenses or any other form of compensation to participate in athletics competition (while not representing an educational institution) from a sponsor other than an individual upon whom the athlete is naturally or legally dependent or the nonprofessional organization that is sponsoring the competition.

12.1.1.1.4.6 *Expenses for Parents/Legal Guardians of Participants in Athletics Competition.* Expenses received by the parents or legal guardians of a participant in athletics competition from a nonprofessional organization sponsoring the competition in excess of actual and necessary travel, room and board expenses, or any entertainment expenses, provided such expenses are made available to the parents or legal guardians of all participants in the competition.

12.1.1.1.5 *Payment Based on Performance.* Any payment, including actual and necessary expenses, conditioned on the individual's or team's place finish or performance or given on an incentive basis, or receipt of expenses in excess of the same reasonable amount for permissible expenses given to all individuals or team members involved in the competition.

12.1.1.1.6 *Preferential Treatment, Benefits or Services.* Preferential treatment, benefits or services because of the individual's athletics reputation or skill or pay-back potential as a professional athlete, unless such treatment, benefits or services are specifically permitted under NCAA legislation.

12.1.1.4 Exceptions to Amateurism Rule

12.1.1.4.1 *Exception for Prize Money Prior to Full–Time Collegiate Enrollment.* Prior to full-time collegiate enrollment, an individual may accept prize money based on his or her place finish or performance in an open athletics event (i.e., an event that is not invitation only). Such prize money may not exceed actual and necessary expenses and may be provided only by the sponsor of the open event.

12.1.1.4.1.1 *Exception—Olympic/National Teams.* It is permissible for an individual to participate on Olympic or national teams that are competing for prize money or are being compensated by the governing body to participate in a specific event, provided the student-athlete does not accept prize money or any other compensation (other than actual and necessary expenses).

12.1.1.4.2 *Exception for Insurance against Disabling Injury or Illness.* An individual may borrow against his or her future earnings potential from an established, accredited commercial lending institution exclusively for the purpose of purchasing insurance (with no cash surrender value) against a disabling injury or illness that would prevent the individual from pursuing a chosen career, provided a third party (including a member institution's athletics department staff members, its professional sports counseling panel or representatives of its athletics interests) is not involved in arrangements for securing the loan. . . .

12.1.2 Amateur Status if Professional in Another Sport. A professional athlete in one sport may represent a member institution in a different sport. However, the student-athlete cannot receive institutional financial assistance in the second sport unless the student-athlete: (a) Is no longer involved in professional athletics; (b) Is not receiving any remuneration from a professional sports organization; and (c) Has no active contractual relationship with any professional athletics team. . . .

12.1.2.1 *Professional at Later Date.* If the individual later becomes involved in professional athletics while still a student-athlete with remaining eligibility, the individual would be considered to have violated the principles of ethical conduct per Bylaw 10, thus rendering the individual ineligible for intercollegiate competition.

12.2 INVOLVEMENT WITH PROFESSIONAL TEAMS

12.2.1 Tryouts

12.2.1.1 *Tryout Before Enrollment.* A student-athlete remains eligible in a sport even though, prior to enrollment in a collegiate institution, the student-athlete may have tried out with a professional athletics team in a sport or received not more than one expense-paid visit from each professional team (or a combine including that team), provided such a visit did not exceed 48 hours and any payment or compensation in connection with the visit was not in excess of actual and necessary expenses. A self-financed tryout may be for any length of time.

12.2.1.2   *Tryout After Enrollment.* A student-athlete shall not try out with a professional athletics team in a sport or permit a professional athletics team to conduct medical examinations during any part of the academic year ... while enrolled in a collegiate institution as a regular student in at least a minimum full-time academic load, unless the student-athlete has exhausted eligibility in that sport. The student-athlete may try out with a professional organization in a sport during the summer or during the academic year while not a full-time student, provided the student-athlete does not receive any form of expenses or other compensation from the professional organization [see Bylaw 14.7.3.2–(e)].

12.2.4   Draft and Inquiry

12.2.4.1   *Inquiry.* An individual may inquire of a professional sports organization about eligibility for a professional-league player draft or request information about the individual's market value without affecting his or her amateur status.

12.2.4.2   *Draft List.* Subsequent to initial full-time collegiate enrollment, an individual loses amateur status in a particular sport when the individual asks to be placed on the draft list or supplemental draft list of a professional league in that sport, even though: (a) The individual asks that his or her name be withdrawn from the draft list prior to the actual draft; (b) The individual's name remains on the list but he or she is not drafted; or (c) The individual is drafted but does not sign an agreement with any professional athletics team.

12.2.4.2.1   *Exception—Professional Basketball Draft—Four–Year College Student–Athlete.* An enrolled student-athlete in basketball may enter a professional league's draft one time during his or her collegiate career without jeopardizing eligibility in that sport, provided the student-athlete is not drafted by any team in that league and the student-athlete declares his or her intention to resume intercollegiate participation within 30 days after the draft. The student-athlete's declaration of intent shall be in writing to the institution's director of athletics.

12.2.4.2.3   *Exception—Division I–A and Division I–AA Football.* An enrolled student-athlete ... in Division I–A or I–AA football may enter the National Football League draft one time during his collegiate career without jeopardizing eligibility in that sport, provided the student-athlete is not drafted by any team in that league and the student-athlete declares his intention to resume intercollegiate participation within 72–hours following the National Football League draft declaration date. The student-athlete's declaration of intent shall be in writing to the institution's director of athletics.

12.2.4.3   *Negotiations.* An individual may request information about professional market value without affecting his or her amateur status. Further, the individual, his or her legal guardians or the institution's professional sports counseling panel may enter into negotiations with a professional sports organization without the loss of the individual's amateur status. An individual who retains an agent shall lose amateur status.

12.3 USE OF AGENTS

12.3.1 General Rule. An individual shall be ineligible for participation in an intercollegiate sport if he or she ever has agreed (orally or in writing) to be represented by an agent for the purpose of marketing his or her athletics ability or reputation in that sport. Further, an agency contract not specifically limited in writing to a sport or particular sports shall be deemed applicable to all sports, and the individual shall be ineligible to participate in any sport.

12.3.1.1 *Representation for Future Negotiations.* An individual shall be ineligible per Bylaw 12.3.1 if he or she enters into a verbal or written agreement with an agent for representation in future professional sports negotiations that are to take place after the individual has completed his or her eligibility in that sport.

12.3.1.2 *Benefits from Prospective Agents.* An individual shall be ineligible per Bylaw 12.3.1 if he or she (or his or her relatives or friends) accepts transportation or other benefits from: (a) Any person who represents any individual in the marketing of his or her athletics ability . . . ; or (b) An agent, even if the agent has indicated that he or she has no interest in representing the student-athlete in the marketing of his or her athletics ability or reputation and does not represent individuals in the student-athlete's sport.

12.3.2 Legal Counsel. Securing advice from a lawyer concerning a proposed professional sports contract shall not be considered contracting for representation by an agent under this rule, unless the lawyer also represents the individual in negotiations for such a contract.

12.3.2.1 *Presence of a Lawyer at Negotiations.* A lawyer may not be present during discussions of a contract offer with a professional organization or have any direct contact . . . with a professional sports organization on behalf of the individual. . . .

12.3.4 Professional Sports Counseling Panel. It is permissible for an authorized institutional professional sports counseling panel to: (a) Advise a student-athlete about a future professional career; (b) Provide direction on securing a loan for the purpose of purchasing insurance against a disabling injury; (c) Review a proposed professional sports contract; (d) Meet with the student-athlete and representatives of professional teams; (e) Communicate directly (e.g., in-person, by mail or telephone) with representatives of a professional athletics team to assist in securing a tryout with that team for a student-athlete; (f) Assist the student-athlete in the selection of an agent . . . ; or (g) Visit with player agents or representatives of professional athletics teams to assist the student-athlete in determining his or her market value. . . .

12.5 PROMOTIONAL ACTIVITIES

12.5.2 Nonpermissible

12.5.2.1 *Advertisements and Promotions Subsequent to Enrollment.* Subsequent to becoming a student-athlete, an individual shall not be eligible for participation in intercollegiate athletics if the individual:

(a) Accepts any remuneration for or permits the use of his or her name or picture to advertise, recommend or promote directly the sale or use of a commercial product or service of any kind, or

(b) Receives remuneration for endorsing a commercial product or service through the individual's use of such product or service.

12.5.2.2 *Use of a Student–Athlete's Name or Picture without Knowledge or Permission.* If a student-athlete's name or picture appears on commercial items (e.g., T-shirts, sweatshirts, serving trays, playing cards, posters, photographs) or is used to promote a commercial product sold by an individual or agency without the student-athlete's knowledge or permission, the student-athlete (or the institution acting on behalf of the student-athlete) is required to take steps to stop such an activity in order to retain his or her eligibility for intercollegiate athletics.

12.5.2.3 *Specifically Restricted Activities.* A student-athlete's involvement in promotional activities specified in this section is prohibited.

12.5.2.3.2 *Athletics Equipment Advertisement.* A student-athlete's name or picture may not be used by an athletics equipment company or manufacturer to publicize that the institution's team utilizes its equipment.

12.5.2.3.4 *Appearance in Commercial Films.* Footage of an institution's intercollegiate game or event or of the individual performance of a student-athlete may not be used in a commercial movie unless all individuals appearing in the footage have exhausted their seasons of eligibility.

Art. 14. Eligibility: Academic and General Requirements

14.01.2 Academic Status. To be eligible to represent an institution in intercollegiate athletics competition, a student-athlete shall be enrolled in at least a minimum full-time program of studies, be in good academic standing and maintain progress toward a baccalaureate or equivalent degree. A waiver of the minimum fulltime enrollment requirement may be granted for a student enrolled in the final term of the baccalaureate program. Also, a student may represent the institution while enrolled as a graduate or professional student or while enrolled and seeking a second baccalaureate degree at the same institution (see Bylaw 14.1.9).

14.02.9 Qualification Status

14.02.9.1 *Qualifier.* A qualifier is a student who, for purposes of determining eligibility for financial aid, practice and competition, has met all of the following requirements (see Bylaw 14.3): (a) Graduation from high school; (b) Successful completion of a required core curriculum consisting of a minimum number of courses in specified subjects; (c) Specified minimum grade-point average in the core curriculum; and (d) Specified minimum SAT or ACT score.

[The following Bylaw 14.02.9.2 was deleted at the October 31, 2002, NCAA Division I Board of Directors meeting, effective August 1, 2005:

14.02.9.2   *Partial Qualifier.* A partial qualifier is a student who does not meet the requirements for a qualifier but who, at the time of graduation from high school, presents the core-curriculum grade-point average and the corresponding ACT or SAT score set forth in Bylaw 14.3.2.1.]

14.02.9.3   *Nonqualifier.* A nonqualifier is a student who has not graduated from high school or who, at the time specified in the regulation (see Bylaw 14.3), presented neither the core-curriculum grade-point average and SAT/ACT score required for a qualifier.

14.1.8   Full–Time Enrollment

14.1.8.1   *Requirement for Practice.* To be eligible to participate in organized practice sessions, a student-athlete shall be enrolled in a minimum full-time program of studies leading to a baccalaureate or equivalent degree as defined by the regulations of the certifying institution. The violation shall be considered an institutional violation per Constitution 2.8.1; however, it shall not affect the student-athlete's eligibility.

14.2   SEASONS OF COMPETITION: FIVE–YEAR RULE.   A student-athlete shall not engage in more than four seasons of intercollegiate competition in any one sport (see Bylaws 14.02.6 and 14.3.2)....

14.2.1   Five–Year Rule. A student-athlete shall complete his or her seasons of participation within five calendar years from the beginning of the semester or quarter in which the student-athlete first registered for a minimum full-time program of studies in a collegiate institution, with time spent in the armed services, on official church missions or with recognized foreign aid services of the U.S. government being excepted. For foreign students, service in the armed forces or on an official church mission of the student's home country is considered equivalent to such service in the United States.

14.3   FRESHMAN ACADEMIC REQUIREMENTS

14.3.1   Eligibility for Financial Aid, Practice and Competition. A student-athlete who enrolls in a member institution as an entering freshman with no previous full-time college attendance shall meet the following academic requirements, as certified by an initial-eligibility clearinghouse approved by the Executive Committee, and any applicable institutional and conference regulations, to be considered a qualifier and thus be eligible for financial aid, practice and competition during the first academic year in residence....

[Note: Those student-athletes first entering a collegiate institution on or after August 1, 2003, shall meet the current standard [which has been deleted] or the standard that is effective August 1, 2005 (see below). The following Bylaw 143.1.1(a) applies to those student-athletes first entering a collegiate institution on or after August 1, 2005.]

14.3.1.1 *Qualifier.* A qualifier is defined as one who is a high-school graduate and who presented the following academic qualifications:

(a) A minimum cumulative grade-point average as specified in Bylaw 14.3.1.1.1 (based on a maximum 4.000) in a successfully completed core curriculum of at least 14 academic courses per Bylaw 14.3.1.2, including the following: English—4 years; Mathematics (two years of mathematics courses at the level of Algebra I or higher)—2 years; Natural or physical science (including at least one laboratory course if offered by the high school) (Computer science courses containing significant programming elements that meet graduation requirements in the area of natural or physical science also may be accepted.)—2 years; Additional courses in English, mathematics, or natural or physical science—1 year; Social science—2 years; Additional academic courses [in any of the above areas or foreign language, computer science, philosophy or nondoctrinal religion (e.g., comparative religion) courses]—3 years. The record of the above courses and course grades must be certified by the initial-eligibility clearinghouse using an official high-school transcript or official correspondence forwarded directly from the high school or upon a high-school transcript forwarded by an institution's admissions office, and

[The following Bylaw 14.3.1.1(a) applies to those student-athletes first entering a collegiate institution on or after August 1, 2008.]

14.3.1.1 *Qualifier.* A qualifier is defined as one who is a high-school graduate and who presented the following academic qualifications:

(a) A minimum cumulative grade-point average as specified in Bylaw 14.3.1.1.1 (based on a maximum 4.000) in a successfully completed core curriculum of at least 16 academic courses per Bylaw 14.3.1.2, including the following: English - 4 years; Mathematics (three years of mathematics courses at the level of Algebra I or higher)—3 years; Natural or physical science (including at least one laboratory course if offered by the high school) - 2 years; Additional courses in English, mathematics, or natural or physical science—1 year; Social science—2 years; Additional academic courses (in any of the above areas or foreign language, philosophy or nondoctrinal religion (e.g., comparative religion courses). . . . , and

(b) A minimum combined score on the SAT verbal and math sections or a minimum sum score on the ACT as specified in Bylaw 14.3.1.1.1. The required SAT or ACT score must be achieved under national testing conditions on a national testing date [i.e., no residual (campus) testing or regional testing dates].

14.3.1.1.1 *Initial-Eligibility Index.* Freshmen may establish eligibility using the following eligibility index:

Core GPA	SAT	Sum ACT
3.550 & above	400	37
3.525	410	38
3.500	420	39

[the sliding scale continues through 58 more steps (not shown here) with declining GPA and increasing SAT or ACT test score, ending with . . .]

2.050	990	84
2.025	1000	85
2.000	1010	86

14.3.1.2 *Core-Curriculum Requirements.* For purposes of meeting the core-curriculum requirement to establish eligibility at a member institution, a "core course" must meet all the following criteria:

(a) A course must be a recognized academic course and qualify for high-school graduation credit in one or a combination of the following areas: English, mathematics, natural/physical science, social science, foreign language or nondoctrinal religion/philosophy;

(b) A course must be considered college preparatory by the high school. College preparatory is defined for these purposes as any course that prepares a student academically to enter a four-year collegiate institution upon graduation from high school;

(c) A mathematics course must be at the level of Algebra I or a higher level mathematics course;

(d) A course must be taught by a qualified instructor as defined by the appropriate academic authority (e.g., high school, school district or state agency with authority of such matters); and

(e) A course must be taught at or above the high school's regular academic level (i.e., remedial, special education or compensatory courses shall not be considered core courses). However, the prohibition against the use of remedial or compensatory courses is not applicable to courses designed for student's with learning disabilities (see Bylaw 14.3.1.2.1.1).

14.3.1.2.1 *Core-Curriculum Time Limitation.* Generally, only courses completed in grades nine through 12 may be considered core courses, ...

14.3.1.2.1.1 *Students with Learning Disabilities.* The Academics/Eligibility/Compliance Cabinet may approve, for a student diagnosed with a learning disability, the use of all core courses completed prior to initial full-time enrollment at a collegiate institution. The determination as to whether courses taken at a high school are core courses shall be made on the basis of the 48–H confirmation statement issued to the high school where the student completed the classes. Courses taken at a collegiate institution must be approved by the Academics/Eligibility/Compliance Cabinet.

14.3.1.2.1.2 *International Students.* A student from a foreign country is subject to the core curriculum time limitations as set forth in the NCAA Guide to International Academic Standards for Athletics Eligibility. A student who graduates from a foreign educational system may repeat a regular term or academic year only within his or her home system and is not required to repeat the term or year at the secondary school from which he or she graduated. All other provisions of Bylaw 14.3.1.2.1 apply.

14.3.1.2.2 *Nontraditional Courses.* Courses taught via the Internet, distance learning, independent study, individualized instruction, correspondence, and courses taught by similar means may be used to satisfy NCAA core-course requirements if all of the following conditions are satisfied: (a) The course meets all requirements for a core course as defined in Bylaw 14.3.1.2; (b) The instructor and the student have access to one another during the duration of the course for purposes of teaching, evaluating and providing assistance to the student; (c) Evaluation of the student's work is conducted by the appropriate academic authorities in accordance with the high school's established academic policies; and (d) The course is acceptable for any student and is placed on the high-school transcript.

14.3.1.2.5 *Courses for Students with Disabilities.* High-school courses for students with disabilities may be used to fulfill the core-curriculum requirements, even if such courses appear to be taught at a level below the high school's regular academic instructional level (e.g., special education courses), if the high-school principal submits a written statement to the NCAA indicating that the courses are substantially comparable, quantitatively and qualitatively, to similar core course offerings in that academic discipline and the courses appear on the high-school's list of approved core courses. Students with disabilities still must complete the required core courses and achieve the minimum required grade-point average in this core curriculum. The fact that the title of a course includes a designation such as "remedial," "special education," "special needs," or other similar titles used for courses designed for students with learning disabilities does not, in and of itself, disqualify a course from satisfying core-curriculum requirements.

14.3.1.2.7 *Pass-Fail Grades.* Courses that are awarded pass-fail grades may be used to satisfy core-curriculum requirements. The NCAA Initial–Eligibility Clearinghouse shall assign the course the lowest passing grade that the high school assigns for a pass-fail course.

14.3.1.2.8 *Repeat Courses.* A repeated course may be used only once to satisfy core-curriculum requirements. The best grade in that course may be used to calculate the grade-point average in the core curriculum.

14.3.1.3.2 *Combined Test Scores.* For students utilizing the SAT examination, the highest scores achieved on the verbal and mathematics sections of the SAT from two different national testing dates may be combined in determining whether the student has met the minimum test score requirements. For students utilizing the ACT examination, the highest scores achieved on the individual subtests of the ACT from more than one national testing date may be combined in determining whether the student's sum score has met the minimum test-score requirement.

14.3.1.3.3 *Nonstandard Test Administration.* Students with disabilities may use scores achieved during a nonstandard administration of the SAT or ACT. A student who takes a nonstandard SAT or ACT still must achieve the minimum required test score; however, the test does not have to be administered on a national testing date.

14.3.2　Eligibility for Financial Aid, Practice and Competition—Partial Qualifier and Nonqualifier

[The bylaws defining a "partial qualifier" and describing the effect of such classification were deleted at the October 31, 2002, NCAA Division I Board of Directors meeting, effective August, 1, 2005.]

14.4　PROGRESS TOWARD DEGREE REQUIREMENTS

14.4.1　Progress Toward Degree Requirements. To be eligible to represent an institution in intercollegiate athletics competition, a student-athlete shall maintain progress toward a baccalaureate or equivalent degree at that institution as determined by the regulations of that institution. As a general requirement, "progress toward degree" is to be interpreted at each member institution by the academic authorities who determine the meaning of such phrases for all students, subject to controlling legislation of the conference(s) or similar association of which the institution is a member.

14.4.1.2 *Temporary Student.* A student-athlete having the status of temporary, transient or exchange student shall not represent an institution in intercollegiate athletics competition unless such status is specifically allowed and governed by provisions adopted by the membership.

14.4.2　Eligibility for Financial Aid and Practice. Eligibility for institutional financial aid and practice during each academic year after a student-athlete's initial year in residence or after the student-athlete has utilized one season of eligibility in a sport shall be based upon the rules of the institution and the conference(s), if any, of which the institution is a member.

[The following bylaws apply to those student-athletes who first enrolled in a collegiate institution fulltime prior to August 1, 2003.]

14.4.3　Eligibility for Competition

14.4.3.1 *Fulfillment of Credit–Hour Requirements.* Eligibility for competition shall be based upon the following requirement:

(a) Satisfactory completion of six-semester or-quarter hours of academic credit the preceding regular academic term in which the student-athlete has been enrolled at any collegiate institution, ...

14.4.3.1.3 *Hours Earned during Regular Academic Year.* A student-athlete shall earn at least 75 percent of the minimum number of semester or quarter hours required for progress toward degree during the regular academic year. The student-athlete shall earn no more than 25 percent of the minimum number of semester or quarter hours required for progress for degree during the summer or through correspondence courses taken during the 1993–94 academic year and thereafter.

14.4.3.1.4 *Designation of Degree Program.* A student-athlete shall designate a program of studies leading toward a specific baccalaureate degree at the certifying institution by the beginning of the third year of enrollment (third semester or fourth quarter) and thereafter shall make progress toward that specific degree. This provision shall be applicable to the eligibility not only of a continuing student, but also of a transfer student from a four-year or two-year collegiate institution who is entering his or her third year of collegiate enrollment, even if the student has not yet completed an academic year in residence or utilized a season of eligibility in a sport at the certifying institution. . . .

14.4.3.2 *Fulfillment of Percentage of Degree Requirements.* A student-athlete who is entering his or her third year of collegiate enrollment shall have completed successfully at least 25 percent of the course requirements in the student's specific degree program. A student-athlete who is entering his or her fourth year of collegiate enrollment shall have completed successfully at least 50 percent of the course requirements in the student's specific degree program. A student-athlete who is entering his or her fifth year of collegiate enrollment shall have completed successfully at least 75 percent of the course requirements in the student's specific degree program. The course requirements must be in the student's specific degree program (as opposed to the student's major).

14.4.3.3 *Fulfillment of Minimum Grade–Point Average Requirements.* A student-athlete shall meet the "satisfactory completion" provision of this requirement by maintaining a grade-point average that places the individual in good academic standing, as established by the institution for all students who are at an equivalent stage of progress toward a degree.

14.4.3.3.1 *General Rule.* A student-athlete who is entering his or her third year of collegiate enrollment shall present a cumulative minimum grade-point average (based upon a maximum of 4.000) that equals at least 90 percent of the institution's overall cumulative minimum grade-point average required for graduation. A student-athlete who is entering his or her fourth or subsequent year of collegiate enrollment shall present a cumulative minimum grade-point average (based upon a maximum of 4.000) that equals 95 percent of the institution's overall cumulative minimum grade-point average required for graduation. If the institution does not have an overall grade-point average for graduation, it is permissible to utilize the lowest grade-point average required for any of the institution's degree programs in determining the cumulative minimum grade-point average. The minimum grade-point average must be computed pursuant to institutional policies applicable to all students.

14.5 TRANSFER REGULATIONS

14.5.1 Residence Requirement—General Principle. A student who transfers (see Bylaw 14.5.2) to a member institution from any collegiate institution is required to complete one full academic year of residence at the certifying institution before being eligible to compete for or to receive travel expenses from the member institution (see Bylaw 16.8.1.2), unless the student satisfies the applicable transfer requirements or receives an exception or waiver as set forth in this bylaw. In the sport of basketball, a transfer student athlete who satisfies the applicable transfer requirements or receives an exception or waiver as set forth in this section, but initially enrolls as a full-time student subsequent to the first term of the academic year shall not be eligible for competition until the ensuing academic year.

Art. 16. Awards, Benefits and Expenses for Enrolled Student–Athletes

16.01 GENERAL PRINCIPLES

16.01.1 Eligibility Effect of Violation. A student-athlete shall not receive any extra benefit. Receipt by a student-athlete of an award, benefit or expense allowance not authorized by NCAA legislation renders the student-athlete ineligible for athletics competition in the sport for which the improper award, benefit or expense was received. If the student-athlete receives an extra benefit not authorized by NCAA legislation, the individual is ineligible in all sports.

16.01.1.1 *Restitution for Receipt of Impermissible Benefits.* For violations of Bylaw 16 in which the value of the benefit is $100 or less, the eligibility of the student-athlete shall not be affected conditioned upon the student-athlete repaying the value of the benefit to a charity of his or her choice. The student athlete, however, shall remain ineligible from the time the institution has knowledge of receipt of the impermissible benefit until the student-athlete repays the benefit. Violations of this bylaw remain institutional violations per Constitution 2.8.1, and documentation of the student-athlete's repayment shall be forwarded to the enforcement staff.

16.02 DEFINITIONS AND APPLICATIONS

16.02.1 Award. An award is an item given in recognition of athletics participation or performance. Such awards are subject to the limitations set forth in Bylaw 16.1.

16.02.2 Excessive Expense. An excessive expense is one not specifically authorized under regulations of the Association concerning awards, benefits and expenses.

16.02.3 Extra Benefit. An extra benefit is any special arrangement by an institutional employee or a representative of the institution's athletics interests to provide a student-athlete or the student-athlete's relative or friend a benefit not expressly authorized by NCAA legislation. Receipt of a benefit by student-athletes or their relatives or friends is not a violation of NCAA legislation if it is demonstrated that the same benefit is generally available to the institution's students or their relatives or friends or to a particular segment of the student body (e.g., foreign students, minority students) determined on a basis unrelated to athletics ability.

16.02.4 Pay. Pay is the receipt of funds, awards or benefits not permitted by governing legislation of the Association for participation in athletics. (See Bylaw 12.1.1.1 for explanation of forms of pay prohibited under the Association's amateur-status regulations.)

Art. 19. Enforcement

19.02 DEFINITIONS AND APPLICATIONS

19.02.2 Types of Violations

19.02.2.1 *Violation, Secondary.* A secondary violation is a violation that is isolated or inadvertent in nature, provides or is intended to provide only a minimal recruiting, competitive or other advantage and does not include any significant recruiting inducement or extra benefit. Multiple secondary violations by a member institution may collectively be considered as a major violation.

19.02.2.2 *Violation, Major.* All violations other than secondary violations are major violations, specifically including those that provide an extensive recruiting or competitive advantage.

19.4 NOTICE OF CHARGES AND OPPORTUNITY TO APPEAR

19.4.1 For Major Violations. A member under investigation for major violations shall be given the following : (a) Notice of any specific charges against it and the facts upon which such charges are based; and (b) An opportunity to appear before the Committee on Infractions (or the Infractions Appeals Committee per Bylaw 19.2) to answer such charges by the production of evidence (see Bylaw 19.6.2).

19.4.2 For Secondary Violations. A member under investigation for secondary violations shall be given the following: (a) Notice of any specific charges against it and the facts upon which such charges are based; and (b) An opportunity to provide a written response to the vice-president for enforcement services (or to appear before the Committee on Infractions upon appeal) to answer such charges by the production of evidence (see Bylaw 19.6.1).

19.4.3 New Findings. When an institution and involved individual appears before the committee to discuss a response to the notice of allegations, the hearing shall be directed toward the general scope of the notice of allegations but shall not preclude the committee from finding any violation resulting from information developed or discussed during the hearing.

19.5 PENALTIES

19.5.1 Penalties for Secondary Violations. The vice-president for enforcement services, upon approval by the chair or another member of the Committee on Infractions designated by the chair, or the committee may determine that no penalty is warranted in a secondary case, that an institutional-or conference-determined penalty is satisfactory or, if appropriate, impose a penalty. Among the disciplinary measures are: [lengthy list of possible penalties deleted].

19.5.2 Penalties for Major Violations

19.5.2.1 Presumptive Penalty. The presumptive penalty for a major violation, subject to exceptions authorized by the Committee on Infractions on the basis of specifically stated reasons, shall include all of the following:

(a) A two-year probationary period (including a periodic in-person monitoring system and written institutional reports);

(b) The reduction in the number of expense-paid recruiting visits to the institution in the involved sport for one recruiting year;

(c) A requirement that all coaching staff members in the sport be prohibited from engaging in any off-campus recruiting activities for u p to one recruiting year;

(d) A requirement that all institutional staff members determined by the committee knowingly to have engaged in or condoned a major violation be subject to: (1) Termination of employment; (2) Suspension without pay for at least one year; (3) Reassignment of duties within the institution to a position that does not include contact with prospective or enrolled student-athletes or representatives of the institution's athletics interests for at least one year; or (4) Other disciplinary action approved by the committee.

(e) A reduction in the number of financial aid awards;

(f) Sanctions precluding postseason competition in the sport, particularly in those cases in which: (1) Involved individuals remain active in the program; (2) A significant competitive advantage results from the violation(s); or (3) The violation(s) reflect a lack of institutional control.

(g) Institutional recertification that the current athletics policies and practices conform to all requirements of NCAA regulations.

19.5.2.2 *Disciplinary Measures.* In addition to those penalties prescribed for secondary violations, among the disciplinary measures, singly or in combination, that may be adopted by the committee (or the Infractions Appeals Committee per Bylaw 19.2) and imposed against an institution for major violations are: [lengthy list of possible disciplinary measures deleted].

19.5.2.2.1 *Opportunity to Appear.* In the event the committee considers additional penalties to be imposed upon an institution in accordance with Bylaw 19.5.2.2–(*l*) above, the involved institution shall be provided the opportunity to appear before the committee; further, the institution shall be provided the opportunity to appeal (per Bylaw 19.6.2) any additional penalty imposed by the committee.

19.5.2.3 *Repeat Violators*

19.5.2.3.1 *Time Period.* An institution shall be considered a "repeat" violator if the Committee on Infractions finds that a major violation has occurred within five years of the starting date of a major penalty. For this provision to apply, at least one major violation must have occurred within five years after the starting date of the penalties in the previous case. It shall not be necessary that the Committee on Infractions' hearing be conducted or its report issued within the five-year period.

19.5.2.3.2 *Repeat-Violator Penalties.* In addition to the penalties identified for a major violation, the minimum penalty for a repeat violator, subject to exceptions authorized by the Committee on Infractions on the basis of specifically stated reasons, may include any or all of the following:

(a) The prohibition of some or all outside competition in the sport involved in the latest major violation for one or two sports seasons and the prohibition of all coaching staff members in that sport from involvement directly or indirectly in any coaching activities at the institution during that period;

(b) The elimination of all initial grants-in-aid and all recruiting activities in the sport involved in the latest major violation in question for a two-year period;

(c) The requirement that all institutional staff members serving on the Board of Directors, Management Council, Executive Committee or other committees of the Association resign those positions, it being understood that all institutional representatives shall be ineligible to serve on any NCAA committee for a period of four years; and

(d) The requirement that the institution relinquish its voting privilege in the Association for a four-year period.

19.6 RIGHTS OF MEMBER TO APPEAL

19.6.1 Appeal of Secondary Violations. A member shall have the right to appeal actions taken by the vice-president of enforcement services in reference to secondary violations. To appeal, the member must submit written notice of appeal to the Committee on Infractions. The Committee on Infractions must receive the written notice of appeal and any supporting information within 30 days of the date the institution receives the enforcement staff's decision.

19.6.2 Appeal of Major Violations. A member shall have the right to give written notice of appeal of the committee's findings of major violations (subject to Bylaw 32.10.2), the penalty, or both to the Infractions Appeals Committee per Bylaw 19.2.

19.6.3 Appeal by an Institutional Staff Member. If any current or former institutional staff member participates in a hearing (either in person or through written presentation) before the Committee on Infractions and is involved in a finding of a violation against that individual, the individual shall be given the opportunity to appeal any of the findings in question (subject to the conditions of Bylaw 32.10.2) or the committee's decision to issue a show-cause order to the Infractions Appeals Committee. Under such circumstances, the individual and personal legal counsel may appear before the appeals committee at the time it considers the pertinent findings.

19.6.4   Student–Athlete Appeal. If an institution concludes that continued application of the rule(s) would work an injustice on any student-athlete, an appeal shall be submitted to the Committee on Student–Athlete Reinstatement and promptly reviewed.

19.6.4.1 *Obligation of Institution to Take Appropriate Action.* When the committee (or the Infractions Appeals Committee per Bylaw 19.2) finds that there has been a violation of the constitution or bylaws affecting the eligibility of an individual student-athlete or student-athletes, the institution involved and its conference(s), if any, shall be notified of the violation and the name(s) of the student-athlete(s) involved, it being understood that if the institution fails to take appropriate action, the involved institution shall be cited to show cause under the Association's regular enforcement procedures why it should not be disciplined for a failure to abide by the conditions and obligations of membership (declaration of ineligibility) if it permits the student-athletes to compete.

19.8   RESTITUTION

If a student-athlete who is ineligible under the terms of the constitution, bylaws or other legislation of the Association is permitted to participate in intercollegiate competition contrary to such NCAA legislation but in accordance with the terms of a court restraining order or injunction operative against the institution attended by such student-athlete or against the Association, or both, and said injunction is voluntarily vacated, stayed or reversed or is finally determined by the courts that injunctive relief is not or was not justified, the Management Council may take any one or more of the following actions against such institution in the interest of restitution and fairness to competing institutions: (a) Require that individual records and performances achieved during participation by such ineligible student-athlete shall be vacated or stricken; (b) Require that team records and performances achieved during participation by such ineligible student-athlete shall be vacated or stricken; (c) Require that team victories achieved during participation by such ineligible student-athlete shall be abrogated and the games or events forfeited to the opposing institutions; (d) Require that individual awards earned during participation by such ineligible student-athlete shall be returned to the Association, the sponsor, or the competing institution supplying same; (e) Require that team awards earned during participation by such ineligible student-athlete shall be returned to the Association, the sponsor, or the competing institution supplying same; (f) Determine that the institution is ineligible for one or more NCAA championships in the sports and in the seasons in which such ineligible student-athlete participated; (g) Determine that the institution is ineligible for invitational and postseason meets and tournaments in the sports and in the seasons in which such ineligible student-athlete participated; (h) Require that the institution shall remit to the NCAA the institution's share of television receipts (other than the portion shared with other conference members) for appearing on any live television series or program if such ineligible student-athlete participates in the contest(s) selected for such telecast, or if the Management Council concludes that the institution would not have been selected for such telecast but for the participation of such ineligible student-athlete during the season of the telecast; any such funds thus remitted shall be devoted to the NCAA postgraduate scholarship program; and (i) Require that the institution that has been represented in an NCAA championship by such a student-athlete shall be assessed a financial penalty as determined by the Committee on Infractions.

PROFESSIONAL GOLFERS ASSOCIATION (PGA) PLAYER HANDBOOK AND TOURNAMENT REGULATIONS (2003)

III. ELIGIBILITY FOR TOURNAMENT PLAY

A. PGA TOUR

Subject to the approval of PGA TOUR and to the availability of places in particular tournament fields as determined by PGA TOUR, players eligible to compete in cosponsored tournaments shall be PGA TOUR members (including temporary members) and qualified amateurs in the following categories:

1. Eligible Players, listed in order of the priority that shall be used to complete the starting field in open cosponsored tournaments:

a. Special Exemptions

(1) Winners of PGA Championship or U.S. Open prior to 1970 or in the last 10 calendar years through the 1997 winner. Beginning with the 1998 winner, winners are exempt for the remainder of the calendar year in which they win, and also for five years following the end of the calendar year in which they win.

NOTE: Winners of PGA Championship or U.S. Open prior to 1970 must have made at least one cut in a cosponsored or approved tournament within the five calendar years preceding the tournament such member has entered in order to retain a normal spot in the starting field of such open cosponsored tournament. If such member has not made at least one such cut, the member shall be added to the field in any of the open tournaments in each calendar year until the calendar year immediately following the year in which the member last made a cut in a cosponsored or approved tournament.

(2) Winners of THE PLAYERS Championship in the last 10 calendar years through the 1997 winner. Beginning with the 1998 winner, winners are exempt for the remainder of the calendar year in which they win, and also for five years following the end of the calendar year in which they win.

(3) Winners of the NEC World Series of Golf in the last 10 calendar years through the 1997 winner. Beginning with the 1998 winner, winners are exempt for the remainder of the calendar year in which they win, and also for three years following the end of the calendar year in which they win.

(4) Winners of the Masters Tournament in the last 10 calendar years through the 1997 winner. Beginning with the 1998 winner, winners are exempt for the remainder of the calendar year in which they win, and also for five years following the end of the calendar year in which they win.

(5) Winners of the British Open in the last 10 calendar years through the 1997 winner. Beginning with the 1998 winner, winners are exempt for the remainder of the calendar year in which they win, and also for five years following the end of the calendar year in which they win.

(6) Winners of THE TOUR Championship for three calendar years following the year in which they win.

(7) Winners of official money World Golf Championship events for the remainder of the calendar year in which they win, and also for three years following the end of the calendar year in which they win.

(8) The leader from the final Official PGA TOUR Money List in each of the last five calendar years.

(9) Winners of PGA TOUR cosponsored or approved tournaments, whose victories are considered official, in the last two calendar years or during the current year.

NOTE: Winners are exempt for two years following the end of the calendar year in which they win, except that: (a) Winners of two cosponsored or approved tournaments in a calendar year are exempt for three years following the end of the calendar year in which they win their tournaments;(b) Winners of three tournaments in a calendar year are exempt for four years; and (c) Winners of four or more tournaments in a calendar year are exempt for five years.

NOTE: A player who earns a multiple year exemption for winning the PLAYERS Championship, Masters, U.S. Open, British Open, PGA Championship, TOUR Championship, an official money World Golf Championship event or two or more cosponsored tournaments in a calendar year shall have his multiple year tournament winner exemption extended by one year for each official victory in the subsequent calendar year(s), but in no case shall it be extended beyond five years from the current calendar year.

NOTE: If a player under 18 years of age wins a PGA TOUR cosponsored or approved event, such player, upon reaching age 18 and joining the PGA TOUR, would be entitled to the remainder of the exemption provided as a result of such win, which shall be determined as if it commenced on the date of such win.

(10) Playing members of the last-named United States Ryder Cup team.

(11) Players on the Official PGA TOUR Career Money List, as follows:....

[*This list of "special exemptions" continues through nineteen categories in order of their priority*]

b. Top 125—If not otherwise exempt ... those PGA TOUR members within the top 125 money leaders on the previous year's Official PGA TOUR Money List in order of their positions on the list; ....

e. Leading Money Winner and Three–Time Winners from Nationwide Tour

The leading money winner from the previous year's Official Nationwide Tour Money List, and those players, if any, from the previous year who won three Nationwide Tour events awarding official victory status, in chronological order of their third win.

f. Top 10 from Previous Tournament—....

g. Top 35 and Ties from Qualifying Tournament/2 through 15 from Nationwide Tour—....

h. Players Winning Three Nationwide Tour Events in the Current Year—Those players who win three Nationwide Tour events awarding official victory status in the current year, in chronological order of their third win.

[*To fill the remainder of the field, a tournament may use special members and temporary members in order of their position on the money list, as well as players holding medical extensions, lifetime members, and tour veterans.*]

V. CONFLICTING EVENTS; MEDIA AND MARKETING RIGHTS

A. CONFLICTING EVENTS

1. Obligations of the PGA TOUR— On a date on which any golf tournament or event cosponsored by PGA TOUR is being played, PGA TOUR will not cosponsor or approve any other similar golf tournament or event without the advance written consent of the tournament of the first scheduled PGA TOUR tournament or event, which consent shall not be reasonably withheld. . . .

2.Obligations of PGA TOUR Members— To contribute to the success of a PGA TOUR tournament or event and to permit PGA TOUR to fulfill its contractual obligations concerning representative fields, no PGA TOUR member shall participate in any other golf tournament or event on a date when a PGA TOUR (Regular TOUR) cosponsored tournament or event for which such member is exempt is scheduled, except for the following tournaments or events:

> *[Nine major categories of exceptions are listed, including most of the major golf tournaments or events like the four "major" tournaments, the Ryder Cup, the World Cup, all Senior PGA TOUR events, and all Nationwide Tour events.]*

B. MEDIA AND MARKETING RIGHTS

1. Media Rights.

a. The television, radio, motion picture and all other media rights of all players participating in PGA TOUR cosponsored and coordinated tournaments, pro-ams or any other golf event conducted in conjunction with PGA TOUR cosponsored and coordinated tournaments (e.g., clinics, long-drive contests), or any portion thereof, shall be granted and assigned to PGA TOUR. Based upon this grant and assignment, all such rights shall be the property of and expressly reserved by and to PGA TOUR, and any use thereof without the express written consent of PGA TOUR shall be forbidden.

b. No PGA TOUR member shall participate in any live or recorded television golf program without the prior written approval of the Commissioner, except that this requirement shall not apply to PGA TOUR cosponsored, coordinated or approved tournaments, wholly instructional programs or personal appearances on interview or guest shows. . . .

VI. CONDUCT OF PLAYERS

Players participating in PGA TOUR cosponsored, approved or coordinated tournaments shall observe these *Regulations* and the applicable rules of play while engaged in tournament play, and at all times shall conduct themselves in a manner becoming professional golfers that will not reflect unfavorably on PGA TOUR, its members, officers or representatives, tournaments and sponsors.

To this end, players shall use their best efforts to play golf of the caliber and with the skill befitting professionals, and to show respect for the game of golf. Any player who violates any of the foregoing or any of the provisions of this Article VI may be subject to a fine, suspension from play in PGA TOUR cosponsored and coordinated tournaments, permanent disbarment from such play or any appropriate combination thereof.

A. NO GUARANTEE FOR APPEARANCE

Neither players nor other individuals acting on such players' behalf shall solicit or accept any compensation, gratuity or other thing of value offered for the purpose of guaranteeing their appearance in any PGA TOUR cosponsored, approved or coordinated tournament, ...

Conversely, neither players nor other individuals acting on such players' behalf shall offer anything of value to a PGA TOUR cosponsored, approved or coordinated event in return for an invitation to the tournament . . . .

B. FINANCIAL INTEREST BY A PLAYER IN ANOTHER PLAYER; GAMBLING; BRIBES; GIFTS

A player shall not have any financial interest, either direct or indirect, in the performance or the winnings of another player in any event cosponsored, coordinated, approved or otherwise sanctioned by the PGA TOUR, whether through purse-splitting, prize money "insurance," financial assistance, bets or otherwise. Any player who violates the provisions of this paragraph shall be subject to a suspension from tournament play for a minimum period of two years.

A player shall not do any of the following:

1. Fail to give his best efforts in competition.

2. Gamble or play cards on the premises where a PGA TOUR cosponsored or coordinated tournament is being played.

3. Associate with or have dealings with persons whose activities, including gambling, might reflect adversely upon the integrity of the game of golf.

4. Bet money or anything of value on a golf tournament or similar event, whether or not the player is in such competition.

5. Offer or give a bribe, gift, payment, reward or anything of value to any player with the intention of influencing his efforts in a competition.

6. Solicit, agree to accept or accept a bribe, gift, payment, reward or anything of value offered or given with the intention of influencing the player's efforts in a competition.

7. Fail to report promptly to the Commissioner any known or suspected offer, bribe, gift, payment, reward or anything of value, or any agreement or acceptance or bet described in the foregoing.

C. MEDIA COMMENTS, PUBLIC ATTACKS

The favorable public reputation of PGA TOUR and its tournaments are valuable assets and create tangible benefits for all PGA TOUR members. Accordingly, it is an obligation of membership to refrain from comments to the news media that unreasonably attack or disparage tournaments, sponsors, fellow members, players or PGA TOUR. Responsible expressions of legitimate disagreement with PGA TOUR policies are not prohibited. However, public comments that a member knows, or should reasonably know, will harm the reputation or financial best interests of a tournament sponsor or charity are expressly covered by this section. Any violation of this section shall be considered conduct unbecoming a professional.

ATP [MEN'S TENNIS] TOUR OFFICIAL RULEBOOK (2002)

TOURNAMENTS

ATP—The ATP is the official international circuit of men's professional tennis tournaments governed by ATP Tour, Inc.

Categories of Tournaments—In official men's professional tennis, there are four (4) categories of Tournaments.... [(1) Grand Slams; (2) ATP Tournaments; (3) Challenger Series Tournaments; and (4) Satellite Series Circuits and Futures].

* * *

PLAYERS

Special Events—Exhibitions

Restrictions

1. Special Events are those other than Grand Slams, ATP Tournaments, Challenger Series Tournaments, Futures and Satellite Series Circuits. A player may not compete in a Special Event if it is scheduled as follows:

a. Within the Tournament weeks of any Tennis Masters Series Tournament, International Series Gold Tournament, the Tennis Masters Cup or the ATP World Doubles Championship....

b. Within thirty (30) days before or after the Tournament weeks of any Tennis Masters Series Tournament, International Series Gold Tournament, the Tennis Masters Cup or the ATP World Doubles Championship, if the Special Event is located within: (i) One hundred (100) miles or one hundred sixty (160) kilometers of the same; or (ii) The same market area of the city where the Tournament is located as determined by the CEO.

c. Within the period of any International Series Tournament (qualifying competition and main draw) if the Special Event is located within: (i) One hundred (100) miles or one hundred sixty (160) kilometers of the same; or (ii) The same market area of the city where the Tournament is located as determined by the CEO.

d. Within the Tournament Week of any ATP Tournament in which he is entered including the Sunday night after such Tournament final, ...

Players Eligibility—

1. Pursuant to the ATP Bylaws, a player shall be entitled to become an active ATP Player Member as follows:

a. Division One Player membership in the ATP shall be open to any individual who, on the date of his application for membership, shall be positioned among the top 200 players in the ATP Singles Entry System or among the top 100 players in the ATP Doubles Entry System and pays ATP dues.

b. Division Two Player membership in the ATP shall be open to any individual who does not qualify for Division One membership and who, on and as of the date of his application for membership, shall be positioned among the top 500 players in the ATP Singles Entry System or among the top 250 players in the ATP Doubles Entry System and pays ATP dues.

* * *

Promotional Fees—

1. Except as expressly permitted in subsection 2 below, a player shall not accept money or anything of value that is given from any source, directly or indirectly, to influence or assure his competing in any ATP Tournament, or Challenger Series Tournaments, other than prize money unless authorized by the ATP.

2. International Series Tournaments and the ATP World Team Championship have the option to offer fees for promotional services. No other ATP or Challenger Series Tournament owner, operator, sponsor or agent is permitted to offer, give or pay money or anything of value, nor shall the Tournament permit any other person or entity to offer, give or pay money or anything of value to a player, directly or indirectly, to influence or assure a player's competing in a Tournament, other than prize money, unless authorized to do so by the ATP.

———

TENNIS [MEN'S] ANTI–DOPING PROGRAM

A. General Statement of Policy—

1. The purpose of the Tennis Anti–Doping Program is to maintain the integrity of tennis and protect the health and rights of all tennis players. The scope of the Program includes:

a. Doping tests in and out of competition;

b. The imposition of penalties for Doping Offenses;

c. Providing support and assistance to players when applicable.

B. Covered Players and Events—

1. Any player who enters or, participates in an event organized, sanctioned or recognized by the ATP or who is an ATP member or is

listed in the Singles or Doubles ATP Entry System, shall comply with and be bound by the provisions of this Program. . . .

D. Prohibited Substances and Doping Methods

1. In this Program, the expressions "Prohibited Substances" and "Doping Methods" shall mean the classes of substances and doping methods set out in Appendix B.

Appendix B

For the purpose of this Program, the Prohibited Substances and Doping Methods are categorized under the following Classes: (See Addendum for examples of Prohibited Substances and Doping Methods.)

Class I: Anabolic Agents and Related Substances, Diuretics and Related Substances, Peptide Hormones, Mimetics and Analogues. Doping Methods (Blood doping, pharmacological, chemical and physical manipulation of urine).

Class II: Stimulants and Related Substances. Narcotics and Related Substances.

Class III: The following compounds are subject to certain restrictions: Caffeine, Glucocorticosteriods, Local Anesthetics (injectable)

The Addendum is not an exhaustive list of Prohibited Substances. Many substances that do not appear on this list are prohibited under the phrase "and Related Substances".

G. In–Competition Testing

2. The timing of on-site testing, and the selection of players to be tested, will be within the discretion of the APA or his designee. However, in addition to any players selected for testing, all finalists and losing semi-finalists will ordinarily be tested. . . .

3. Any player who withdraws from the main draw after the first main draw match has commenced must submit to on-site testing at the time of the withdrawal. . . .

4. If a player fails or refuses to submit to testing at any time as provided herein or otherwise fails or refuses to comply with the provisions of this Program pursuant to an in-competition test, then the APA shall notify the ATP that such player has failed or refused to submit to the provisions of the Program and that, subject to section L, the player has committed a Doping Offense in violation of section C2b of this Program. The ATP shall notify the player and inform him that, subject to his entitlement to have his case heard by an Anti–Doping Tribunal, he shall be subject to the penalties set out under the provisions of the

Program. A failure or refusal to submit to testing or to comply with the provisions of the Program shall be treated as a Doping Offense involving a Class I Prohibited Substance and the player shall, subject to his entitlement to have his case heard by an Anti–Doping Tribunal, be subject to the penalties set out in section M1a or M1b of this Program, as appropriate, and section N.

H. Out–Of–Competition Testing

2. Except as provided in section H3, players will be randomly selected for out-of-competition testing by the APA and the Administrator of Rules and Competition. Selection of the player by the APA and the Administrator of Rules and Competition shall remain confidential to all persons except those with a reasonable need to know of such testing in order to facilitate the testing procedures.

M. Penalties

1. Class I Prohibited Substances and Doping Methods

a. First Doping Offense

A player who is found through the procedures set forth in this Program to have committed a Doping Offense involving a Class I Prohibited Substance or Doping Method shall be suspended from participation in any and all ATP sanctioned or recognized tournaments or events for a two (2) year period

b. Second Doping Offense

A player who commits a second Doping Offense under the Program involving a Class I Prohibited Substance or Doping Method shall be permanently disqualified from participation in or association with any ATP sanctioned or recognized tournaments or events.

3. Class III Prohibited Substances

a. First Doping Offense

A player who is found through the procedures set forth in this Program to have committed a Doping Offense involving a Class III Prohibited Substance, subject to minimum levels set by the Program, shall be notified by the ATP and advised by the ML of the medical effects and risks of such usage.

b. Second Doping Offense

A player who commits a second Doping Offense under the Program involving any Class III Prohibited Substance shall be suspended from participation in any and all ATP sanctioned or recognized tournaments or events for a three (3) month period.

c. Third and Subsequent Doping Offense

a. A player who commits a third or subsequent Doping Offense under the Program involving any Class III Prohibited Substance shall be suspended from participation in any and all ATP sanctioned or recognized tournaments or events for a one (1) year period.

————

WOMEN'S TENNIS ASSOCIATION (WTA) TOUR RULES AND REGULATIONS

[Similar to the ATP Tour, the WTA Tour uses a tiered system of allocating players to tournaments, which are classified according to the amount of prize money offered. The WTA Tour also contains similar drug-testing procedures, explicitly prohibits all promotion fees or guarantees, and imposes penalties for participation in exhibitions within geographical proximity to a WTA tournament during any tournament week. The WTA Tour, open only to women, also contains a unique provision for determining tournament qualifiers:]

XII. ENTRIES, WITHDRAWALS, DRAWS, SCHEDULING

A. ENTRIES AND ACCEPTANCES

1. Tour Responsibility

The WTA Tour is responsible for processing all player applications for any Tour Tournament, including Grand Slam events and notifying individual Tournaments of their player field in a timely fashion. (The Grand Slam events at Wimbledon and the U.S. Open also require players to sign their individual Tournament entry forms prior to playing their first match.)

1. *Femininity Test*

The Tour shall be comprised of women's tennis Tournaments open to women tennis players only. If there is any question as to the eligibility of an applicant for entry into a Tournament, * * * based on the applicant's sex, notice shall be given to the WTA Tour which reserves the right to require the Tournament Director to request a physical examination, Barrbody or Buccal smear test to determine the sexual status of a player competing in a Tournament. * * * Should a player fail or refuse to take the test, her application for entry into women's Tournaments will be denied by the WTA Tour until such time as she has successfully passed such tests. All tests will be at the expense of the player.

————

THE OLYMPIC CHARTER

Chapter I—THE OLYMPIC MOVEMENT

1. Supreme Authority

1—The IOC is the supreme authority of the Olympic Movement.

2—Any person or organization belonging in any capacity whatsoever to the Olympic Movement is bound by the provisions of the Olympic Charter and shall abide by the decisions of the IOC.

3. Belonging to the Olympic Movement

1—In addition to the IOC, the Olympic Movement includes the International Federations (IFs), the National Olympic Committees (NOCs), the Organizing Committees of the Olympic Games (OCOGs), the national associations, clubs, and persons belonging to them, particularly the athletes.... It also includes other organizations and institutions as recognized by the IOC.

9. Olympic Games

1—The Olympic Games are competitions between athletes in individual or team events and not between countries. They bring together the athletes designated for such purpose by their respective NOCs, whose entries have been accepted by the IOC, and who compete under the technical direction of the IFs concerned.

2—The authority of last resort on any question concerning the Olympic Games rests in the IOC.

3—The Olympic Games consist of the Games of the Olympiad and the Olympic Winter Games. Both take place every four years subject to the provisions of paragraph 4 below.

Chapter II—THE INTERNATIONAL OLYMPIC COMMITTEE

19. Legal Status

1—The IOC is an international non-governmental non-profit organization, of unlimited duration, in the form of an association with the status of a legal person, recognized by the Swiss Federal Council.

4—The decisions of the IOC, taken on the basis of the provisions of the Olympic Charter, are final. Any dispute relating to their application or interpretation may be resolved solely by the IOC Executive Board and, in certain cases, by arbitration before the Court of Arbitration for Sport (CAS).

20. Members

1. *Composition of the IOC—Recruitment, election, admittance and status of IOC members*

1.1 The members of the IOC are all natural persons. The IOC includes among its members active athletes and presidents or senior leaders of IFs, organizations recognized by the IOC ... and NOCs. The total number of IOC members may not exceed 115....

1.2 The IOC recruits and elects its members from among such persons as it considers qualified....

28. IOC Resources

1—The IOC may accept gifts and bequests and seek all other resources enabling it to fulfill its tasks. It collects revenues from the exploitation of rights, including television rights, as well as from the celebration of the Olympic Games.

2—The IOC may grant part of the revenues derived from the exploitation of television rights to the IFs, NOCs including Olympic Solidarity, and the OCOGs.

Chapter III—THE INTERNATIONAL FEDERATIONS

30. Role

1—The role of the IFs is to:

1.1   establish and enforce, in accordance with the Olympic spirit, the rules concerning the practice of their respective sports and to ensure their application;

1.2   ensure the development of their sports throughout the world;

1.3   contribute to the achievement of the goals set out in the Olympic Charter . . .;

1.4   establish their criteria of eligibility to enter the competitions of the Olympic Games in conformity with the Olympic Charter, and to submit these to the IOC for approval;

1.5   assume the responsibility for the technical control and direction of their sports at the Olympic Games and at the Games under the patronage of the IOC;

1.6   provide technical assistance in the practical implementation of the Olympic Solidarity program.

Chapter IV—THE NATIONAL OLYMPIC COMMITTEES

31. Mission and Role of the NOCs

1—The mission of the NOCs is to develop and protect the Olympic Movement in their respective countries, in accordance with the Olympic Charter.

2—The NOCs:

2.1   propagate the fundamental principles of Olympism at [the] national level within the framework of sports activity and otherwise contribute, among other things, to the diffusion of Olympism in the teaching programs of physical education and sport in schools and university establishments. They see to the creation of institutions which devote themselves to Olympic education. In particular, they concern themselves with the establishment and activities of National Olympic Academies, Olympic Museums and cultural programmes related to the Olympic Movement;

2.2   ensure the observance of the Olympic Charter in their countries;

2.3   encourage the development of high performance sport as well as sport for all;

2.4 help in the training of sports administrators by organizing courses and ensure that such courses contribute to the propagation of the Fundamental Principles of Olympism;

2.5 commit themselves to taking action against any form of discrimination and violence in sport;

2.6 shall fight against the use of substances and procedures prohibited by the IOC or the Ifs, in particular by approaching the competent authorities of their country so that all medical controls may be performed in optimum conditions.

3—The NOCs have the exclusive powers for the representation of their respective countries at the Olympic Games and at the regional, continental or world multi-sports competitions patronized by the IOC. In addition, each NOC is obliged to participate in the Games of the Olympiad by sending athletes.

33. The National Federations—To be recognized by an NOC and accepted as a member of such NOC, a national federation must be affiliated to an IF recognized by the IOC and conduct its activities in compliance with both the Olympic charter and the rules of its IF.

Chapter V—THE OLYMPIC GAMES
39. Organizing Committee

1—The organization of the Olympic Games is entrusted by the IOC to the NOC of the country of the host city as well as to the host city itself. The NOC shall form, for that purpose, an Organizing Committee (OCOG) which, from the time it is constituted, communicates directly with the IOC, from which it receives instructions.

40. Liabilities—The NOC, the OCOG and the host city are jointly and severally liable for all commitments entered into individually or collectively concerning the organization and staging of the Olympic Games, excluding the financial responsibility for the organization and staging of such Games, which shall be entirely assumed jointly and severally by the host city and the OCOG, without prejudice to any liability of any other party, particularly as may result from any guarantee given pursuant to Rule 37, paragraph 6. The IOC shall have no financial responsibility whatsoever in respect thereof.

45. Eligibility Code—To be eligible for participation in the Olympic Games a competitor must comply with the Olympic Charter as well as with the rules of the IF concerned as approved by the IOC, and must be entered by his NOC. He must notably: *respect the spirit of fair play and non violence, and behave accordingly on the sports field; *refrain from using substances and procedures prohibited by the rules of the IOC, the IFs or the NOCs; *respect and comply in all aspects with the Olympic Movement Anti–Doping Code.

Bye-Law To Rule 45

1—Each IF establishes its sport's own eligibility criteria in accordance with the Olympic Charter. Such criteria must be submitted to the IOC Executive Board for approval.

2—The application of the eligibility criteria lies with the IFs, their affiliated national federations and the NOCs in the fields of their respective responsibilities.

3—Except as permitted by the IOC Executive Board, no competitor who participates in the Olympic Games may allow his person, name, picture or sports performances to be used for advertising purposes during the Olympic Games.

4—The entry or participation of a competitor in the Olympic Games shall not be conditional on any financial consideration.

49. Entries

1—Only NOCs recognized by the IOC may enter competitors in the Olympic Games. The right of final acceptance of entries rests with the IOC Executive Board.

2—An NOC shall only exercise such attributions upon the recommendations for entries given by national federations. If the NOC approves thereof, it shall transmit such entries to the OCOG. The OCOG must acknowledge their receipt. NOCs must investigate the validity of the entries proposed by the national federations and ensure that no one has been excluded for racial, religious or political reasons or by reasons of other forms of discriminations.

51. Olympic Sports—The sports governed by the following IFs are considered as Olympic sports:

1—*Games of the Olympiad*:

—International Amateur Athletic Federation (IAAF);

—International Rowing Federation (FISA);

—International Badminton Federation (IBF);

—International Baseball Federation (IBAF)

—International Basketball Association (FIBA);

—International Amateur Boxing Association (AIBA);

—International Canoeing Federation (FIC);

—International Cycling Union (UCI);

—International Equestrian Federation (FEI);

—International Fencing Federation (FIE);

—International Association Football Federation (FIFA);

—International Gymnastics Federation (FIG);

—International Weightlifting Federation (IWF);

—International Handball Federation (IHF);

—International Hockey Federation (FIH);

—International Judo Federation (IJF);

—International Amateur Wrestling Federation (FILA);

—International Amateur Swimming Federation (FINA);

—International Union of the Modern Pentathlon (UIPM);

—International Softball Federation (ISF);

—World Taekwondo Federation (WTF);

—International Tennis Federation (ITF);

—International Table Tennis Federation (ITTF);

—International Shooting Sport Federation (ISSF);

—International Archery Federation (FITA);

—International Triathlon Union (ITU);

—International Sailing Federation (ISAF);

—International Volleyball Federation (FIVB);

2—*Olympic Winter Games*:

—International Biathlon Union (IBU);

—International Bobsleigh and Tobogganing Federation (FIBT);

—World Curling Federation (WCF)

—International Ice Hockey Federation (IIHF);

—International Luge Federation (FIL);

—International Modern Pentathlon and Biathlon Union (UIPMB);

—International Skating Union (ISU);

—International Skiing Federation (FIS).

STATUTES OF THE BODIES WORKING FOR THE SETTLEMENT OF SPORTS-RELATED DISPUTES

(The Constitution of the Court of Arbitration For Sport)

A. Joint Dispositions

S1.   In order to settle, through arbitration, sports-related disputes, two bodies are hereby created : **the International Council of Arbitration for Sport (ICAS), and the Court of Arbitration for Sport (CAS).** The disputes referred to in the preceding [sentence] include, in particular, those connected with doping. The disputes to which a federation, association or other sports body is party are a matter for arbitration in the sense of this Code, only insofar as the statutes or regulations of the said sports bodies or a specific agreement so provide. The seat of the ICAS and the CAS is established in Lausanne, Switzerland.

S2.   The task of the ICAS is to facilitate the settlement of sports-related disputes through arbitration or meditation and to safeguard the independence of the CAS and the rights of the parties. To this end, it looks after the administration and financing of the CAS.

S3. The CAS, which has a list of arbitrators, procures the arbitral resolution of disputes arising within the field of sport through the intermediary of arbitration provided by Panels composed of one or three arbitrators. It comprises an Ordinary Arbitration Division and an Appeals Arbitration Division. The CAS can also procure the resolution of sports-related disputes through mediation. The mediation procedure is governed by separate rules.

B. The International Council of Arbitration for Sport (ICAS)

1. Composition

S4. The ICAS is composed of twenty members, namely high-level jurists appointed in the following manner:

a. four members are appointed by the International Sports Federations ("IFs"), viz. three by the Summer Olympic IFs (ASOIF), one by the Winter Olympic IFs ("AIWF"), chosen from within or from outside their membership;

b. four members are appointed by the Association of the National Olympic Committees ("ANOC"), chosen from within or from outside its membership;

c. four members are appointed by the International Olympic Committee ("IOC"), chosen from within or from outside its membership;

d. four members are appointed by the twelve members of the ICAS listed above, after appropriate consultation with a view to safeguarding the interests of the athletes;

e. four members are appointed by the sixteen members of the ICAS listed above and chosen from among personalities independent of the bodies designating the other members of the ICAS.

S5. The members of the ICAS are appointed for a renewable period of four years. Upon their appointment, the members of the ICAS sign a declaration undertaking to exercise their function in a personal capacity, with total objectivity and independence, in conformity with this Code. They are, in particular, bound by the confidentiality obligation which is provided in Article R43. The members of the ICAS may not appear on the list of arbitrators of the CAS nor act as counsel to one of the parties in proceedings before the CAS. If a member of the ICAS resigns, dies or is prevented from carrying out his functions for any other reason, he is replaced, for the remaining period of his mandate, in conformity with the terms applicable to his appointment.

2. Attributions

S6. The ICAS exercises the following functions :

1. It adopts and amends this Code; . . .

3. It appoints the personalities who are to constitute the list of arbitrators and the list of mediators of CAS (Article S3); . . . .

C. The Court of Arbitration for Sport (CAS)

1. Mission

S12. The CAS sets in operation Panels which have the task of providing for the resolution by arbitration of disputes arising within the field of sport in conformity with the Procedural Rules (Articles R27 et seq.). To this end, the CAS attends to the constitution of Panels and the smooth running of the proceedings. It places at the disposal of the parties the necessary infrastructure. The responsibility of such Panels is, inter alia:

a. to resolve the disputes that are referred to them through ordinary arbitration;

b. to resolve through the appeals arbitration procedure disputes, (including doping-related disputes) concerning the decisions of disciplinary tribunals or similar bodies of federations, associations or other sports bodies, insofar as the statutes or regulations of the said sports bodies or a specific agreement so provide;

c. to give non-binding advisory opinions at the request of the IOC, the IFs, the NOCs, the associations recognized by the IOC and the Olympic Games Organizing Committees ("OCOGs").

2. Arbitrators

S13. The personalities designated by the ICAS . . . appear on the list of arbitrators for a renewable period of four years. There are at least one hundred and fifty of these arbitrators.

S14. In establishing the list of CAS arbitrators, the ICAS shall call upon personalities with a legal training and who possess recognized competence with regard to sport and respect, in principle, the following distribution :

- 1/5th of the arbitrators selected from among the persons proposed by the IOC, chosen from within its membership or from outside;

- 1/5th of the arbitrators selected from among the persons proposed by the IFs, chosen from within their membership or outside;

- 1/5th of the arbitrators selected from among the persons proposed by the NOCs, chosen from within their membership or outside;

- 1/5th of the arbitrators chosen after appropriate consultations with a view to safeguarding the interests of the athletes;

- 1/5th of the arbitrators chosen from among persons independent of the bodies responsible for proposing arbitrators in conformity with the present article.

3. Organization of the CAS

S20. The CAS is composed of two divisions, the Ordinary Arbitration Division and the Appeals Arbitration Division.

a. **The Ordinary Arbitration Division** constitutes Panels, the mission of which is to resolve disputes submitted to the ordinary procedure, and performs, through the intermediary of its President, all other functions in relation to the smooth running of the proceedings conferred upon it by the Procedural Rules (Articles R27 et seq.).

b. **The Appeals Arbitration Division** constitutes Panels, the mission of which is to resolve disputes (including doping-related disputes) concerning the decisions of disciplinary tribunals or similar bodies of federations, associations or other sports bodies insofar as the statutes or regulations of the said sports bodies or a specific agreement so provide. It performs, through the intermediary of its President, all other functions in relation to the smooth running of the proceedings conferred upon it by the Procedural Rules (Articles R27 et seq.). Arbitration proceedings submitted to the CAS are assigned by the Court Office to one of these two Divisions according to their nature. Such assignment may not be contested by the parties or raised by them as a cause of irregularity.

S21. The President of one or other of the two Divisions of the CAS may be challenged if circumstances exist that give rise to legitimate doubts with regard to his independence vis-à-vis one of the parties to an arbitration assigned to his Division. He shall spontaneously disqualify himself when, in arbitration proceedings assigned to his Division, one of the parties is a sports body to which he belongs, or when a member of the law firm to which he belongs is acting as arbitrator or counsel. When the President of one of the two Divisions is challenged, the functions relating to the smooth running of the proceedings conferred upon him by the Procedural Rules (Articles R27 et seq.), are performed by the President of the CAS and the President of the Division may not receive any information concerning the activities of the CAS regarding the arbitration proceedings which led to the disqualification.

†